Transforming Aggression

Psychotherapy with the Difficult-to-Treat Patient

Frank M. Lachmann, Ph.D.

JASON ARONSON INC.
Northvale, New Jersey
London

This book was set in 11 pt. Berkeley Book by Pageworks of Old Saybrook, CT, and printed and bound by Book-mart Press, Inc. of North Bergen, NJ.

10 9 8 7 6 5 4 3 2 1

Library of Congress Cataloging-in-Publication Data

Lachmann, Frank M.
    Transforming aggression : psychotherapy with the difficult-to-treat patient. / Frank M. Lachmann.
        p.   cm.
    Includes bibliographical references and index.
    ISBN 0-7657-0293-2
    1. Aggressiveness. 2. Psychotherapy. I. Title.
    [DNLM: 1. Psychotherapy. 2. Aggression—psychology. WM 420 L138t 2001]
  RC569.5.A34L33 2001
  6.6.89'14—dc21
                                        00-038963

Printed in the United States of America on acid-free paper. For information and catalog write to Jason Aronson Inc., 230 Livingston Street, Northvale, NJ 07647-1726, or visit our website: www.aronson.com

To Annette, Suzanne, and Peter

Contents

	Preface	vii
	Acknowledgments	xv
1.	Self Psychology Strikes Back	1
2.	The Aggressive Toddler and the Angry Adult	25
3.	The View from Motivational Systems Theory	47
4.	State Transformations in Psychoanalytic Treatment	73
5.	State Transformations and Trauma	87
6.	State Transformations through Creativity	103
7.	The Transformation of Reactive Aggression into Eruptive Aggression	119
8.	It's Better to Be Feared Than Pitied	149
9.	The Empathy That Enrages	173
10.	A Requiem for Countertransference	191
11.	A Systems View	209
12.	Self Psychology and the Varieties of Aggression	221
	References	239
	Credits	255
	Index	257

Preface

Coming of age as a psychologist in the field of psychoanalysis just before its domination by the medical establishment declined presented an extraordinary challenge: how to get training in psychotherapy and psychoanalysis when many doors to analytic training were closed to nonmedical candidates. Among the reasons for this exclusion was the belief that psychoanalysis required a knowledge of medicine.

My graduate school education had emphasized psychological testing and research, but my fellow intern at Bellevue Hospital, Lloyd Silverman, whetted my interest in psychoanalytic theory. I was able to find psychotherapy training in the mid-1950s at a Veterans Administration outpatient clinic. Later, at the Postgraduate Center for Mental Health in New York, my training broadened to include psychoanalysis.

In those years, by training and temperament, I was an ego psychologist. Even then, as a psychologist, psychotherapist, and psychoanalyst, I was part of a distinct, still restricted minority. Likening this experience to having grown up as a Jew in Germany in the 1930s is a stretch, but being part of a discriminated-against minority was not unfamiliar to me. So, my reaction of frustration at being a psychologist when the practice of psychotherapy and psychoanalysis was open mainly to physicians is perhaps one, among my several motives, for writing a book on "reactive" aggression.

In the 1960s I became acquainted with the work of Heinz Kohut in a seminar on the development of psychoanalytic thought taught by Martin Bergmann, the consummate teacher, scholar, and practitioner of psychoanalysis. In the years I spent in one of his study groups I became acquainted with the vast and exciting literature of psychoanalysis.

I liked Kohut's challenge to the prevailing clinical and theoretical wisdom of psychoanalysis. In his early papers, I found a blueprint for a truly widening scope for psychoanalytic treatment. The attacks on Kohut's work by the psychoanalytic establishment that followed his writing for the next several years surprised and outraged me. Here, I believe, arose another motive for writing about aggression from the vantage point of Kohut's contributions.

In the 1980s, after Bob Stolorow and I had published *Psychoanalysis of Developmental Arrests,* I was invited to become a member of the Program and Publications Committee, the forerunner of the International Council for Psychoanalytic Self Psychology. Thereby my participation in the development of self psychology was assured, and, ironically, I became an even more active and committed member of an out-of-favor minority.

In the past two decades I have been struck by the combination of half-truths as well as by the valid questions that have characterized the criticism of self psychology in the psychoanalytic literature, case conferences, and especially in the meeting rooms and corridors at psychoanalytic conferences. The voices of relational psychoanalysis joined the chorus of classical Freudian analysts in looking askance at the theory of self psychology, and especially the clinical implications that grew out of the theory. Furthermore, relational analysts, whose ranks have swelled during the past decade, have been more radical than their classical analytic counterparts. They have advocated, if not actually "throwing away the book," then deconstructing it, at least in the postmodern sense. Once again, I find myself swimming against the current. In my desire to maintain some continuity with the past, I am not prepared to join that chorus either.

Perhaps I am still clinging to a minority status. However, as I see it, I am primarily interested in the leading edge of theories rather than in examining them from a trailing-edge perspective. I have borrowed these edge terms from Heinz Kohut's view of interpretation. In making interpretations, Kohut advised, the leading edge addresses what the person is striving to achieve, and the trailing edge addresses the contents and conflicts that are avoided, repressed, or disavowed. Both edges are important in psychoanalytic treatment and in theory evaluation. But life among the trailing edges can be grim, whereas the leading edge carries hope and points to a direction for the future. In the course of this book I articulate the leading edge of self psychology in psychoanalytic treatment. To be able to do so provides me with another motive for writing this book. Contrary to the assumptions of its detractors, trailing-edge interpretations are not avoided in self psychology, but neither are they privileged.

A friend asked me if it had been difficult for me to switch to self psychology from my classical psychoanalytic beginnings. My friend remembered that I had taught the contributions of Arlow, Brenner, Greenson, and Jacobson, and the work of many other ego psychologists at the Postgraduate Center for Mental Health in New York. In responding, it struck me how easy that shift had been for me. In truth, I had been practicing as a self psychologist all along. I found in self psychology the framework that fit the way I had already been working in my practice.

The conservative in me has held on to aspects of the conflict model that I found useful as an ego psychologist. However, I think of conflict as a subjective experience that captures what a person is struggling to express, suppress, disavow, or attribute to others. I am not referring to conflict as the theoretical assumption that explains motivations and leads to compromise formations. The question of drives, what is innate, especially when it comes to aggression and destructiveness, is another matter and that will occupy the pages to follow.

Self psychology places its emphasis on individual uniqueness and on the uncanny resourcefulness and survival strivings of people. I like Kohut's focus on self-experience, thereby giving these strivings and resources a legitimate theoretical and clinical status. So I consider myself a self psychologist. Out of my history, my clinical experience, my theoretical biases and beliefs, and my desire to explain and extend self psychology, I strike back at its detractors.

For a theory of psychology to remain clinically applicable it must continue to evolve. This has been true for practitioners of classical Freudian analysis as well as those following in the tradition of Melanie Klein. Today's Freudians (for example, Adler and Bachant 1998) and Kleinians (see Schafer 1997) have attempted to maintain a continuity with their past. Furthermore, they have absorbed later influences from other psychoanalytic perspectives as well as from the cultural context in which we all practice. I differ with the results of their integration of their past with the present, but I applaud and admire their maintenance of continuity. Similarly, self psychologists have maintained a continuity with Kohut's seminal formulations. In addition, there have been theoretical advances and clinical reformulations that have stirred lively controversy among self psychological practitioners (see *Psychoanalytic Dialogues* 1995).

My aim in this book is to explore and to illustrate Kohut's contributions specifically with respect to aggression as I have applied them in my clinical work. I indicate how and where this theory has been criticized, and how and where it can be expanded and modified. Wherever I describe Kohut's theory, it is my version of Kohut's theory. Like all phenomena of the clinical situation, for example, transference, the theoretical positions I discuss are also co-constructed through my contributions and biases and the specific bent of the theoretician that I cite. Furthermore, the modifications I offer are to my version of Kohut's clinical theory. Specifically, I focus on the area of Kohut's work that has been most useful to me and most vehemently criticized in the wider analytic community: Kohut's theory of aggression, or, as he termed it, narcissistic rage.

In my graduate school training I became fascinated by psychological research, an interest I have been able to bring to self psychology through my collaboration with Beatrice Beebe. Together, we have explored the relationship between the empirical infant research and the analysis of adult patients. My immersion in these studies has seeped into my clinical work, and appears in some of the chapters. However, in this book I focus predominantly on the treatment of adults.

It is risky to describe how I work, how I think about the way I work, and what I have been doing in my work with patients. The risk is that my adherence to self psychology will give its detractors a field day, whereas my departures from self psychology will turn off its adherents. I know you can't please everyone. Perhaps the next best possibility is to displease these two groups equally.

This book is not intended as a scholarly examination of the vicissitudes of aggression, but an anecdotal personal account of my clinical interests, a clinical journey. I have gathered together, revised, and updated some previously published papers, elaborated my published cases, added new case vignettes, spelled out some long-held convictions, and organized this material around the question: how can aggression or narcissistic rage be inherently reactive (secondary) to deprivation, frustration and injury, and yet become "eruptive," that is, appear primary and drive-like? In this book I present what I have learned, examine the direction in which I want to go, and invite you to join me.

I have given the patients in the case vignettes first names so that the reader can identify them as I discuss aspects of their treatment in subsequent chapters. I am not providing complete descriptions of these analyses, but rather highlights relevant to the topic of the chapter. I use the terms *analyst* and *therapist*, and *analysis* and *psychotherapy*, and *treatment* interchangeably. There is debate as to the equivalence and difference among these terms. However, my discussions of aggression and transformation are applicable to psychoanalytically informed treatment whether conducted on a one-session-per-week basis or more frequently, whether the patient sits in a chair or lies on the couch, and whether the patient is in psychoanalysis or psychotherapy.

THE PLAN OF THE BOOK

What are the implications for psychoanalytic treatment when aggression is viewed as reactive to threats, frustrations, and injuries to one's

pride and self-esteem? In Chapter 1 I outline the self psychological terms
that are relevant to a discussion of aggression, and distinguish between
those criticisms of self psychology that are based on a theoretical model
that differs fundamentally from self psychology, and those criticisms that
I believe do require a more careful assessment by self psychologists. To
explore the developmental and clinical implications of the view that aggression is primary and a drive, and the view that aggression is a secondary phenomenon and a reaction, I describe two contrasting depictions
of toddlers in Chapter 2. One view emphasizes innate aggression, and
the other draws on systems theory and self- and interactive regulations
in the development of aggressive reactions. The treatment of an adult
patient follows and illustrates the clinical applicability of the constructs
of self- and interactive regulation in working with an angry adult.

A self psychological model of the mind, amended and expanded
by motivational systems theory, is presented next. Its relevance to understanding and working with aggression and assertion is illustrated in
the treatment of a patient who fluctuated between flare-ups of rage and
frightening doubts about his ability to take care of himself. In this analysis, aggressive outbursts are interpretively related to the context that contributed to their organization. The motivational systems framework is
described and expanded through the construction of model scenes by
analyst and patient.

In the middle chapters of this book I consider the ways in which
reactive aggression can be transformed. To do so, the concept of *transformation of self-states* is explicated, and such transformations are described in two directions. They occur throughout life, and through psychoanalytic interventions. However, transformations also occur through
physical and emotional deprivation and abuse, as well as through a variety of adverse developmental experiences. Self-states include affects and
cognition, as well as contributions from bodily and physiological sources.
For example, trauma can transform expectations of encountering a reasonable, responsive, or admiring environment into rigid self-states of
anxious anticipation, irritability, and a dominant propensity toward expressions of anger.

Central to the argument of this book is this question: Even if aggression is understood to be reactive to a threat, injury, or frustration, can it come to appear innate, or with barely noticeable provocations, or as I will term it, eruptive? My answer is yes! A reconsideration of the clinical theory of self psychology and the treatment implications derived therefrom then follows. Thus, I ultimately consider the transformation of reactive into eruptive aggression through the study of violent men drawn from clinical and nonclinical sources. Among the latter I draw on the plays, biography, and autobiography of Henrik Ibsen and from biographies of serial killers. In both instances I am using illustrations of extremes of the varieties of aggression.

The value of placing a patient's rage reaction into the context in which it was evoked is demonstrated in numerous clinical illustrations throughout this book. However, I shall also challenge this formulation by discussing the analysis of a patient who found that my embedding her rageful outbursts in the contexts in which she experienced narcissistic injuries, as well as their historical antecedents, did not enable her to feel better understood by me, or provide her with a broader understanding of her own experience. Instead it produced rage outbursts toward me. This patient responded to the reactivity implied in my context-embedding interventions as yet another insult that brought forth increased contempt and distrust toward me. I will utilize my correspondence with a member of the British Independent Group of analysts about this patient to address her paradoxical response.

Tilting away from a confrontational stance and its iatrogenic consequences, has, I believe, led to the neglect of the enlivening and self-affirming aspect of rage. Accordingly, I will consider the extent to which acknowledging a person's murderousness can be vitally needed to confirm a sense of integrity, as a source of pride, and as an antidote to shame and depression. Following this, I return to the vexing questions of countertransference and projective identification. In place of these concepts, I propose a systems theory perspective. I conclude in the final chapter with a synthesis of self psychology, the theoretical and clinical modifications I have proposed, and the implications of this treatment model in addressing the varieties of aggression.

Acknowledgments

My students, colleagues, the members of my study groups, and my peer group were generous with their time and comments as they critiqued various versions of this book. I am grateful to them not only for these efforts but also for challenging and inspiring me as we discussed psychoanalytic theory and treatment. I want to thank Phyllis Ackman, Linda Beeler, Robert Broad, Annabel Brodie, Girard Franklin, Arthur A. Gray, Diane Greene, Ruth Gruenthal, Dianne Heller Kaminsky, Linda Klempner, Tom Menaker, Ann Morris, Harriet Pappenheim, Pauline Pinto, Gertrude Schwartzman, Manny Shapiro, Doris Silverman, Dorienne Sorter, Ann Sullivan, Ellen Synan, Shake Topalian, Harriet Werner, Jane Wilkins, and Annette Lachmann.

Self Psychology Strikes Back

A university professor sought analysis because of his inability to control his temper, especially his critical and destructive outbursts toward his students. Although his preparation of lectures is extensive, his ambivalent relationship with his students and colleagues deprives him of the professional status to which his competence entitles him. He described similar flare-ups of rage toward his friends, wife, and children, usually prompted by his sense that they were less competent, reasonable, or conscientious than he expected them to be. Afterward, he would feel remorseful, contrite, ashamed, and guilty. Many years of prior analysis with another analyst diminished this pattern considerably, but not sufficiently to enable him to function better. His unsuccessful attempts at self-control continued to evoke painful self-reproaches and prompted him to try analysis again. After our initial consultation he told a friend who knew him well that he was going to begin analysis with me, a self psychologist. His friend said, "How could you? They don't know anything about aggression."

My patient's friend turned out to be a Kleinian psychoanalyst. He voiced one of the many criticisms of self psychology that have been spread in the psychoanalytic literature and by word of mouth since Heinz Kohut published *The Analysis of the Self* in 1971. However, although the comment that self psychology does not deal with aggression is a misconception, it does point to clinical and theoretical questions with respect to self psychology that demand clarification.

I use the term *aggression* as it is used in ordinary language and defined as "the first attack in a quarrel; an assault, an inroad, the practice of setting upon someone; the making of an attack or assault" (*Oxford English Dictionary* 1982). From the dictionary entry I left out the first definition—"an unprovoked attack"—because that is the specific aspect of aggression that self psychology challenges. The attack is not unprovoked when understood from the vantage point of the aggressor's subjectivity. Kohut (1972) proposes that aggression is *not* a primary motive, but is reactive to a narcissistic injury. Thus, the circumstances in which a person acts aggressively may appear to an observer to be unprovoked, but when understood from within that person's perspective or within his subjective experience, a context for the attack can be discerned. This view of aggression does not excuse the attack in a normative sense, but makes it understandable in a psychological sense. Psychoanalytic treatment then focuses on the context in which aggression is evoked and the injury, deprivation, and/or frustration to which it is reactive.

Kohut came to his views on aggression through his study of narcissism and his experience as clinician, supervisor, and teacher. The first generation of self psychology patients included many who had been traumatized in prior analyses where their narcissism was relentlessly confronted. When narcissism is diagnosed as a defense or an ego-syntonic character trait, treatment often entails confronting the patient's self-centeredness, arrogance, and self-aggrandizement, and focusing on the patient's inability to relate to other people as separate objects. From some theoretical perspectives, the rage with which patients react to such confrontations is seen as confirmation that aggression underlies narcissistic defenses. However, from the vantage point of self psychology, when confrontation constitutes a narcissistic injury, then rage is a plausible response.

Merton Gill's (1994) description of his experience as an analysand in one of his classical analyses illustrates the kind of treatment approach that Kohut addressed in his theory and in his technical innovations. Gill reported, "One of my analysts once said that if my parents' behavior accounted for 95% of my troubles and it was my experience of their behavior that accounted for the remaining 5%, it was only that 5% in which he was interested. I see his point more clearly now than I did then, but I still think I was right to become enraged" (p. 31). Gill did not reveal how his rage reaction was interpreted. However, if his analyst applied the same principle to the analysis of transference as he did to the shaping of Gill's early experience, then he may have focused on Gill's rage rather than on the context, the analyst–patient interaction, from which the rage emerged. Placing rage, or other expressions of aggression, into the past and current context in which they were evoked reconnects them with the patient's broader affective life. Furthermore, it enables the patient to appreciate and understand the totality of the experience that motivated the rage, rather than feeling himself to be defined as rageful.

Self psychology is not alone in claiming that it is essential to place aggressive reactions into the contexts in which they were evoked. However, the central focus placed by self psychology is on understanding the patient from within the patient's subjectivity, that is, the patient's frame of reference, which is co-constructed by analyst and patient and provides the context for the patient's reactions of rage. By "co-construction" I mean that both participants, analyst and patient, contributed to the organization of the interaction, but not similarly or equally. For example, by dismissing 95 percent of the contribution of Gill's parents to his troubles, the analyst dismissed, out of hand, Gill's perception of his childhood experience. In this way the analyst made a contribution to the context in which Gill became enraged.

Gill's vignette captures the connection between injured narcissism and rage. However, the differences between the self psychological view of narcissism and aggression and other psychoanalytic views point to fundamental questions about human nature: Is aggression an innate drive that must be mastered? Is the task of managing sexual and aggressive drives a basic challenge that we must be helped to face? Is the task of facing one's infantile anxieties, and overcoming the propensity to attribute one's painful and conflicted affect states to others, the position from which we must move? Or is aggression a reaction to massive deprivation, frustration, and narcissistic injuries that obstruct self-development? Is striving toward self-integration the fundamental human task?

I believe that these positions, innate versus reactive aggression, are mutually exclusive and fundamentally irreconcilable. Posed in these extreme terms they also revive the bankrupt nature–nurture controversy. For example, the fetus in utero can change its state, dampen its arousal, and put itself to sleep to cope with aversive stimulation (Brazelton 1992). Already in utero "the fetus can regulate the level of arousal and responsivity as a function of the nature of the stimulation provided" (Beebe and Lachmann 1994, p. 138). We know now that nurture, environmental influences, begin in utero, and that nature, biological and genetic influences, may emerge at varying times in a person's life (see, for example, Field 1981, Thelen and Smith 1994). However, the innate versus reactive aggression controversy is relevant with respect to the guiding theory used by a psychoanalytic clinician. The clinician who adheres to a theory that aggression is innate will make clinical choices that differ from those of the clinician who adheres to a theory that requires searching for the context in which aggression has been triggered in reaction to a narcissistic injury, frustration, or disappointment.

From my point of view, a person's rage, hostility, contempt, or other variant of aggression is a reaction. However, the observation of drive theorists and object relations theorists of rage outbursts that appear unprovoked or proactive captures aspects of how aggression can be experienced by some people. The phenomenology of ragefulness or unprovoked anger, disdain, or contempt is thus of interest to self psychology. Later, I will elaborate on these varieties of aggression, with special attention to patients whose outbursts of rage, contempt, and murderousness evoke more rage when the analyst searches for the patient's subjective context that can house the aggression. But first, I review Kohut's formulations about aggression and self-development along with the criticisms and attacks from the psychoanalytic community that his proposals brought forth.

Kohut proposed that obstructions in self-development were derived from disruptions in a child's needed connection to a caregiver. As one consequence of chronic disruptions in this connection, the sense of self remains vulnerable and is prone to breakdown. Rage as well as sexual pathology can be a consequence of that breakdown, of that self-disintegration.

Nowhere is the distinction between Freud's and Kohut's theories of development clearer than in their differing formulations of the Oedipus complex. Kohut (1984) contrasted oedipal conflicts with an oedipal phase. He distinguished between two paths of development that centered on how the oedipal child experienced his or her parents. If the parents are experienced as supporting the developmental achievements of this phase, then a normal, joyful oedipal period follows. If the parents are experienced as responding seductively or with counteraggression to the child's phase-appropriate oedipal exhibitionism and sexual strivings, then castration anxiety and oedipal conflict follow.

Kohut's postulation of a normal oedipal phase that can become conflicted due to parental pathology and misattunement stands in stark contrast to the Oedipus complex postulated by Freudian theory, in which the way the person manages powerful erotic and aggressive feelings toward the parents, that is, the characteristics of the Oedipus complex, is basic to subsequent personality organization. These differences point to irreconcilably different visions of human nature that lead to diverging clinical theories. To a large extent, different treatment approaches have evolved from these distinctions, with different conceptualizations of narcissism and aggression and different theories of therapeutic action in the treatment of pathology derived from aggression.

THE DEBATE OVER THE SELF PSYCHOLOGICAL TREATMENT OF AGGRESSION

There have been numerous excellent reviews and summaries of the literature on aggression (for example, Leider 1998). Hartmann and colleagues (1949) provided an early review and elaboration of Freud's theory of aggression. Although they did consider aggression a reaction to deprivation and frustration, they attributed entirely internal sources to these two triggers. In an illustration of their theory, they described the state of the child when fed and when not fed, when gratified and when frustrated.

> Food intake permits gratification of libidinal needs both through zonal pleasure and . . . through the libidinal significance of the incorporation of the "source" of satisfaction; giving of food at this stage also means giving of love. . . . The biting of food, its disappearance, its incorporation, affords aggressive satisfactions early in development. . . . The absence of food deprives the child of an opportunity to discharge aggressive tension in its incorporation. [p. 29]

In this view, deprivation leads to a buildup of aggressive tensions and a frustration of the aggressive drive. The child's angry response is then *not* a reaction to having been deprived, but an accumulation of anger that did not have the usual or normal channels for discharge. This theory of aggression as an internal accumulation of tension has lingered in psychoanalytic practice. It is exemplified in treatments that encourage the outward expression of aggression as a way of divesting oneself of it.

Freud's view of aggression was already questioned by Bernfeld (1935, cited by Stepansky 1977). He disputed "Freud's claim that biology was at the source of his drive theory," and that the "final drive theory in no sense originates from biological considerations" (p. 188). Nevertheless, an insistence on the biology of drives, specifically as related to aggression, has been a central canon of the critics of self psychology. The publication of *The Restoration of the Self* (Kohut 1977) provided the critics with a field day. Although the hand-to-hand combat that followed Kohut's three major publications has died down, the smell of gunpowder has remained in the air. Volleys of criticism expectedly came from drive theorists, interpersonalists, and object relationalists. For example, Rothstein (1980) faulted Kohut for "de-emphasizing the instinctual biological underpinnings of the aggressive drive." Such de-emphasis ran counter to Rothstein's conviction that "a well of basic rage . . . is part of every human being" (p. 433). Years later, at a symposium on the central-ity of aggression in clinical psychoanalysis, Rothstein (1999, cited in Singer 1999) reiterated that "a successful analysis will necessarily need to have patients take 'responsibility for their sadistic, vengeful, and mur-derous desires'" (p. 1184). In a similar vein, Curtis (1985) faulted Kohut for ignoring "the child's drive-motivated fantasies and distortions of pa-rental behavior" (p. 361).

The number of published attacks has indeed diminished, but lone critical voices can still be heard. Even fifteen years after the first assaults, Raphling (1998) criticized a self psychological treatment by reiterating that aggression is innate, that it is "an intrinsic psychic motivation: a primary, obligatory appetite of an instinctual nature modified by the ego into complex drive derivatives" (p. 100).

To attack the theoretical underpinnings of self psychology for not recognizing instinctual drives is bizarre. Of course, self psychology is not based on a dual drive theory. That is exactly what it aims not to be. But implicit in this critique of the role self psychology accords to aggres-sion is this question: If there are no endogenous, biologically based drives, how does self psychology account for motivation? And, even more to the point, how can a person come to terms with his or her destructive-ness? Even this frequently reiterated question assumes that destructive-ness, a derivative of aggression, is an entity, is *there*, and must be ac-cepted as part of oneself.

By not considering aggression and sadistic behavior to be biologi-cally rooted, self psychologists are depicted as abdicating individual re-sponsibility in favor of traumatically induced, and environmentally pro-duced, deficits and reactions. In fact, Kramer (1994) specifically argued that because self psychology uses a deficiency model, it is confined to dealing with "surface material and fails to recognize the necessity for frustration, rather than the avoidance of frustration for development" (pp. 9–10).

In the background of these debates is this question: What kind of evidence can sway the adherents of either view, reactive or innate aggression, to consider the other's perspective? When we buttress our arguments with clinical illustrations, we are usually applauded by the partisans of the approach illustrated, and dismissed by those who hold another opinion. Research evidence could help, but there is the problem of formulating studies that do justice to the complexities of a theory and simultaneously avoid the potential bias of the investigator. And even then, Raphling (1998) held that research evidence is inadmissible in addressing these controversies. He specifically dismissed infant observation and other research methods as incapable of revealing the complex verbal meaning encoded in aggressive behavior. In dismissing research evidence, Raphling implicitly dismissed the seminal studies of Henri Parens (1979), whose conversion from drive theory to a view of aggression as reactive will be considered later.

From a clinical standpoint, the self psychological view of aggression has also been contrasted with treatment approaches derived from Kleinian object relations theories. While Fairbairn (1952) considered aggression reactive to frustration, aggression as a basic constituent of human nature was central to the work of Melanie Klein. This emphasis has been continued by modern Kleinians, for example, Betty Joseph (1985, 1992).

About the origin of aggressiveness, Melanie Klein (1975) asserted that "some babies experience strong resentment about any frustration and show this by being unable to accept gratification when it follows on deprivation" (p. 249). She contrasted children who she believed show strong innate aggressiveness and greed with children whose outbursts of rage were occasional. In addition, she believed that an innate aggressive component in a child would also result in strong persecutory anxiety, frustration, and greed. These predispositions contribute to the child's difficulty in tolerating frustration and dealing with anxiety. Finally, she concluded that the interaction of the strength of the destructive impulse with libidinal impulses "provides the constitutional basis for the intensity of greed" (p. 62).

Both Klein and Joseph accepted Freud's (1914b) seesaw relationship between narcissism and object love. As one increased, the other would decrease. In their view, narcissism and problems with aggression noted in a patient were closely linked. A similar connection between narcissism and aggression is found in the theories of Kernberg (1975) and other object relational theorists. They hold to the traditional psychoanalytic dictum that an increase in narcissism, an early libidinal stage, is linked to a failure to achieve the developmental level of object love. The treatment they espouse attempts to reverse this situation—to diminish archaic narcissism and thereby raise the person to the level of object love.

The treatment implications of a link between narcissism and aggression are clear in non–self psychological approaches. The analyst confronts and analyzes the patient's negative transference, the repository of the patient's aggression and narcissism, and confronts and analyzes the patient's resistance and the inability to relate to the analyst as a separate object. These treatment strategies share a common emphasis: to identify and analyze the negative transference.

FAILURES IN EMPATHY AND SELFOBJECT RUPTURES

In presenting his views on aggression, Mitchell (1993) criticized both drive theorists and those who have abandoned drives, among whom he includes self psychologists. Specifically, he attacked self psychology for portraying aggression as though it is always "provoked and *therefore* as avoidable and peripheral to the development and structuralization of the self" (pp. 157–158, italics added). In contrast, he believes that aggression is spontaneous, inevitable, and central in human interactions. Mitchell is among those analysts (see also Harris 1998) who have distanced themselves from a drive version of aggression but have embraced aggression as central to an understanding of human nature, and central to the analytic enterprise. That is, they do not believe that aggression should be given the status of a drive, but they do argue that it is a central human motivation.

The problem with Mitchell's depiction of self psychology is the word *therefore*. To claim, as self psychologists do, that aggression is reactive and provoked does not mean it is avoidable. It does not mean that analysts are advised to walk on eggshells to avoid stirring up a patient's aggression. It does mean that the context in which aggression has been experienced by the patient requires exploration. Mitchell, as have other critics of self psychology, also erroneously equates failures in empathy with selfobject ruptures. Before distinguishing between the effects of empathic failures and ruptures of selfobject transferences, a word about selfobject transferences.

Selfobject Transference

Selfobject transference pertains to "that dimension of our experience of another person that relates to this person's functions in shoring up our self" (Kohut 1984, p. 49). Developmentally, selfobject transferences derive from the ties between the infant and his or her parents. To the extent that the child's longings for needed experiences of feeling mirrored and being included within the protective orbit of an idealized parent are met, these longings evolve into a set of guiding ideals and ambitions and a cohesive sense of self. In treatment, the patient may derive selfobject experiences in which the analyst is felt to be a source of self-coherence, affect regulation, and self-continuity. That is, the analyst is experienced as a "function" that maintains and organizes the sense of self, and not used as a target for the patient's affects, or to work over projected fantasies and displaced experiences with significant people from the past. Rather, the selfobject experience is a vitalizing, affective, self-restorative, or self-enhancing experience. It can be derived from a variety of sources, not necessarily only from the analyst, or from "good-enough" parents. A selfobject experience is defined by the positive, self-sustaining, self-maintaining, or self-restoring quality of a person's subjective experience and is distinguished from the interpersonal or environmental context in which the experience is evoked. A variety of contexts may be the breeding grounds of selfobject experiences. Not all of these contexts would be considered positive or healthy. These contexts include sports, love, fantasies, and friendships, as well as sources such as sadomasochistic relationships, drugs, addictions, and violence.

Empathy

Kohut considered empathy as a mode of observation, the way in which we gather information about the subjective life of another person. Through vicarious introspection, what it feels like to live in that person's shoes, the analyst grasps the subjective life and experiences of the patient. To be so exquisitely attended to and understood, to be the object of this "empathic listening perspective" (P. Ornstein 1985, p. 43) is felt to be a beneficial experience by many, but not by all patients, as I will illustrate in Chapters 8 and 9. However, Kohut was clear in not giving empathy a value. He exemplified the dark side of empathy by referring to a hoodlum standing at a street corner and sensing who would be a good mugging prospect (P. Ornstein, personal communication, 2000), and in the Nazis adding sirens to their buzz bombs when they bombed London during World War II, knowing that these sounds would increase the terror and confusion of the populace (Kohut 1981). They were using empathy, sensing themselves into the subjective experience of other people and attacking where they sensed the greatest vulnerability. In Shakespeare's *Othello*, Iago's empathy enables him to manipulate Othello because he is able to sense with uncanny accuracy just how and where Othello is vulnerable (A. Lachmann 1999).

Although failures in empathy and selfobject ruptures may coincide, failures in empathy can be traced to aspects of the therapeutic relationship where there has been a misunderstanding, a misinterpretation, or a tactless response by the analyst (see Stolorow et al. 1987). The extent to which this disruption was due to the analyst's insensitivity or the patient's specific hypersensitivity can then be investigated. In these instances, the therapeutic interaction in the here and now is explored more fully. Identifying the empathic failure restores the therapeutic interaction. The patient's specific vulnerability contributes to the occurrence of these failures.

In selfobject ruptures the accent falls on the specific vulnerability and sensitivity of the patient to a greater extent. The presence of this vulnerability makes such ruptures an everyday event of treatment. Investigating the basis for the rupture constitutes its repair. In neither case can failures and ruptures be avoided. In both instances the patient may provide the crucial signal. This signal may be a verbal recognition that something went awry, or an increase in symptomatology that may range from a slight cold withdrawal to a flare-up of flamboyant behavior.

Exploration of failures of empathy and selfobject ruptures accrue to the stability of the patient's self organization. Such exploration and interpretation can lead the patient toward expectations of being understood and the further expectation that when a dialogue is disrupted, the patient can expect the analyst to be motivated to try to understand the basis for the disruption and thereby restore the dialogue.

WHAT ABOUT PROJECTION AND DISTORTION?

The place accorded to frustration as the impetus for aggressive reactions is a distinguishing factor in contrasting self psychology with other psychoanalytic approaches. For self psychologists, attention given to frustration is closely connected with the attention given to the investigation of empathic ruptures in the transferences. This emphasis places the patient's frustration-generated anger into a context through which the threat, the disruption that triggered the anger, can be understood. Placing frustration-generated anger into a context in which the patient's reaction becomes understandable has led numerous critics such as Kernberg (1974) and Bromberg (1989) to claim that self psychology fails to deal with the extent to which patients distort their experience of the analyst and contribute to the failure of the analyst to understand them (Tuch 1997). Kernberg argued that the self psychological focus on the patient's disappointment, whether in the analyst or in other people, fails to recognize how narcissistic patients will "totally devaluate the transference object for the slightest reason" and that the self psychology perspective "fails to recognize the narcissistic patient's intense, overwhelming . . . aggression against the object" (p. 232). These arguments between proponents of innate and reactive aggression resemble political debates. One side accuses the other of being soft on aggression, and the other retorts, "You are hard on the vulnerable."

Some critics of self psychology see the emphasis on the analyst's empathic immersion in the patient's experience as a deprivation for the patient. That is, Bromberg (1998), from an interpersonal point of view, argues that in a self psychologically informed treatment the patient does not get to hear from the analyst what it feels like for another person to be the target of the patient's needs and demands. Curtis (1983), from the position of classical Freudian theory, faulted self psychology because he believes that a focus on "empathic responses to build the self crowds out other experiences and affects of anger, sexuality, and sadism" (p. 284). Modell (1986) joins this line of criticism by faulting Kohut for not acknowledging the "dark side to empathy" and thereby "seriously inhibit[ing] the patient's own creative powers" (p. 375).

In essence, self psychology is being criticized for not according patients the powers of projection and distortion. These mechanisms play a major role in both understanding psychopathology and in analyzing transference resistances in other psychoanalytic approaches. When the accent is placed on the reactivity of aggressive motivations and the co-construction of the analytic process, a burden is placed on the analyst. Nothing can be explained as residing solely within the patient. Rather the analyst investigates what in the analyst–patient interaction may have contributed to triggering the patient's aggressive reaction. Of course, whatever the trigger, rage is certainly not the only possible response a patient can have. The patient's potential for reacting with rage, rather than reacting in another way, can then lead to an investigation of the roots of the patient's vulnerability to rage reactions.

The close association between narcissistic pathology and aggression, captured in Kohut's term *narcissistic rage*, will dog us throughout these chapters. Both theoretically and clinically we know that narcissistic pathology provides a fertile field for the growth of aggressive reactions.

Freud's (1914b) proposal of a seesaw relationship between narcissism and object love is central to numerous treatment approaches to narcissism, not only that of Melanie Klein and her followers. In contrast, one of Kohut's earliest contributions was to unlink this connection between narcissism and object love and argue that narcissism and object love follow independent lines of development—independent but certainly not unrelated to each other. In unlinking this connection, Kohut voted against the imposition of a "relationships are healthy" morality as part of a mental health ethic. As a separate sector of the personality, Kohut proposed that narcissistic pathology can be explored without simultaneously imposing a goal.

Kohut also challenged the assumption that narcissistic patients are unable to form analyzable transferences. He proposed that these transferences reflect the patient's striving to (re)establish or restore necessary, sustaining ties to parental figures, ties that had been traumatically and repeatedly disrupted in childhood. These disruptions led to the failure of these ties to become abstracted and depersonified as symbolic processes. In consequence, as such a child becomes an adult, the literal presence of another person is required to sustain a cohesive sense of self and to feel attended to and loved. Conversely, even the temporary absence and certainly the loss of that person can lead to anxiety and despair, emotional coldness, or bodily symptoms.

Inevitably, a patient's strivings to establish selfobject ties to the analyst are prone to be disrupted through (1) failures of empathy on the part of the analyst, (2) selfobject ruptures, (3) the patient's requirements for exquisite attention, or (4) the slings and arrows of everyday life. Sustaining the ongoing selfobject tie and the analysis of ruptures promote self restoration and self integration. In a therapeutic milieu informed by this vision of narcissism, a patient can develop a more cohesive, temporally continuous, and affectively more positive sense of self (Stolorow and Lachmann 1980). In turn, as a consequence of a better integrated sense of self, an increase in the capacity to regulate strong affects, such as rage, follows. Increased affect regulation links the treatment of narcissistic pathology with the diminution of rage outbursts.

NARCISSISTIC RAGE, AMBITION, AND ASSERTION

Although narcissistic rage, ambition, and assertion are discussed in greater detail in subsequent chapters, some preliminary comments are in order.

Kohut distinguished between rage, which he labeled narcissistic rage, and healthy aggression. By healthy aggression, he meant ambitions and assertiveness as expressions of a cohesive sense of self. He considered narcissistic rage and hostile destructiveness to be breakdown products of an enfeebled self. That is, the fundamental pathology lay in the lack of self-cohesion or, put differently, in ready self-fragmentation. Under these conditions, in the absence of a responsive milieu, narcissistic rage and perverse or driven compulsive sexuality would predominate. The therapeutic implication of this proposal is to restore the sense of self and the selfobject ties by addressing the transference ruptures that inevitably occur, and as they occur, in the course of treatment. The restored sense of self can then become a functional unity, an independent center of initiative (Kohut 1977).

I believe that Kohut's illumination of narcissistic rage constituted one of his major contributions to the analysis of the pathology associated with aggression. However, theoretical and clinical problems are also introduced into psychoanalysis in this contribution. First, he distinguished healthy aggression and pathological aggression *not* on the basis of subjective experience. A person may feel assertive or may be expressing aggression in a healthy way, but others may view him or her as a pathologically aggressive bully. Or, the reverse, a person may feel like, or, in his or her eyes, act like, a bully, but others may be admiring of the display of force and determination. Thus, the distinction between healthy and pathological aggression is based on the judgment of an outside observer. The distinction thus overrides the subjectively experienced similarity between healthy and pathological aggression. Second, assertion and aggression are provided with a common origin. Kohut's distinction between healthy and pathological aggression gives healthy aggression a proactive status. It is linked with ambitions and assertiveness, whereas pathological aggression or narcissistic rage is deemed reactive. Third, pathological aggression is linked to and is indicative of a lack of self-cohesion. Linking pathological aggression to a breakdown of the self does not do justice to the extent to which feeling enraged, hostile, or fantasizing sadistically can enliven the sense of self. That is, in Kohut's formulation, aggression is not credited with maintaining a person's sense of cohesion. These are important issue to which I will return later in this book.

From Kohut's vantage point, narcissistic rage is always a consequence of self pathology. And indeed, clinically, in many instances, therapeutic restoration of self-cohesion does address the underlying basis for rage outbursts. When the sense of self is strengthened through analysis, eruptions of narcissistic rage decrease. Healthy aggression, assertion, and ambitions can then become expressions of a cohesive self. Indirectly then, healthy aggression rather than narcissistic rage becomes the handmaiden of a cohesive self.

In psychoanalytic treatment, narcissistic rage is diminished by attention to disruption and repair of the transference tie. The context for the patient's rage is addressed when the analyst tries to understand the patient's need to have grandiosity mirrored, and the patient's need to have idealizations of the analyst accepted. When these needs remain unfulfilled, aggressive reaction can coagulate on the surface of the analysis. Recognition of these needs, and recognition of disappointment at their nonfulfillment, constitutes meeting necessary developmental requirements. Thus, according to Kohut's theory of development, these "arrested" structures, the patient's archaic grandiosity and idealizations, can then resume development and mature on their own.

Earlier I cited references to highlight the theoretical positions from which self psychology has been criticized, and the nature of these criticisms. The differences noted between Kohut and his critics delineate a great divide that is unlikely to be bridged. These differences have distinct clinical corollaries that can be illustrated through a summary of Kohut's essential contributions to psychoanalytic practice. Particularly relevant in the treatment of aggressive pathology, these contributions are "(1) the unwavering application of the empathic-introspective mode of observation as defining and delimiting the domain of psychoanalytic inquiry, (2) the central emphasis on the primacy of self experience, (3) the concepts of selfobject function and selfobject transference" (Stolorow 1986, p. 388).

The critics of self psychology have claimed that the analyst's empathic focus on the patient's experience, and thus on the patient's subjectivity and self-experience, deprives the patient of an experience of the analyst as an other, a separate observer/interpreter of the patient's experience. Since there are circumstances when experiencing the analyst in this way is instrumental in furthering the treatment, Kohut has suggested that interpretations be framed with leading and trailing edges (Miller 1985).

THE LEADING AND THE TRAILING EDGE OF INTERPRETATIONS

In the framing of interpretations, Kohut described leading-edge interpretations that capture the patient's strivings, the quality of self-experience the patient is attempting to attain or maintain, and trailing-edge interpretations that refer to the dynamic and historical basis underlying the patient's motivations and defenses. Complete interpretations contain both of these edges. A leading-edge interpretation can stand alone for a considerable time in treatment. A trailing-edge interpretation, without recognition of the leading edge, can be experienced as confrontational and injurious by the patient, as an iatrogenic injury. At its best, a trailing-edge interpretation can offer the patient a feeling of being understood, can be felt as relieving and enlightening, and can construct a broader current and historical context for an experience.

A combination of a leading-edge and trailing-edge interpretation, and its consequences, can be illustrated in a case described by Peter Fonagy (1999).

His patient was a depressed, anxious man with pervasive feelings of inadequacy and an arrogant manner. Fonagy found the arrogance enraging. In a session before a weekend break, the patient spoke in a particularly boastful manner, "listing the properties he owned and suggesting that my consulting room could be moved with advantage to one of the large houses owned by the patient" (p. 4). Fonagy interpreted that the patient wanted "me to be close to him over the weekend (the leading edge) and also under his control, so he could avoid the humiliation of having to miss me" (p. 4) (the trailing edge). The patient responded contemptuously that if that had been his intention he would simply have bought the house that Fonagy was in. He said he was quite fed up with Fonagy's monotonous whining—and was considering an extended break from the analysis during the coming week.

In addition to providing an illustration of leading- and trailing-edge interpretations, Fonagy's example highlights the difficulty in choosing one or both of these edges at any given point. Would a more productive interchange have evolved had Fonagy only made the leading edge part of the intervention? The situation would certainly have been different. But would the patient have become so engaged and enraged? And was it to the patient's benefit or detriment that he became so enraged? Was the patient's hostility and contempt, although present from the first moments of the analysis, also called forth and even reinforced by the trailing-edge portion of the interpretation? Was the patient's hostility a reaction to Fonagy's confrontation of the patient's needs and shameful exposure of his vulnerability? Was the patient's contempt an ever-present latent aspect of his manner that would have emerged under any circumstances? Or was it a refreshing experience for the patient to be tacitly recognized as a contender? These are clinical questions and decisions that are relevant to the place accorded to aggression, contempt, and hostility in the therapeutic dialogue.

Leading-edge interpretations have a shady reputation in the psychoanalytic community. At best they are viewed by some analysts as useful in a preparatory phase of analysis, providing support for the patient or temporarily siding with the defenses or the resistances. In self psychology they are positioned on a par with interpretations that aim toward reconstructing childhood experiences, as well as feelings, memories, and contents that have been disavowed or repressed. It is self psychology's use of leading-edge interpretations that has contributed to its reputation among classical, Kleinian, and relational psychoanalysts as avoiding a patient's aggression and as failing to deal with a patient's devaluation, rage, or withdrawal from the analyst.

COMPARING TREATMENT APPROACHES

A case report by Gail Reed (1996) can illustrate the clinical implications of the many differences between self psychology and classical defense analysis, particularly in treating psychopathology rooted in aggressive conflicts. These differing organizing concepts and beliefs point to basically and irreconcilably different assumptions about human nature. In making these principles explicit, I believe, differences can be clarified and sharpened. Furthermore, I believe that at present such comparisons can only be impressionistic and anecdotal. Until such evaluations have been systematically applied, who knows which theory produces the better outcome?

In contrast to self psychology, Reed (1996) adhered to the classical psychoanalytic theory and treated her patient's narcissism as a defense against aggression. "For the better part of five years," her patient "came to each session precisely on time, lay down and recited, in detail and impregnably, the facts of her work situation" (p. 74). The patient spoke little about her private life, brought neither dreams, daydreams, nor for that matter, any irrational thought or behaviors to the sessions. Reed reported that this patient made "*no acknowledgment that I existed*" (emphasis added). "If I questioned the meaning of this dry recital *as an action*, she reacted with high-handed but ever polite frustration. She was doing what she was supposed to do, wasn't she, saying what came to mind?" (p. 74, italics in original). Reed interpreted the patient's behavior as "doing something" to her. This interpretation did not alter the patient's behavior in the analysis, making Reed "feel helpless, frustrated, bored, and trapped by the unending march of details, a victim pinned to the wall by her words" (p. 75). Reed realized that her patient's behavior had "aroused my hostility. . . . If I did intervene, my interventions led to labyrinthine, rationalized discussions during which I felt like a rat trapped in the maze of her narcissistic defenses. . . . I was aware, of course, that these intense reactions were data, something she wanted me or needed me, at some level, to feel" (p. 75).

Contained in Reed's description, understanding, and treatment of her patient is a theory and treatment that provides a clear contrast to the self psychological perspective. First, the patient is described and evaluated from the analyst's perspective. In contrast, self psychology would propose attempting to see the patient and her complaints from *her* frame of reference, a perspective within *her* subjectivity. From the vantage point of the primacy of the patient's self-experience, a leading-edge interpretation of her dry recital might emphasize her effort to secure her safety. Furthermore, she might be understood as dreading to be pulled into a perhaps all-too-familiar irrational world. Reed's wish that the patient present dreams and irrational material could be understood as Reed's contribution to the dry recital, a possible demand that veered the patient even further into her dry retreat. Hence, a stalemate may have ensued. The analyst's pull toward the expression of unconscious material would contribute to the patient's retention of her dry-recital resistance. The repetitive dry recital, although no doubt a behavior with which this patient was quite familiar in other circumstances, has thus also been co-constructed by analyst and patient in the analytic setting.

Second, in her report, Reed emphasizes what the patient does not provide for the analyst. The patient fails to adhere to her analyst's expectations. In contrast, a leading-edge interpretation would mirror the patient's desperate strivings and necessary attempts to protect her vulnerable sense of self.

Third, Reed expected her patient to acknowledge her and thus form an object-related transference. Thus, the selfobject dimension of the transference that the patient *is* attempting to establish is not recognized. The patient attempts to provide the analyst with what she understands the analyst to require of her. It comes across as a compliant, dry recital. But, from the vantage point of the leading edge, the patient's presentation requires acceptance. Not to criticize or dismiss the dry recital but to accept it as the patient's participation in the analytic dialogue constitutes the analyst's contribution to the mirroring selfobject experience. Through its recognition and noninterference, the patient may feel understood, as a totality, rather than having aspects of herself subjected to scrutiny and criticism. The analyst's acceptance of the mirroring selfobject tie constitutes the analyst's participation in its transformation, its depersonification, and its abstraction. The safety and security that is part and parcel of the establishment, and the repair of disruptions in the selfobject tie, then opens up possibilities for the revival and establishment of other affective relationships in the analysis.

Fourth, Reed described her countertransferences of feeling hopeless, frustrated, trapped, and bored. She interprets this as the patient's attempt to arouse the analyst's hostility. The countertransferences she described are typical of those felt by analysts who believe that what they experience is not only a clue to the transference but has been evoked in them by the patient. When an analyst resents being experienced by a patient as fulfilling a selfobject function, the patient's need for the analyst may then be interpreted as an attempt to control, devalue, or negate the presence, aliveness, or goodness of the analyst. From a self psychological perspective, the analyst's ability to tolerate being experienced as a selfobject function is posited to be crucial for the eventual transformation of pathological narcissism.

Fifth, although Reed (1996) states that "classical theory puts us in the humbling position of not knowing anything about the patient's meaning from the manifest content, including the manifest content of the transference" (p. 142), she equates her own manifest experience of feeling "trapped like a rat" as indicative of the patient's motivation. She assumes that how she feels is how the patient made her feel or intended her to feel. However, from the assumption that any experience of the analyst or the patient in the context of the analysis has been organized by both, though not similarly or to an equal extent, the contributions of each participant would be investigated.

Sixth, Reed views narcissism as a defense to be analyzed and resolved. In contrast, self psychology views narcissism as serving vitally needed self-sustaining and self-restorative functions. In the context of the sustained selfobject transference, the patient's narcissism would be expected to evolve from concrete forms to more abstract and depersonified forms. For example, one might anticipate that the patient's rigid self-protection would eventually yield to a greater resilience in her perception of herself and others.

Seventh, from Reed's vantage point, the patient's protestations that she was trying to do what was required of her in analysis were viewed as resistive and an aspect of her character pathology. In contrast, from the standpoint of the leading-edge strivings of the patient, the patient's concretized (Atwood and Stolorow 1984) efforts to comply with and connect with her analyst require recognition. Subsequently, trailing-edge interpretations derived from her associations and the meaning and implications of her specific method of complying and connecting could be investigated.

Eighth, according to classical psychoanalytic theory (Freud 1914b) narcissistic patients are assumed to be unable to form genuine interpersonal relationships. Thus, the patient's positive feelings were suspect. Reed understood her experience of frustration and hostility as a consequence of the patient's projections. In contrast, when these strivings for self integration and selfobject experiences are understood and affirmed as legitimate efforts on the part of the patient to maintain or sustain herself, other (leading-edge) motivations can be investigated with less potential iatrogenic resistance and defensiveness.

Reed concluded her account of this analysis by stating that the patient became aware of who she was, developed stable relationships, married, and gave birth to a child. Numerous somatic symptoms (e.g., dermatitis) decreased or disappeared. Just as classical Freudian or relational analysts cannot argue that a patient treated by a self psychologist would have received a better analysis from a treatment guided by their position, self psychologists cannot argue the reverse. As I will discuss later, in any treatment, analyst and patient form a system, and it is this analyst–patient system that can reveal the processes that account for therapeutic change. My point in contrasting Reed's treatment approach with a self psychological one was to highlight the major differences in assumptions, both theoretical and clinical, and spell out the domain of self psychology, which I explore and enlarge as well as modify.

Reed's treatment of her patient illustrates a theory of narcissism and therapy in which hostility is inferred, and assumed to be concealed beneath positive, idealizing feelings. This inference constitutes one of the traditional analytic assumptions; others are that beneath feelings of inadequacy there is unbridled grandiosity, beneath grandiosity there lies inadequacy, and beneath love there lurks hate. Within this perspective, good psychoanalytic treatment demands that the message is never the message (compare to Lichtenberg et al. 1996, principle of technique, "the message contains the message," p. 94). These assumptions that the patient has concealed rage, envy, and grandiosity, require stringent application. They place the analyst in the role of explorer at best, and in the role of surgeon, onion peeler, or sledgehammer wielder at worst.

In the view of some treatment approaches to narcissism, a patient's self-centeredness and infantile sense of entitlement constitutes an attack by the patient on his or her love objects—past, present, and transferential. On Kohut's couch, such meanings are not ruled out, but must be arrived at in each particular case. However, a patient's expectation of perfection and feelings of defectiveness are not, a priori, viewed as defensive and to be analyzed and relinquished, but as analyzable selfobject transferences. An emphasis on the reactive nature of aggression and on the self-maintaining function of narcissism leads to the view that self-centeredness constitutes a person's striving to attain or maintain a sense of self-cohesion, continuity, and vitality.

Especially when it comes to problems with aggression, there is a close connection between how treatment is conducted and how aggression is understood. However, I do not believe that there is only one treatment approach that emerges from a particular theoretical perspective. The exquisite varieties of human nature, specifically, the variations of aggression, challenge any treatment approach that presents itself as cast in stone. Thus, I believe there is validity to the criticism that self psychology needs to put forward a more comprehensive, coherent view of the variety of functions, meanings, manifestations, and expression of, and defenses against the expression of, aggression in analysis.

The controversy between those following a theory of treatment that assumes innate aggression and those following a theory of reactive aggression will reemerge in the chapters to follow. However, to conflate the legitimate debate over the clinical application of the theory of reactive versus innate aggression with attacks on and criticism of the theory and clinical application of self psychology is a different matter.

Contrary to the opinion of the analyst who said to my patient that self psychologists don't know anything about aggression, self psychology as a theory attempts to neither minimize nor ignore rage. Rather, in its clinical application, the self psychologist strives to place rage into the context of self-experience. Though as a group, we are often accused of needing to be nice and empathic, I react badly to having my theoretical views misunderstood, or worse, distorted. Therefore, I offer a final word to the critics of self psychology, illustrating my reactive aggression. In a footnote in *Civilization and Its Discontents*, Freud (1930) quotes the German poet, Heinrich Heine:

> Mine is a most peaceable disposition. My wishes are: a humble cottage with a thatched roof, but a good bed, good food, the freshest milk and butter, flowers before my window, and a few fine trees before my door; and if God wants to make my happiness complete, he will grant me the joy of seeing some six or seven of my enemies hanging from those trees. Before their death I shall, moved in my heart, forgive them all the wrong they did me in their lifetime. One must, it is true, forgive one's enemies—but not before they have been hanged. [p. 110]

2

The Aggressive Toddler and the Angry Adult

Armed with the fundamental principles of self psychology; the centrality of self experience, empathy, and introspection as tools of observation; the selfobject dimension of the transference; repairing of empathic ruptures and selfobject failures; and the twin edges, leading and trailing; we are prepared to examine the development and analysis of aggressive reactions. When aggression is seen as the well of rage that is part of every human being, there is a parallel assumption that at birth the well is already well supplied. The case for aggression as an innate drive in full swing in toddlers, and the case for aggression as reactive, are illustrated in two vignettes, one from a paper by Anna Freud and the other from the work of Gerald Stechler. Each analyst illustrated aggression in a toddler. First, Anna Freud's vignette from her 1972 critique, "Comments on Aggression":

> Toddlers are not easy to control in groups, since they are extremely aggressive towards each other. To take hold of a toy, food, sweets, to get attention, to move an obstacle whether human or material, or for no obvious reason at all, they will bite, scratch, pull hair, throw

over, hit out, kick, etc. Nevertheless what emerges is not a physical fight between two hostile partners as it would with older children. Instead, the victim of attack dissolves into tears, runs for protection or stands helpless and needs to be rescued. What puzzles the observer is the fact that this attacked child may have been an aggressor himself a short time previously or may be soon afterwards, i.e., that he is by no means without aggression and its tools himself. He has both but is unable still to employ them in the service of defence. [pp. 169–170]

From these observations Anna Freud inferred that aggression develops in a sequence, a developmental line along which the ability to attack others is primary and a direct expression of the aggressive drive. Defending oneself is an acquired response, a defense mediated by the ego.

To Anna Freud toddlers appeared to be extremely aggressive. The primacy of their aggressive attacks is evident in their taking hold of a toy and "*for no obvious reason at all*" (p. 169, italics added) biting, scratching, or hitting another child. The sequence of aggression dissolving into tears is seen as indicative of aggression as primary, whereas aggression as a defense is reactive, learned, and therefore secondary. In contrast, I quote the following vignette offered by Gerald Stechler (1987):

We are in an infant and toddler day care center. On the floor, in the center of a well-lighted playroom, a young but experienced childcare worker is sitting with a newly enrolled eight-month-old girl, Laura. About three feet away a 14-month-old girl, Jane, is also sitting on the floor looking at the other two. Jane has a push-toy with a musical wheel at the end of it. She is moving it with her left hand, slowly and then more forcefully advancing it toward Laura. The worker responds by first positioning her body to protect Laura, and then by reaching out and removing the toy from Jane's hand. As she does this, she says to Jane, "Why don't you do it with your other hand?" At that point she brings the toy around and puts it in Jane's right hand. Jane has plenty of open space on her right side, and starts to push the toy in that direction with increasing vigor. Her facial expression becomes more joyfully excited. Finally she stands up and walks the toy across the room, pleasantly vocalizing. [p. 348]

Stechler described the act of moving the toy as primarily joyful, assertive, and exploratory. Should Laura have appeared as an obstacle in Jane's path, had there been no child-care worker present, Jane would surely have pushed the toy into Laura. At that point Jane and Laura might have pushed each other or cried, as Anna Freud described. To Stechler, however, self-protection is primary and an aggressive attack is a consequence of a misregulated infant–caregiver system in which normal assertion becomes attack aggression.

DIFFERENCES IN HISTORICAL CONTEXTS

Among the numerous differences between these two vignettes are the different models of early development. Stechler's illustration dates from the era of Sander (1977) and Stern (1985), when the empirical studies of infancy had already made an impact on psychoanalytic theorizing. In contrast, at the time of Anna Freud's writing, the most important empirical contributions to early development came from Spitz's (1965) work. In the developmental theory of Spitz, the neonate lived in an "objectless stage, a world in which there is neither an object nor an object relation" (p. 35). Spitz contended that not until about age 3 does a rudimentary ego organization coalesce. Prior to that time, as the neonate is stimulated, energy is discharged in a random and diffuse manner.

Beginning at about 3 months, according to Spitz, the neonate is able to "discharge energy" through more controlled action. Then "directed action proper becomes not only an outlet for the discharge of libidinal and aggressive energy, but also a device to acquire mastery and control. The infant shifts from passivity to directed activity at the stage at which the smiling response appears. The emergence of the smiling response initiates the beginning of social relations in man" (pp. 106–

107). Spitz emphasized that aggressive energy is not limited to the expression of aggression, but serves as the motor of every movement and activity, and of life itself.

This is the essence of the model of aggression from which Anna Freud observed her toddlers, and which still, implicitly and explicitly, underlies much psychoanalytic theorizing and treatment. The crucial assumptions of this model are that aggressive energy refers to a life force *and* is also linked to the expression (discharge) of hostility, rage, sadism, anger, and destructiveness. Furthermore, according to Spitz, aggression as a driving force predates the organization of an ego. It also predates attachment to objects since for Spitz social relations began with the smiling response, not at birth.

When aggression is seen as the motor of life itself, a life force, and is conflated with destructive aggression, survival requires aggression (and sexuality). In contrast, Kohut proposed that survival hinges on the quality of the selfobject tie between the infant and its parents. Kohut thus singled out an inborn attachment motivation as necessary for ensuring survival. Although it may be argued that these two visions of human nature do not have to be either/or, I believe a more encompassing question is: Are these motivations *sufficient* to capture the panoply of human motivations? In the next chapter a number of other basic motivations will be described that are implicated in survival.

Mahler and colleagues (1975) entered the nursery with assumptions similar to those of Anna Freud and René Spitz. They attributed children's early, severe temper tantrums and ambivalent reactions, especially upon loss or separation from the mother, to a too sudden and too painful deflation of their omnipotence. They proposed that trauma from external sources is certainly implicated, but ego development must be such that drive discharge is regulated and effective. They held that ego immaturity characterized by infantile grandiosity can eventuate in the discharge of aggression as a tantrum. For Mahler and colleagues, development hinged directly on the deployment of the aggressive drive and the fusion of libido and aggression.

Using empirical studies of infants and viewing Mahler's films as a point of departure, Karlen Lyons-Ruth (1991) challenged Mahler's formulations and thereby the entire theoretical edifice upon which they were built. Lyons-Ruth concurred with Mahler's stress on the clinical significance of the ambivalence she noted in toddlers. After separation from the mother, Mahler observed, the toddlers would shriek and push away from their mother, bang on the door through which the mother left, collapse on the floor, and cry. But, Lyons-Ruth questioned, "Are these behaviors tied to the mother's 'too sudden deflation of omnipotence' or failure to remain available to the child as a source of comfort and 'refueling' after toddlerhood begins?" Lyons-Ruth suggested that "the anger, distress, and avoidance directed by these infants toward their mothers at 18 months is part of a more deep-seated disturbance of the caregiving relationship" (p. 8).

Lyons-Ruth's (1991) challenge to traditional psychoanalytic thinking about early development goes even further. She noted the conceptual contradiction in the traditional developmental theory of psychoanalysis that infants lack the ability to organize separate psychological representations of self and other, but can keep separate their representations of good mother/self and bad mother/self. She reasoned that it would follow that the ambivalent, angry behaviors of infants alternating with positive behaviors would underlie such early psychological organizations. However, such behavior is not prevalent among infants prior to 15 months of age during the time when split object representations are hypothesized to exist. It is specifically among children at serious social risk that ambivalent angry behaviors become increasingly prominent. Thus, Lyons-Ruth argued that the developmental evidence is more congruent with the notion that, under conditions of adequate caregiver regulation, the infant develops smoothly integrated behavior patterns and representations, involving both positive and negative components. By contrast, when caregiver regulation is inadequate, the infant develops increasingly well-articulated and distinct negative representations of self and other, which are poorly integrated with representations of positive interactions. "Poorly integrated positive and negative representations are not intrinsic to early infant functioning, but a gradual developmental acquisition under conditions of disturbed regulation" (p. 13).

Lyons-Ruth stated that the central difficulty with Mahler's theory of infant behavior during the rapprochement period lies not with her rich behavioral observations but with her failure to distinguish clearly between normative and deviant developmental pathways. In retrospect, that Mahler saw disturbed behavior as normative for a particular developmental period was consistent with the psychoanalytic developmental theory of her time. Typically, early developmental periods were seen as having characteristics of adult psychopathology.

GENDER DIFFERENCES

In addition to the differences in historical contexts and in the theoretical perspectives underlying Anna Freud's and Gerald Stechler's vignettes, there are other noteworthy differences. They embody different philosophies of human nature, different theories of motivation, and different assumptions about the relationship between assertion and aggression. Differences in the gender of the toddlers in the two vignettes may also be implicated. Anna Freud seemed to be describing boys, whereas Stechler's illustration is of two girls.

In discussing the cases included in this book, I do not make gender comparisons. I use selected cases to illustrate specific points, and to do so I use more illustrations from the analyses of men than of women. Although it is possible that inferences about the varieties of aggression are gender linked, I hesitate to use my highly selected anecdotal material to generalize about the relationship between expressions of aggression and gender difference. This is clearly an area in need of rigorous empirical and clinical studies.

I will also leave aside differences in temperament, such as different predispositions to various affective responses. For example, in Stechler's illustration Jane might simply have been a particularly cooperative toddler. In similar circumstances another toddler might have responded more aggressively to Laura and to the child-care worker. However, the point of this disussion is not how to produce happy, cooperative toddlers, but to recognize that whatever transpires in the playroom has been co-constructed. Whatever transpires is an emergent behavior, organized between the toddlers and the present or absent child-care worker.

Anna Freud tells her story from the vantage point of a noninterfering, neutral observer. Gerald Stechler includes the active participation of the child-care worker. In fact, a toddler playroom without an intervening child-care worker might indeed come to resemble the situation described by Anna Freud. In the absence of such an observer-participant, an attack scenario might have been played out. From Stechler's vantage point, however, the attack would not be an indication of primary aggression, but a consequence of an unregulated or misregulated toddler–caregiver system. For example, if the child-care worker's attention to the new girl, Laura, had prompted Jane to try to draw the child-care worker's attention, Jane might have attempted to attack Laura. However, that expression of aggression would then have been reactive and a product of the child–caregiver system.

In Stechler's illustration, Jane was interested in exploring her environment, in her efficacy, and in the pleasure of her adventure. Territoriality and self-assertion did not seem to be top priorities for her. Another toddler, with a different history or temperament, might have been more intent on asserting her dominance in that situation, and a different interaction would have been organized. However, the presence and interventions of the child-care worker would still be crucial in the interaction. She contributed by directing Jane's activities toward exploration and enabling her to enjoy her efficacy, rather than toward facing an obstacle and dealing with a potentially competitive, aggressive scenario. The difference between the two vignettes that I want to focus on is the presence of the intervening observer who co-constructs and regulates the interaction.

The intervening observer makes a crucial difference, both in the playroom and in psychoanalysis, and both in theory and practice. It follows that what is labeled "aggression" and what is observed to be aggressive is crucially dependent on interventions made or not made, their context, and the theory in the mind of the observer, whether child-care worker or analyst.

DESTRUCTIVE AND NONDESTRUCTIVE AGGRESSION

The intertwining of normal and pathological behavior has been a continuing vexing problem in the evolution of psychoanalytic theory and practice. This problem is particularly evident in the theories of aggression so that destructive and nondestructive aggression must be phenomenologically distinguished, and assertion and aggression require disentangling. I now consider the distinction between nondestructive and destructive aggression in the context of Henri Parens's (1979) work. (The relationship between assertion and aggression is considered in the next chapter.) Generally, analytic observations express the preferred theory of the observer. An exception is provided by Parens, who assumed, when he began to study toddlers, that aggression was an innate drive. In the course of his observations, he changed his mind. He emerged from these studies with the conclusion that destructive aggression is reactive for both boy and girl toddlers although expressed differently by these two groups.

Parens wrote within a psychoanalytic tradition that required him to consider the range of "aggression from self-assertiveness through mastery, rage and hate" (1979, p. 99). He reported that his findings were consistent with the reports of psychoanalysts who have argued for an inherently nondestructive trend in human aggression. He recommended that aggression be considered to range from inherently nondestructive to destructive.

Parens characterized nondestructive aggression as "compelling peremptory exploration, examination and manipulation of everything. Its aim [is] the exploration, asserting oneself upon, control, assimilation, and mastery of the self and environment" (p. 101). In contrast to destructive aggression, nondestructive aggression "has a spontaneous origin. From the first weeks of life, the awake, sated infant explores, searches visually more or less intently, in what may be inferred to be his first efforts to control and assimilate the environment" (p. 102).

In his discussion Parens linked the nondestructive form of aggression to self-assertion. A further discussion of the relationship between aggression as reactive and assertion as proactive will be found in the next chapter. Destructive aggression or hostile destructiveness, however, according to Parens, "requires an underlying, excessively felt unpleasure experience for its mobilization" (pp. 110–111).

SELF- AND INTERACTIVE REGULATION

The question of how aggression emerges from a regulated or misregulated interaction is at the heart of studies of self- and mutual regulations. Understanding the bases for assertiveness and reactive destructiveness requires a prior discussion of the regulatory processes that provide the context for these varieties of aggression and assertion. Self- and mutual regulations depict a basic level of interaction patterns that underlie the organization of experience in infancy as well as in subsequent development (Beebe and Lachmann 1988a,b, 1994).

Optimally, self- and interactive regulation between infant and caregiver, toddler and parent, and patient and analyst are in some balance (Beebe and McCrorie in press, Lachmann and Beebe 1996a). In the absence of needed parental responsivity, the developing child may turn to solitary self-regulation. Then the child's expectations may become organized around distinct negative images of self and other. Poorly modulated expressions of aggression will then predominate, as illustrated by Lyons-Ruth (1991).

In infants, self-regulation refers to the capacity to regulate arousal; to activate arousal to maintain alertness and engagement with the world, and to dampen arousal in the face of overstimulation; and to calm or soothe oneself or to put oneself to sleep. Self-touching, looking away, and restricting the range of facial expressiveness are examples of infant self-regulation strategies during face-to-face play. In adults, self-regulation includes symbolic elaborations, fantasies, identifications, and defenses. In infancy as well as adulthood, self-regulation is a critical component of the capacity to pay attention and to engage with the partner (Beebe and Lachmann 1994, Lachmann and Beebe 1996a,b).

Sander (1977) was the first to introduce the idea that self-regulation in the infant is successfully established only through adequate

mutual regulation between infant and caregiver. The ease and intactness of the infant's self-regulation, and the particular patterning of
mutual regulation, both develop hand in hand, each affecting the success of the other.

Mutual regulation is often misconstrued as referring to positive
interaction and mutuality, and as implying a desirable outcome. Instead,
mutual regulation means that each partner's behavior affects, that is,
can be predicted by, that of the other. My colleague Beatrice Beebe and I
thus prefer the term *interactive regulation* since it is less likely to be mis-
used as implying a positive or desirable interaction. Patterns of self and
interactive regulation come to be expected by the infant (Beebe and
Lachmann 1988b, 1994, Stern 1985, 1995). Expecting reciprocal
responsivity, as well as anticipating nonresponsivity, and expecting an
optimal range of closeness and distance in one's interactions, as well as
being, or fearing to be, intruded upon, are all interactively regulated.
Furthermore, interactively organized expectations as well as
disconfirmations of the expected are all represented and internalized.
The processes of self- and interactive regulations lead to developmental
transformations and to therapeutic transformations (Lachmann and Beebe
1996a).

When self- and interactive regulation are in balance, neither pre-
dominates or is exclusive in organizing the dyad's interactions. In this
balance there is a flexible foreground–background relationship between
the two, and interactive regulation is in the midrange, neither excessive
nor insufficient. This balance can be tilted toward either pole. At one
extreme there may be excessive interactive vigilance at the expense of
access to the person's inner state. At the other extreme there may be preoccupation with self-regulation at the expense of engagement with the
partner. When the balance between self- and interactive regulation tilted
toward solitary self-regulation, drastic efforts were required to compen-
sate for the tilt, as in the case of David, below. His treatment illustrates
the necessity for understanding a fundamental problem in self-regulation as a central factor in the development of his hostile, sullen, angry
state, and his propensity to provoke and react angrily.

THE TREATMENT OF DAVID:
SELF- AND INTERACTIVE REGULATION

The treatment of a young adult, David, can illustrate the consequences of an early tilt in development toward solitary self-regulation. Problematic interactive regulations veered David's development toward a singular reliance on self-regulation, and sullen, angry, provocative behaviors, especially toward authority figures.

My first meeting with David was at my last session before my summer vacation. I had informed him of that, and offered to refer him to a therapist with whom he would be able to start to work immediately, should that be indicated. Nevertheless, he wanted to make an appointment. When we met, he was surly, demanding, depressed, and belligerent during the consultation. He asked me to charge him a higher fee than the one I quoted so that he could submit that bill to his insurance company. They would pay 50 percent of the fee, which would then cover the total bill and he would not have to pay anything in addition. When I refused this request he became furious, and called me a hypocrite because he did not believe that I was always this honest.

I suspected that he might have been on drugs. He described his depressions as cyclical and that he was at the moment in one of his lowest troughs ever. He then mentioned his heavy marijuana use, but that he did not consider it a problem.

David was angry at his employer, who pressured him about the deadlines that he had been failing to meet at his work. He thereupon informed his boss that he was quitting, but his boss suggested that he find another job before quitting the present one. He advised David that it was not prudent to quit a job until you have another. Angered, David called his boss patronizing. As the session drew to a close, I suggested that because he was so visibly angry, depressed, clearly unable to function, and suffering, he should have a consultation with a psychopharmacologist. I told him to call me in the fall. Privately, I did not think we had made a great connection, and I did not expect to hear from him again.

When I returned in the fall, I received a call from David asking me whether I would be willing to work with him. Not to be outdone by his sadomasochism, I agreed. At our next meeting a strikingly different David appeared. He was well related, civil, more relaxed, and clearly sober. We agreed to meet twice a week.

This dramatic change in David's manner lasted throughout the entire time we worked together. I discovered later in his treatment that this change coincided with the decrease in his use of marijuana. What remained evident outside of his treament, however, was a provocative version of his hostile manner. In the sessions, I could only see subtle, passive-aggressive manifestations of his angry, sullen side. For example, as we explored his tendency to procrastinate, it became clear that he would almost finish a paper for school and then go through a series of requests for deadline extensions and failures to comply with the extensions, through which he would taunt his professors. In the sessions he reported these "successes" in maintaining his passive-aggressive stance as a way of indicating to me that our work had not altered this pattern.

When David was 11 years old he made a discovery that profoundly affected his life. He, his parents, younger sister, and older brother usually had Sunday lunch at the house of his paternal grandparents. One day as the family sat around the dining room table and talked, David explored the house. He came upon the room that had once been occupied by his uncle, his father's younger brother. The room, long vacant, had been left intact just as his uncle had left it when he moved out many years ago. In it he discovered a treasure trove of pornography, including bondage and sadomasochistic literature. After that, visits to Grandpa and Grandma were never the same. David would sit quietly waiting for lunch to be over. Time passed slowly until he could, unobtrusively, make his way up to his uncle's room to spend the afternoon. Then time flew as he thumbed through the books and magazines.

No one in the family noticed David's absence or seemed concerned about where he spent the afternoon. Typically, no one paid attention to him, and his secret was never discovered. These visits continued until his early teen years. They provided a seamless transition into a fantasy life to which masturbation was added. His masturbation fantasies were derived from the imagery of the books and magazines he read.

In his fantasy life, David identified with the women. He imagined himself dressed in silk clothes, highly desirable, and subjected to torture, bondage, and discipline. His view of himself as an alluring, sadistically treated woman stood in stark contrast to his daily life. There he felt and appeared masculine, although he increasingly became a severely depressed, angry, and rebellious young man. His academic potential and intellectual resources were constantly imperiled by his debilitating depression and obstinate procrastination of academic requirements, but mostly by his sullen, angry defiance toward authority.

David was born with impaired hearing, which was not recognized by his parents. It was not corrected until he was about 5, when the impairment was recognized in school. Until that time he also had speech problems. David stated that, according to his mother, she and he developed a private sign language. This communication did not develop into a substantial intimacy with his mother, but was probably more associated with her neglect of his actual problem. When David recounted this material, halfway through the first year of therapy, we characterized his early life as isolated and lonely. In addition to his hearing and speech impairments, he had to make sense out of his experience and feelings, mostly on his own. As a result of the school's attention to his problems, he was given speech lessons and reading remediation, and a myringotomy was performed, in which a hole is created in the tympanic membrane to drain fluid from the ear. His hearing and reading improved rapidly, as did his speech. To this day a very slight speech impairment is noticeable. However, most important, regulation of states of over- and underarousal, and organizing his experience became his task, alone. A tilt toward solitary self-regulation in the absence of participation by his family characterized his early development. Solitary self-regulation was reinforced and repeated throughout his later development and eventuated as his characterisitc seething, hostile withdrawal.

Going to school had been anxiety arousing for David from the start. He recalled daily, early morning stomachaches. To deal with his anxiety, he developed a "curative" self-regulatory ritual. He would set his alarm

clock to awaken him two hours before he needed to get up in the morning. A portion of these two hours would be spent watching the clock. By
watching the clock he felt he could slow down the passage of time. He
said, "You know it works. When you watch the clock, time does seem to
pass more slowly." Watching the clock, slowing down time, succeeded
in restoring his sense of mastery. His anxiety decreased and his stomachaches vanished.

David's experience in his uncle's room brought together a number
of prior themes, which reinforced his solitary self-regulation. That is,
David had found a way of arousing and stimulating himself, and escaping from his feelings of resentful isolation and aloneness. The extent to
which he felt that time dragged as he waited to enter his uncle's room
and the speed at which time raced as he examined the pornographic
literature contributed to his feeling that he could control time.

In the opening weeks of therapy, before I had learned of his visits
to his uncle's room, David questioned my trustworthiness. At this early
time in the treatment, I could only connect his question about my trustworthiness with his concern that he would be left alone. Could he trust
me to watch out for him, and make sure that he did not undermine
treatment? Later, I could understand his worry about me: Would I get
off my chair at the dining room table and find out what he was doing
upstairs? Would I offer him some concerned engagement, or would he
repeat with me his experience of abandonment to his own strained resources? Yet, his characteristic defiant stance, it seemed to me, also expressed some hope of countering abandonment by provoking others to
attend to, react to, and thereby acknowledge him. I understood him to
be striving to engage me in his solitary, massive self-regulatory efforts.

The leading edge of David's sadomasochistic fantasies pointed toward their function as self-regulators of affect and arousal, as attempts to
self-stimulate as well as self-soothe, and attempts to dispel his isolation,
chronic anger, and gloom. In singling out and interpreting David's self-
regulation, the more familiar trailing-edge dynamic formulations, for
example, the presumed unconscious implications of his behavior, are
placed into the background. These include his subtle expressions of contempt for and hostile behavior toward authority figures. In the fore-

ground are aspects of self- and interactive regulations that are often taken for granted.

The salient needs that evoked no response from his parents are depicted in his fantasies. That is, the fantasies depicted a highly responsive interactive engagement in which David as a provocative woman evoked hostile attention, which he found sexually arousing. At the same time the fantasies provided David with the means for self-regulation of arousal. In fact, they provided him with a readily obtainable self-administered antidepressant. The fantasies contributed to David's sense of himself as unique, important, and desirable. They served as David's precondition for functioning in the world, outside of his uncle's room.

David had spent most of his childhood in states of friendless withdrawal, angry depression, and preoccupation with regulating his equilibrium by himself, slowing time to stave off anxiety. We believed this to be the precursor of his sullen withdrawal states characteristic of his later years. Once he found his uncle's pornography, the "cure" for his depression resulted in overwhelming, unmanageable overstimulation. Maintaining some separation between the uncle's room and the outside world became urgent. How to deal with the intensified swings in his feelings, always by himself, became his ongoing, self-regulatory challenge.

David reported that his parents were primarily self-absorbed; secondarily they were absorbed with each other. The children came last. By the time he reached adolescence, David was not sure that obtaining his parents' interest was preferable to being ignored. However, his description of his family reflected the extent to which his relationship with his parents left him feeling very much alone. He expected to be unseen, unheard, and abandoned to his withdrawn and isolated state.

David's pattern of solitary self-regulation organized our relationship as well. He anticipated that I, like his parents, would be primarily self-absorbed, and if I did think of him, it would be to criticize him. In light of this, he spoke in a reportorial manner, observing himself without what I would have thought of as self-reflection. I think of self-observation as characterized by a colder and more dispassionate self-view. Self-reflection would be more affectively varied. In fact, the most visible affects in David were depression, chronic unhappiness, and a low level of anger.

In treating David, I had in mind certain assumptions that have been proposed by Loewald (1980) and Kohut (1971) and that were later articulated from a different theoretical perspective by Fonagy (1991). I believe that each of these authors contributed to an elaboration of the interactive context that is crucial for understanding the extent to which solitary self-regulation can lead to aggressive reactions becoming dominant in a person's life. What Fonagy has added to Loewald and Kohut is the importance of feeling oneself to be in the mind of the other as a constituent of interactive regulation.

Loewald held that the mother, in interactions with her child, maintains a somewhat more organized picture of the child than characterizes the child at that particular moment. She thereby furthers the developmental process. With respect to analyst and patient, Kohut suggested that the analyst must necessarily hold a slightly more organized, better integrated view of the patient than the patient holds. In the eyes of Kohut and Loewald, the mother as well as the analyst provides a context of responsivity in which a sense of direction and a feeling of self-integration can develop. In Kohut's and Loewald's terms, David needed a partner who could see him, hold him as he is, and simultaneously hold a somewhat more cohesive, continuous, and positive picture of him (Stolorow and Lachmann 1980).

At the time I treated David, I was not yet familiar with Fonagy's (1991, 1999) work on the link between having experienced oneself in the mind of one's parents and the development of a self-reflective capacity. That David felt his parents did not hold him in their minds emerged implicitly in the course of his treatment. His desperate attempts to counter his anxiety and depression by himself from an early age on, through fantasy and pornography, can be linked to his sense that he was neither felt, seen, nor heard by his parents. A deadening of self-experience followed, leading him to attempt to buttress a sense of visibility and to provide self-cohesion through aggressive outbursts and sexualization.

When David began therapy, he also began graduate studies. He described involving his professors in his very private struggle. He succeeded in evoking their concern: Would this bright student who participated in class get his work in on time? David explained that indirectly he would be saying to the professors, "Fuck you," but simultaneously, to himself, "Work!" He added, "I always need to find the Achilles heel, and provoke. I can't survive in a context in which the right response to 'Jump' is 'How high, sir?'" The similarities between this behavior and the sadomasochistic fantasies became obvious to David and me. That is, he provoked his professors so as to engage them in a sadomasochistic relationship, just as he tried to do at various times in the therapy. His professors had the power to discipline him and he, as the student, was tied up in a helpless position. He then regulated his heightened arousal, anger, and defiant triumph through his withdrawal and by calming himself through detachment. Eventually, the arena shifted to an internal struggle in which he defied authority and would become depressed and self-loathing. To combat his depression and isolation, he would once again try to enliven himself by calling upon his sexual fantasies.

David and I noted the parallels between his behavior with his professors, his sexual fantasies, and his presentation of his provocative procrastination in the therapy. I focused on his need to maintain self-control and his dread that were he to relinquish it, he would be ignored. I said to him that to ignore the sexual fantasies implicit in this pattern with his professors would smack of a repetition of his earlier experience that no one cared what he was up to. Now, as then, he would be abandoned to solitary overstimulating experiences. But to link his behavior and his sexual fantasies too closely by assuming an underlying well of rage that has been sexualized as well as turned against the self would place the fantasies at the root of his difficulties in school. The extent to which he relied on his fantasies as his major or perhaps sole source of excitement might then be in jeopardy. Through his fantasies, David felt alive, passionate, and, at least temporarily, not depressed. I interpreted the sexual fantasies, their role in his procrastinations, and their function in his affective life.

Had I stayed only with the sexual fantasies, David and I would have come close to enacting either his sadomasochistic fantasies or his early abandonment experiences. I would have become the authority who deprived him of his self-control as well as the sadistic figure to whom he wanted to submit. We would have come close to his feeling sexually gratified, enraged, and humiliated. As I learned later, this is what he had expected, and it would have led us into a stalemate with which he was familiar. Had I pursued the fantasies without acknowledging the dilemma that we were facing, we might have tumbled headlong into an enactment that would have iatrogenically evoked aggression.

David could appreciate the dilemma I outlined. He thought that to pursue the issue of his fantasies might be "interesting, and would probably not affect the fantasies very much." Through my description of our dilemma, I attempted to convey to David my sense of him as potentially capable of setting priorities for his sexual and academic needs and motivations, in short, able to initiate, organize, and integrate his experience in the context of our dialogue. That is, I attempted to convey my sense of his potential self-regulatory capacity in the context of our ongoing interaction.

A thread of continuity can be drawn from David's lonesome clock watching and procrastination in grammar school, and his solitary self-regulation in his uncle's room, to his current writing blocks. David concurred, "I have to do it alone. That was certainly true then." Amplifying on the extent to which he felt neither seen nor heard by his parents, he added, "I could not have risked involving my parents because they might not have responded and I couldn't risk finding out." David was clear in his expectations of nonresponsivity. He had resolved to handle things on his own so as not to risk being disappointed.

For David, expectations of nonresponsivity led to his reliance on self-regulation of affect and arousal. Repeatedly he felt unattended to, exploited, and manipulated. In reaction, he sharpened his argumentativeness, an asset when he engaged in controversy, but a liability when his argumentativeness shaded into hostility and led to defiance or procrastination, as occurred in his oral presentations in school.

Toward the end of the first year, David's finances were still quite limited. He had counted on a one-year teaching assistantship for the following year. In spite of "shooting myself in the leg" by delaying applications past the deadline, David was offered a one-term assistantship.

His procrastinations were not as blatant as they had been, and although he had handed in his application for the position past the deadline, it had not been unreasonably late. The one-semester assistantship he received was in recognition of the good work he had done in the class of the professor he would be assisting.

With regret, David spoke of having to cut down to one session per week, but promised to "run the figures again" to see if anything could be done. When I raised the issue a few sessions later, he told me that he could only come once a week; more frequent sessions would not be financially possible. I said, "Well, we'll have to talk as fast as we can." He responded by telling me that he felt criticized. My comment ruptured the selfobject tie that had slowly been engaged. By this time in the treatment, however, David could initiate restoration of the tie by telling me that he felt hurt. He heard me say that I thought he had not been making good use of the time. We explored his reaction. He was reminded of his unpleasant experience with the psychiatrist whom he had seen briefly before he began treatment with me. I told David that I was glad he could tell me directly how he felt, rather than handle his hurt feelings as he did with the psychiatrist, by leaving precipitously.

In a subsequent session David and I came back to the interchange that had left him feeling criticized. I had not wanted to explain or excuse my comment. Nor had I wanted him to feel his response was inappropriate or excessive. When I felt that we had restored our dialogue, I told him the context of my remark. I had thought he might have known it, but he did not. "A man and a woman were dancing at a resort and one says to the other, 'Do you know this is costing us $18 per hour?' The other answers, 'I'm dancing as fast as I can.'"

David laughed and said he enjoyed my telling him this story. He then proceeded to tell me about the origin of a Yiddish word. I asked him about the meaning of his story. He told me that he had just learned about this derivation and thought I might be equally interested. He added, since I told him a story, gave him a present, he wanted to give me one. He called it a "reciprocal communication." In my story I alluded to David and me dancing together. In his story he indicated that we share a common background. We are both Jews. David's treatment ended after about two and a half years when he received a fellowship for graduate studies that required his relocation to another city.

AFTERTHOUGHTS

In retrospect, David's difficulties could have lent themselves to the theory that narcissism precludes a capacity for object relationships. He was a loner and very much engaged in a fantasy world in which he was an object of intense desire. The treatment implications of this view would have pointed toward an essentially confrontational stance vis-à-vis his fanatsies and behavior. David actually had expected me to take that path, and we discussed that he was prepared to stymie me had I done so. But, more important, since I do not believe that a link between self-absorption and social withdrawal coupled with a private grandiosiy is invariably found, I saw no basis for assuming such a connection in David's treatment. Rather I assumed that the more competent he felt about managing his own states, the less he would feel compelled to withdraw into his fantasies and defiant behavior. I had not used the language of interactive regulation in working with him, so his "reciprocal communications" came as a surprise to me. He formed a relationship with me without my having directly pushed for it.

David's life was suffused with the consequences of his propensity to react provocatively and to withdraw. In his life he provoked anger and disappointment toward himself through procrastination and his pointedly defiant behavior, by shooting himself in the leg, as he termed it, by inevitably just failing to meet deadlines, work requirements, and school assignments.

As in the nursery described by Anna Freud, I noted the absence of intervening observers in David's development. The therapeutic process itself became the crucial carrier of a necessary interactive engagement. In this process, through establishing a balance between self- and interactive regulation, self-regulation became somewhat less burdensome for him.

Following Kohut's theory, I kept track of David's self-destructive, passive-aggressive, and provocative behaviors, by consistently exploring what he needed to do to enliven and soothe himself. I focused on his difficulty in maintaining self-control and his struggles in self-regulation. Without mentioning it in the course of our work, David had clearly cut down on his use of marijuana considerably. His self-regulatory problems were probably increased by his decision no longer to use marijuana as an affect regulator.

Shifting the balance between self- and interactive regulation was not directly addressed in the treatment. Rather, the quality of our engagement was a nonspecific aspect of the treatment process and served as a context for his increasing self-regulation of affect. David's social withdrawal diminished as he joined schoolmates in sports and other activities. Thus, by the end of the second year of therapy, David was able to offer me a "reciprocal communication."

3

The View from Motivational Systems Theory

Empathy, my attempt to understand David's experience from within the context of his life, provided my entrée into his difficulties in self-regulation. In my description of my work with him, in addition to the selfobject dimension, I also illustrated a second dimension of the transference without labeling it, a representational dimension. This dimension, akin to Stern's (1983) self-with-other, referred to the revival of experiences, feelings, and expectations in the analysis that were associated with his uncle's room. In this chapter I elaborate these dimensions of the transference further. Both dimensions organize the analyst–patient interaction, the context, and the role of empathy in enabling the analyst to understand this context. The context is further fleshed out, transformed, and broadened through the use of "model scenes." I also address another criticism of self psychology, that it lacks a theory of motivation.

In the post-Kohut self psychology literature, aggression continues to be viewed as reactive. Simultaneously, the context in which aggression has been evoked continues to receive increasing attention. Rather than a "well of rage" residing solely within the patient, or an inborn aggressive propensity, the focus is on the context, and a prime candidate for the context in which rage emerges is the analyst–patient interaction. It provides the analyst with the most immediate access to this context.

THE EXPERIENCE OF AGGRESSION

In their elaboration of Kohut's views of aggression, Paul and Anna Ornstein (1993) have proposed that clinically, we can only meaningfully consider the *experience* of assertion, anger, or rage. These affects and affect states are embedded in a broad context, which must be understood, in each instance, from the empathic vantage point. They offer the illustration of an analyst who interviewed a Vietnam veteran who had killed, in cold blood, suspected Vietcong. From his empathic vantage point, the analyst said, "'It must have been a horrifying experience to watch people die at your own hands.' Whereupon the veteran responded, 'Doctor, you don't understand, I was in ecstasy at those moments. I had an orgasm!'" (p. 104).

How a person experiences his own aggression may not always be captured precisely by an analyst. But, the Ornsteins argue, when the analyst places him- or herself into the patient's subjectivity, the patient might then feel that the therapist has made an effort to understand the nature and meaning of the experience. If the analyst's empathy is off the mark, then the patient can put the analyst on the right track, in this instance, by explaining how he experienced killing others. The analyst's empathic grasp is thereby increased and the patient will be better understood. However, as we explore later, being off the mark, particularly in the direction of *underestimating* a patient's murderousness and sadism, can be experienced by that patient as an enraging lack of understanding on the part of the analyst.

Analysts, I believe, are far better able to enter a patient's experience of vulnerability, rejection, frustration, and neglect than states of grandiose excitement, expressions of sadistic abuse, and vindictive intentions. When we are off the mark, as was the analyst described by the Ornsteins, we may be experienced by patients as needing to see them in a positive light, as though we are saying, "You should have felt scared" or "Normal people feel scared under such circumstances." In this sense the empathic stance is not neutral, but tilts in the direction of normalizing what a patient has presented to us. This is the side of empathy with which the critics of self psychology have had a field day. I will return to this issue later.

In another post-Kohut contribution, Stolorow (1994) focused on aggression as intersubjectively organized in the analytic dyad. In that context it signals obstructions of, or disturbances in, the selfobject transference. Stolorow described a treatment in which he illustrated the importance of emphasizing the restorative, vitality enhancing aspect of aggression, in contrast to the view of aggression as reflection of a shattered sense of self.

ASSERTION AND AGGRESSION

Since the distinction between aggression, which itself can be self-enhancing, and assertion can become blurred, their relationship becomes an important focus for study. For Stechler (personal communication, 1997), assertion becomes aggression in the course of development through "contamination." That is, the child's joyful assertiveness evokes responses from caregivers that label the child "aggressive" or frustrate the child so that he or she becomes more attacking and destructive. Stechler reports, "Focusing on unraveling the contamination between assertion and aggression often works well. The patient's experience of this process is that there is nothing inside that needs to be eliminated or overcome. Both assertion and aggression are legitimate and natural developmental processes. The only problem is that the two have become entangled to their mutual detriment."

For Stechler, the therapeutic process entails the disentangling of assertion and aggression, and freeing each to return to its legitimate developmental function. That is, assertion is restored as a proactive tendency to make oneself felt in the world and to accomplish one's aims, while aggression serves as a primordial protective reactive tendency in the face of threat. The thwarting or frustration of one's assertivness can be felt as a threat and trigger an aggressive, self-protective reaction.

To illustrate the contamination of assertion with aggression, we might imagine two babies in a home in which the caregivers are overly concerned with dangers from objects such as table corners, dirt, and germs. One baby is very energetic and an avid explorer of the surround. The caregivers are often alarmed by the potential dangers that might befall this infant and convey their concern. The infant begins to feel that to explore the environment and to intrude into it is dangerous. The infant feels thwarted and gets angry. In addition, exploration takes on a connotation of "bad," and expectations of being thwarted are organized. The other baby is quiet, low-keyed, and self-contained. He looks around and takes in the world through the eyes and other senses. That baby will have a vastly different experience in that same family. These two illustrations also suggest that in addition to different patterns of exploration and assertion, different experiences of feeling thwarted and responding angrily or withdrawing will be organized. Based on the interactions with respect to activity levels and their consequences, these two babies will have qualitatively different attachments to their caregivers. Like the ripples made by a rock dropped into a pool, how assertion and exploration are handled within an infant–caregiver dyad impacts all aspects of the infant's (as well as the caregiver's) life.

The elucidation of and distinction between assertion and aggression is clinically important. This distinction has also been central to the extension of self psychology through the theory of five motivational systems (Lichtenberg 1989, Lichtenberg et al. 1992, 1996). A summary of the theory of the motivational systems will provide the necessary background for further discussions of the relationship of assertion and aggression.

THE FIVE MOTIVATIONAL SYSTEMS

Joseph Lichtenberg, James Fosshage, and I (Lichtenberg et al. 1992) distinguish between motivations that are organized to express the *need for* assertion and exploration, and motivations that are organized to express the *need to react* aversively by antagonism or withdrawal. Based on the self psychology literature, our clinical experiences, and our reading of a host of empirical studies of infancy, including the work of Stechler and Parens, we also considered assertion and reactive aggression separate and distinct primary motivations. We proposed that they have different developmental origins, are experienced differently, and serve different functions in our lives.

Exploration and assertion are activated by the many, varying levels of stimulation in our environment. For example, the push-toy that figured so prominently in the play of Jane and Laura in Stechler's day-care center (Chapter 2) can activate the curiosity of a toddler and promote mastery through exploration, and efficacy pleasure through assertiveness. In adults, assertion and exploration can be experienced as invigorating challenges that enhance self-experience and vitality. A tennis game with a worthy adversary or a trip through unknown territory can both provide a sense of heightened excitement and be a source of pleasurable tension. In psychoanalytic treatment, experiences of exploration characteristically involve the joint efforts of both therapist and patient in a therapeutic alliance (Greenson 1965, Stone 1961, Zetzel 1956). Expressions of assertion can engage both analyst and patient in an "adversarial relationship" (Lachmann 1986), which can be exhilarating for both participants so long as it remains within tolerable bounds.

An adversarial relationship may be sought by a patient in treatment after prolonged periods during which the patient experienced the treatment as a comfortable, responsive, supportive "holding environment" (Winnicott 1960). Such experiences of feeling attuned to or merged with the analyst can solidify the analyst–patient bond and enable the patient to seek further stimulation through self-assertion and exploration. A patient's need or readiness for such an experience may be ushered in by a complaint and challenge to the analyst: "I want to know what you think about a current political issue," or "I envy my friend who fights with her analyst," or "Perhaps I should go into group therapy. I need to know how other people think of me." In these assertions a patient may be indicating an increased tolerance for differences and a readiness to be taken as a viable adversary or competitor. In these circumstances, as in a well-matched tennis game or debate, each participant feels better when the game is demanding rather than if one wins due to the weaker playing of the other. The readiness to risk competition leads to the possibility of deriving a sense of vitality through an adversarial relationship. It indicates that the patient feels strong and competent enough to risk asserting opinions contrary to the therapist's, or exploring aspects of the therapeutic relationship and the therapist's personality that are challenging or may make the therapist uncomfortable.

Motivations to assert oneself and explore one's surroundings including the dimensions of the analyst–patient relationship are enhanced when these actions are met with responses that confirm that the patient has reached the status of a worthy opponent. These actions on the part of the patient alter the analyst–patient relationship and thus the context, the environment, in which the treatment is conducted.

Assertion and exploration are associated with affects of interest, joy, excitement, exhilaration, and mild, pleasurable anxiety. Their expression enhances the selfobject dimension of the patient's transference. In contrast, aversiveness is reactive but not necessarily to selfobject failure. For example, a feather landing on an infant's face can evoke an aversive reaction of pushing the offending feather away. That is, aversiveness is a reaction to a perceived threat to the integrity of the individual. It includes self-protective reactions, such as an attack aimed at destroying or driving off the perceived source of the threat. It is associated with the affects of fear, distress, and anger, and is particularly responsive to those instances in which a person feels endangered.

Of the three additional motivational systems, one system is organized around needs to regulate physiological arousal and regulation, such as sleep, nutrients, elimination, and tactile and proprioceptive stimulation. Another system is organized around needs for attachment and affiliation. A third system is organized around needs for sexual excitement and sensual pleasure.

Each motivational system is based on a specific inborn need and an associated pattern of response. Each system exists in a state of dialectic tension both internally and with the other systems, and undergoes continual hierarchical rearrangement. The five systems develop interactively through self- and interactive regulation with caregivers. Comparable motivational systems exist in the parents, enabling them to respond to their children. These systems are irreducible, primary motivations that organize the sense of self, and are in turn organized by it. One factor that interferes with an individual's capacity to maintain a balance among these five cooperating, conflicting, or competing motivations is the massive activation, early in life, of the need to react aversively.

The terminology used in describing varieties of aggressive behavior is replete with ambiguous, confusing, and overlapping terms. I adhere to the distinctions proposed in the motivational systems. Aversiveness is reactive and includes antagonism and withdrawal. I use the terms *antagonism* and *aggression* interchangeably to emphasize that aggression, unlike its use in drive theory, is considered to be reactive. Furthermore, in using these terms interchangeably I emphasize that self psychology does deal with the same phenomena that other psychoanalytic theories deal with, but makes different assumptions about their origins and treatment. Included under the rubric of aversiveness and antagonism or aggression are a variety of nuanced reactions such as provocativeness, hostility, anger, rage, and outrage. Aggressive reactions are designed both to remove a felt threat to the self and to restore a sense of pride and self-esteem.

In any act of aggression the person may perceived him- or herself to be in danger, and therefore rage, in words or actions, can invariably be linked to a felt threat. In many instances, this formulation is not only developmentally accurate but also clinically relevant. Analytic interventions to this effect may even resonate with the patient and be felt to be on target. Yet, as a phenomenon, it is sometimes hard to justify aggressive behavior as obviously reactive. Furthermore, this formulation can also lead to treatment problems and be felt by the patient as off the mark, as in the Ornsteins' illustration of the doctor who thought he had grasped the Vietnam veteran's experience of killing.

Whether the analyst's empathic response is on target or off the mark may turn out to be a matter of trial and error. In the case of the Vietnam veteran, the doctor learned from the patient where his empathy was off the mark. Although trial and error frequently leads to a better empathic grasp of the patient's experience, the construction of model scenes provides a more elegant entry into the patient's experience. Model scenes are an instance of elaborating a broader context, constructed by analyst and patient, for embedding a patient's reactions of antagonism or withdrawal.

MODEL SCENES AND SCREEN MEMORIES

A bridge between the theory of five motivational systems and experiences described by a patient is achieved when patient and analyst co-construct model scenes. Here are some examples of model scenes: David thumbing through his uncle's collection of pornographic literature, both fearing and wishing that someone would find him; a young girl, feeling guilty because she believed she caused her horse to be killed, conflicted about whether to remain with her horse or permit her parents to feel that they are protecting her by taking her away from having to witness the ordeal; a young boy, sitting on the toilet, straining to "produce" while fearing his production would be inadequate.

Model scenes integrate a patient's past experience, capture a character style, clarify previously puzzling information, organize the narratives and associations of the patient, illuminate role enactments and the organization of the transference, and focus further explorations of the patient's experience and motivations. Model scenes can be derived from a variety of sources, such as a patient's associations or an analyst's metaphor, that center on a theme from literature, whether Sophocles, Shakespeare, or the psychoanalytic literature. Frequently a patient's memory, a dream image, a conscious or unconscious fantasy or pathogenic belief, a long-standing conflict, or an expectation of the patient can lead to the construction of a model scene. Thus, model scenes simultaneously describe a current state of affairs in the analysis, and shape, influence, limit, or enhance the patient's organization of experience. They contain the subtleties of fantasy and defense, and offer an evocative context that includes transferences and adaptive resources through which to explore the patient's experience. Model scenes entail significant communications from the patient about his or her life, and can epitomize a significant traumatic or developmental experience.

By participating in the construction, interpretation, and working through of model scenes, an analyst accesses a variety of sensory modalities—visual, auditory, and kinesthetic. Whereas the patient is embedded in a past that may color the present as grim, and the future as bleak, the analyst conveys a perspective in which time is fluid; the present is constructed, the past is metaphorically reconstructed, and the future is up for grabs. The very presence of the analyst with a differently constituted perspective sets up an inevitable tension (Lachmann 1998, Loewald 1980) in the analytic dialogue. This tension provides *perturbations* between repetition and transformation (Lachmann 2001), and between hope and dread (Mitchell 1993) that, in turn, provide the impetus for therapeutic action.

Model scenes can be distinguished from screen memories. Screen memories are vivid scenes whose surface content or subject matter is understood to be rather nondescript. For example, a patient's recollection of the shape of a doorknob may conceal a repressed memory of what was observed behind that door. Screen memories focus on what has happened (Kris 1956). Model scenes pay equal attention to what is happening in the analysis at that moment.

> Screen memories are created by the *patient* to depict an indifferent lived experience in order to prevent (defend against) the coming into awareness of something regarded as disturbing to know. In contrast, model scenes are created by *the analyst and patient together* to depict something previously unknown from a reconception of what is known. The purpose of screen memories is to conceal and obscure; the purpose of model scenes is to give full and complete affective and cognitive representation to obscure repetitive configurations of experience. [Lachmann and Lichtenberg 1992, p. 122]

Model scenes include the body, that is, bodily sensations and experiences, in a way that has not always been sufficiently acknowledged in analytic interventions. The physicality of model scenes provides an important dimension to all treatment but especially in work with the more difficult-to-treat patients whose histories include abuse and trauma, and where inhibitions, anesthesia, dissociation, and numerous ways of privileging or nullifying physical experience is a frequent consequence. A model scene can capture the complex web of circumstances that precede, include, and organize the aftermath of crucial themes of the patient's experience, thereby placing bodily experience in a relevant context.

A caveat before I illustrate the application of motivational systems theory and model scenes in action. When we go to the theater, we really don't want to see the ropes that pull up the scenery or the machine that produces the smoke. Similarly, an analytic case should not directly reveal the theory that organized it. However, since I am both illustrating theoretical constructs, motivational systems, and model scenes, and differentiating theoretical constructs from other theories, some visible staginess in the cases presented is inevitable.

THE TREATMENT OF NICK: MODEL SCENES

The treatment of Nick illustrates the contributions to psychoanalytic treatment from motivational systems and model scenes in the analysis of aversive reactions, rage outbursts, and withdrawal. Typically, Nick's rage would burst forth when a salesperson in a store was less than competent or efficient, when a co-worker was less than cooperative, or when a boss was unreasonably demanding. When he purchased an item in a store, and had to wait while the cashier chatted with another salesperson, Nick yelled at her, "You could do the world a favor if you developed terminal cancer!" Before and during the initial years of our work, Nick's hostile outbursts cost him numerous jobs. While rushing along the street, he was once jostled by another pedestrian. He became so outraged at this man that he followed him, and tried to trip him. Ironically, he tripped himself, and broke his ankle. The other man, unaware that he had been the target of the tripping, immediately turned around and came to Nick's aid, adding humiliation to Nick's injury. This level of rage was not expressed toward me in the course of his analysis. His closest expression of rage erupted when I did not have his insurance form ready. Even then his rage toward me appeared in a more muted form. The analysis of Nick illustrates the therapeutic value of embedding rage and withdrawal in a context, a model scene, to capture its reactivity, as well as the trans-formative effect of leading-edge interpretations.

When he began analysis, on a three-sessions-a-week basis, Nick was 36 years old. He described himself as despondent, socially quite fearful, and frequently "hysterical." He elaborated this term later as his outbursts of self-defeating rage. As Nick spoke in our initial meeting, he cried. He said, "I don't know if I can take care of myself." The model scene to be described centers on this doubt.

Nick is homosexual. When he began treatment, he was living with Jeff, whom he described as emotional and possessive. Prominent in the opening phase of the treatment was the question of whether or not to leave Jeff. Over the course of the treatment their relationship solidified.

Nick is the fourth of five children in an Italian Catholic family that lived an economically marginal existence. His father was a quiet, retiring man. His mother appeared to have been severely depressed and fre-quently nonfunctional. In the first year of the analysis, Nick's rage at his mother escalated. Shortly before beginning treatment, Nick had revealed his homosexuality to his family. His father said, "As long as you're happy." The other members of the family responded with mixtures of disbelief, pity, and horror.

In his developing years, Nick was very much of a loner, both at home and outside. He felt shunned and mocked by his siblings because he was the brightest and because he was unlike the other family mem-bers. He increasingly withdrew into a seething, sullen state. During his adolescence Nick tried to emulate the heterosexuality of his older brother by playing high school football. At his graduation he was named "the most unassuming athlete of the year." Occasionally he dated girls and had sex with some, but he had no sexual interest in them. In college, he became actively homosexual.

In the course of his analysis, Nick spoke about his longing for a father who would be his ally in the family, protect him, lead him, as well as admire him and approve of him. However, in relation to his father he felt repeatedly disappointed, unsafe, and unsupported. He felt he could never quite relax.

In his current life, Nick described pervasive feelings of shame, humiliation, anxiety, and rage, which began in his childhood. Scanning the surround became crucial in predicting and avoiding further humiliations. Nick's anxiety often reached extremes in which he experienced himself as rageful, out of control, and "hysterical." What he described as his "hysteria" we came to understand as derived from his inability to control his bodily states and later his affect states. Affect states were felt as physical, sexual tensions that he could not regulate, either by containing or expelling his feelings. He felt unable to soothe or enliven himself. These difficulties in self-regulation had led to impulsive rageful behavior.

I found Nick emotionally open and easy to relate to. His anguish was quite palpable. He had a raucous sense of humor, which occasionally broke through his clouds of despair. At those times I would respond in kind and, for a while, we were able to sustain a playful tone in the session.

An early version of the "I don't know if I can take care of myself" theme appeared in the first year of treatment. As Nick lay on the couch he would twist and turn from side to side as he bemoaned his inability to·talk. He did not ask for my help, but berated himself for his failure to do what he thought I required of him in analysis. I was puzzled by his increasing fear of being criticized and rebuked by me. I thought he was bringing in relevant material. However, he continued to insist that he failed to live up to what he believed to be my expectations of him in the analysis. In this context, his early problem in bowel control emerged in bits and pieces.

At about age 5 and continuing until he was about 7, Nick had occasional accidents in school. He defecated into his underwear, and upon returning home hid his underwear behind a closet. Initially his mother threatened him with enemas unless he exercised better control. Later she ordered him to sit on the toilet and "make" to prevent future accidents.

As Nick associated and recalled these memories, I could easily imagine his experience and its significance, and I could understand its impact. I articulated its details, and we further investigated and explored it. I could imagine Nick, unable to control himself, fearing humiliation from his classmates, shamefully slinking home to hide the evidence. As Nick communicated his toilet trauma, including the physical sensations, I focused on the meaning of these experiences for him and explored their wider implications. My (empathic) grasp and articulation of his experience constituted one of my contributions to the co-construction of the model scene. Analogous to infant and caregiver co-constructing and transforming the infant's (and the caregiver's) experience in development, Nick and I embarked on the process of co-constructing the context for his rage flare-ups and sense of helplessness—"I don't know if I can take care of myself."

Though the underwear "disappeared" after a while, no one expressed much concern about the basis for his accidents. One of the signals the accidents sent, "I need someone to take care of me," was not responded to by anyone in the family. In squirming on the couch, Nick conveyed his bodily, physical discomfort as well as his terror of me as the enema-threatening mother who was angrily demanding immediate productions. We then elaborated this model scene as it organized the transference: Nick's sense that he could not control himself, his terror at having to reveal his shameful behavior or worse, having me discover it, and his expectation of my criticism and fear of me. Given these underlying expectations and dreads, he did not expect help, nor could he ask for it. His wish that someone respond with help and understanding remained concealed.

The model scene depicted an elaboration of his early experience organized as a hierarchy of motivations. Viewed from the perspective of the motivational systems theory, these motivations were an inability to control physiological requirements, leading to shameful withdrawal and outrage; and a sacrifice of self-assertion to conform and accommodate himself to secure some place within his family. Feeling that he could not regulate himself and could not take care of himself, he needed someone to take care of him.

I said to Nick that he seemed to feel on the couch the way he did as a child sitting on the toilet—obliged to produce, straining to comply, enraged about the effort required, feeling criticized for the insufficiency of his productions, and ultimately feeling defeated. I singled out and embellished various aspects of his toilet trauma as analogous to his experience in treatment. I described the physical sensations, the twisting and turning that I noted, and connected these to his general difficulties in self-regulation. In addition, I said that while he had to produce in the toilet, his brother was urinating on the floor of the room they shared, and his depressed mother had let the home become squalid through her neglect and her inability to throw out the newspapers that had accumulated over the years.

The link I make between Nick's early development and his analysis as an adult is not based on a continuity of content. Rather, it is based on analogous experiences in his analysis and experiences prior to, as well as including, the toilet trauma. The patterns of Nick's early experience that predated the toilet trauma at age 5 included escalations of distress and alternations between his mother's lack of interest and her intrusiveness. These early interaction patterns between Nick and his mother are embedded in the model scene. Early interaction patterns may be subsumed within model scenes derived from later phases of a person's life. The analysis of these model scenes then includes their precursors.

Nick and I related this toilet trauma model scene to his doubt as to whether he could take care of himself, his fear of my reaction, his pervasive sense of shame, and to his feeling so pressured to produce material in the sessions. The accidents conveyed his sense that his body might betray him just as it had in school in his childhood. He felt that he could not rely on his own regulation of his physical requirements. His bodily states were overwhelming and mysterious, and could prompt acts of shameful self-expression. To the extent that the accidents were intended as expressions of assertion and defiance, they failed. Rather they succeeded in reinforcing his feelings of impotence.

Producing material in the sessions was also encumbered by his wish to please me and his fear that he would produce "shit." He expected his failure to lead to humiliation. He anticipated that his efforts and accomplishments as an analysand would not be recognized. Thus, the model scenes on the toilet brought together three major themes: (1) a repeated childhood experience, (2) a characterological style (reacting self-critically and resentfully dependent), and (3) transference expectation that included being pressured and humiliated.

Let us first consider the repeated childhood experience. Nick's toilet memories stem from about age 5, the age at which these experiences presumably came into preconscious organization. Its precursors were noted in earlier experiences of maternal intrusions and impingements that set the tone that Nick's privacy, feelings, and safety were of no consequence to the members of his family. The accidents concretized the battle between Nick and his mother in which interactive regulation was characterized by her domination and his submission, albeit with rage, terror, and a desire to retaliate. A sense of efficacy and mastery that would ordinarily be derived from self-regulating bodily functions was thereby subverted. Derailed interactive regulation brought about self-disregulation, and in turn self-disregulation contributed to further de-railing interactive regulation. Although Nick had conscious access to some aspects of these memories, he was not aware of their general, per-vasive effect, and their particular contribution to his conviction that "I don't know if I can take care of myself."

This leads us to his characterological style. Nick's habitual style of organizing his experience was to blame himself for any failures, and to react self-critically and antagonistically, and eventually to withdraw. Through withdrawal, although with poorly suppressed rumblings of anger, he could find a place for himself in his family, with his partner Jeff, as well as in his work relationships. Acceptance was sought, though never really achieved, at the sacrifice of his self-assertion and autonomy. The elaboration of the model scene clarified that he placed himself in resentful, dependent positions in relation to those people he needed to take care of him, since he felt unable to take care of himself.

This model scene contains specific transference expectations. Nick's expectations and dreads, as these emerged in the transference, encom-pass more dimensions of our interactions than is included in the selfobject concept. His selfobject needs were clearly in evidence, but so were the more traditionally encountered transferences of parental relationships. Whereas selfobject needs define one dimension of the transference, my colleagues and I (Lachmann and Beebe 1992, 1998, Stolorow and Lachmann 1984/1985) have proposed a two-dimensional view of transference. In this view, a selfobject dimension and a representational dimension of the transference occupy a figure–ground relationship.

Beatrice Beebe and I (Lachmann and Beebe 1992) initially referred to this dimension as representational configurations of the transference, linking it to Stern's (1985) concepts of self-with-other and representations of interactions that are generalized (RIGs). We shortened the concept to the *representational dimension* of the transference (Lachmann and Beebe 1998). Distinguishing between the selfobject and the representational dimensions of the transference is important in treatment because they address different functions and different qualities of experience. The selfobject dimension includes the experience and maintenance of the tie to the analyst, and the requirements for cohesion, articulation, and vitality of the sense of self. The representational dimension refers to the qualities of self and other and the themes of their interrelationships. The term is intended to encompass those transferences that are usually referred to as "object related" (Bacal and Newman 1990).

Both dimensions of the transference are represented, and contain repetitions of past experiences as well as the seeds for their transformation. The representational dimension provides the context for selfobject experiences, and, in turn, selfobject experiences provide access to representational configurations. Although the representational dimension is shaped by the transactions of important relationships, it also is shaped by the person's efforts to construe experience in such a way that vital selfobject functions can be derived.

These two concurrent transference configurations were already evident in the early phase of Nick's analysis. Nick dreaded and expected that I, like his terrifying mother, would consistently be dissatisfied with his productions and humiliate him for the inadequacy of his performance. This expectation was the representational transference that oscillated, sometimes in the foreground, sometimes in the background, as

Nick tried to find the supportive, protective father he longed for. That longing, a striving for the idealizable father in whose presence he would feel cared for and protected, constituted the selfobject dimension of the transference. The function of this idealizing selfobject transference was *not* to provide Nick with the assurance that I will take care of him, although he may well have felt this at times. Rather, it was to construct a context through which Nick might develop, initially in connection with me, but later on his own, the ability to take care of himself. This idealizing selfobject tie was in the background when the impinging, intruding, enema-threatening mother loomed in the foreground.

The following excerpts from a series of sessions in the first year of Nick's treatment illustrate the engagement of the toilet trauma model scene. In these sessions, the themes of "I don't know if I can take care of myself" and rage at feeling disappointed appeared directly and indirectly. In my interventions I attempted to accompany his affect states, recognize his anxiety about his inability to take care of himself, understand his rage and distress, and articulate parallels between his experience with me and his toilet trauma. The content of my interventions addressed the repetitiveness of his past experiences in the present. In recognizing, articulating, and thereby accompanying his affect states, I added my presence to his previously solitary experiences. Accompanying Nick's affect states is analogous to state sharing, and affect and arousal entrainment as described by Stern (1985). As described in the empirical infant studies, I made no attempt to match the level or intensity of these states. In accompanying the contours of his affects and providing continuity in our affective connection, I altered the repetitive nature of Nick's experience. By accompanying Nick's affect states, I co-constructed a new context, a repetition with a difference, in which his aversive reactions could lead to new expectations. That is, the analyst–patient interaction can constitute a new context that contributes to the transformation of aversive reactions.

Nick said, "I'm trying to be a good boy, responsible, wondering why you thought I should go on the couch. It's a good idea. How did you know? I like dealing with my shit. I take these shits. It keeps coming out. Like when I was little and I couldn't wipe it all off. I can't get it all out. If I don't get it all out, it'll be a mess. I can't get off my ass and I can't get clean."

Picking up on Nick's wish to be taken care of, I said, "You would like me to tidy it all up?" Nick responded, "I don't want to do it, I want to have it all done for me.

In a later session, Nick said, "I couldn't say I was enraged about your not having my insurance form ready, then you won't help me. I do believe that. I want to beat the shit out of you. It's a long time from Thursday to Tuesday. If I'm angry, it's easier to be away." I pursued Nick's attachment to me and his fear of alienating me and said, "It's hard for you to be away from me." Nick responded, "I guess so. I'm not getting enough already and to be away for two weeks—even though I'm going away and I know that."

In a subsequent session Nick complained, "It takes me so long to do things—like defecating." Again I responded to Nick's need for me and his fear that like his mother I want him to produce now, specifically with respect to the analysis. I said, "And I will lose patience?"

In a still later session Nick complained, "I'm resentful of this whole process. Why do I have to come here? I'm boring you anyway. Why don't I give us all a break? I don't like it because it's hard. Effortless is okay. Work is a struggle, discomfort, anxiety, and that I might not be able to do it. It's like twisted shit." I said, "That's the worst kind!"

I responded to Nick's twisted shit reference, rather than to his resentment and anxiety because these communications were repetitions of his characteristic self-devaluation. The twisted shit was a new way of describing his painful process of production, and with some humor. Thus, his repetitive recital of his resentment was momentarily transformed by him.

The foregoing segments from the four sessions in the first year of the analysis track a facet of our work on the model scene. I believe that Nick's potential for rage was intertwined with our joint exploration of the model scene. Exploration of the model scene was sufficiently novel so that the more usual triggers for Nick's rage were not set off. I attempted to maintain an ambience of safety (Lichtenberg et al. 1996, Sandler 1960) for Nick as I acknowledged his need for me, his anticipation of alienating me, his concern that he is wasting my time, and his fear of my losing patience with him. I empathized with his rage at having been and even now being required to take care of himself.

Nick's comment that he wanted to "beat the shit" out of me, even though in the service of diminishing his conflicted need to be taken care of by me, reflected his current analytic experience and its similarities to his mother. He felt safe enough to reexperience feeling pressured, but could now include his rage at being compelled to comply. He could convey his rage directly rather than through his bowel movement accidents.

The analysis made requirements of him similar to his past, but the joint analytic work militated against its rigid repetition in his current analytic experience. Previously, he felt obliged to suppress rage; now his rage could be included. An ambience of safety facilitated the pathway to accessing affects and motivations that had previously been inaccessible.

In the course of these sessions, Nick's imagery of bodily states became more blatant. I contributed to the co-construction of these images and metaphors by resonating with them and thereby amplifying them. The manner in which Nick and I played with words diminished his fear of being humiliated by me. He was able to talk about his fear and rage, rather than act aversively. Previously, he would become withdrawn in the course of a session. Thus, Nick's actions of rage and expressions of need became more pointed. But most important, his self-reflection also increased. For example, he could tell me how angry he was about not getting enough from me, but was also aware that he was the one going away.

I assumed that we had constructed a safe-enough ambience that enabled him to express his wish to "beat the shit" out of me, a side of his conflicted need to be taken care of by me. Thus, in pursuing the exploration of the model scene, I paid attention to the current organization of the threatening-mother transference, and the retention of an idealizing selfobject (background) experience. That is, I understood that Nick needed to see me as powerful and in charge so that through his connection with me he could feel protected. But it is not the function of the idealizing selfobject tie to provide him with the feeling that I will take care of him. Rather, its function is to provide the context, which can enable him to develop the feeling that, initially in connection to me, and later on his own, his ability to take care of himself can develop. In addition, Nick could explore the extent to which he felt invaded and pressured to produce and to conform, as well as to investigate his rage as a reaction to these feelings.

By maintaining an ambience of safety, I contributed toward enabling Nick to access previously inaccessible, shameful material. In my interventions I attempted to recognize and maintain a connection with Nick's helplessness, frustration, and anger, as well as with his longings to be cared for. In tracking Nick's affect, rather than pursuing a particular content, I continued to maintain a connection with him in the present as he relived his past frustrations and humiliations.

In presenting the treatment of Nick and the excerpts from these sessions at a psychoanalytic conference, questions were raised about my responding to his "twisted shit" with "that's the worst kind." In my response I certainly did not investigate Nick's experience or fantasy about producing twisted shit. I accepted and even empathized with his difficulty in expelling it. Doesn't Nick's twisted shit depict a fantasy of hostile, malevolent inner forces that torment him? Isn't his twisted shit a depiction of his unconscious rage that could damage him and could even damage me? Not to investigate the twisted shit reference, I was told at the conference, may ignore an important entry into Nick's unconscious fantasy life. How did the shit get twisted? Or, as some analysts wanted to find out, who is represented by the twisted shit that is so painful to expel? Had I explored the twisted shit as an alien or introjected bad object, or as a derivative of an unconscious fantasy, a different session and indeed a different treatment would certainly have evolved. I would have addressed Nick as the ingestor of bad objects and the producer of twisted shit. Most important, I would have veered away from Nick's current productivity in the analysis. After all, he *was* struggling on the couch and in fact did succeed in talking, associating, and producing material. And, in his twisted shit comment, he no longer repeated his past trauma.

TRANSFORMATION OF NARCISSISTIC
RAGE THROUGH HUMOR

There was an even more important reason for my "that's the worst kind" intervention. In addition to Freud's (1905) discussion of the relationship between humor and the unconscious and Reik's (1935) emphasis on the role of surprise in analysis, Kohut (1966) proposed that both creativity and humor constitute transformations of archaic narcissism. He held this to be relevant in the course of development and by implication in the course of an analysis. Fonagy (1999), in discussing the process of change in psychoanalysis, stated that "the analyst performs the function of the object who enters the child's pretend play, creating a transitional sphere of relatedness [in which] humor is often a critical and underrated component" (p. 24). I believe that in our humor, Nick and I shared a similarity, or perhaps a potential similarity. I refer specifically to how we have each transformed, or can transform, our narcissistic vulnerability and potential for narcissistic rage.

In the course of Nick's analysis there were many humorous exchanges, instances in which I responded to Nick's imagery with humor rather than by reducing his occasional light touches to psychoanalytic rock bottoms. These noninterpretive comments and enactments have been receiving increasing attention in the psychoanalytic literature as the "something more" and "now moments" (Stern et al. 1998) that are crucial in therapeutic action and thus in transforming experiences. Wallerstein (1986) referred to these events as "turning points" in treatment. Beatrice Beebe and I (1994, Lachmann and Beebe 1996a) conceptualized such interactions as heightened affective moments that have an organizing potential far beyond the brief time that they take up. An analysis without such "disciplined spontaneous engagements," as Lichtenberg, Fosshage, and I (1996) termed these interactions, a treatment in which the analyst invariably responds with technically correct interventions, an analysis in which the analyst attempts to avoid any semblance of an enactment, an analysis devoid of improvisations, is likely to be deadly. Such an analysis can turn the patient into a cadaver like his analyst.

The kinds of interactions I have been describing are usually thought of as occurring on the level of procedural knowledge. Stern and colleagues (1998) argue that therapeutic action depends on something more than interpretation, a process in which each partner, analyst and patient, learns something new about what it is like to be with the other. These moments may be short in duration of time but they are crucial for the future of the dyad. These moments are an emergent property of the analyst–patient interaction, of what I will later discuss as the analyst–patient system.

With respect to the dynamics of Nick's analysis, I viewed this phase of the analysis as Nick bringing in his dirty underwear rather than feeling compelled to hide it. From my point of view, Nick was not soiling me. Through our interactions and his sense of me as a steady presence, he gained increasing self-control over his "soiling." Through the procedures of our interaction, implicit in the work on the model scene, his self-regulation in retention and expulsion increased. In addition, needs previously constricted through the dominance of aversive reactions were now becoming increasingly more available for analysis. These included Nick's needs for physiological regulation, as well as for assertion, exploration, and attachment.

The work with the toilet trauma model scene diminished Nick's distrust, as became evident in his ability to reveal more shameful and guilt-laden experiences. In a series of sessions that followed, more aspects of the "I don't know if I can take care of myself" theme were taken up. Nick spoke about stealing money from his mother's purse at ages 9 and 10 and stealing money from his father's cash register with which he bought an artist's easel. He hid the easel behind the same closet behind which he had hidden the soiled underwear, which, by that time, had mysteriously disappeared. I thought, "Where dirty underwear was, there a painting shall be," and in the session I said, "It was your secret hiding place for self-expression. The dirty underwear was replaced by a paint set." Nick continued, "I wanted to learn things on my own. To get away from my parents. I was so frightened. But if I learn it on my own, it can't be taken away from me."

I noted a shift in the theme that Nick felt he could not take care of himself. He now included the prospect of learning. Motivations associated with assertion and exploration had been dominated by fears of losing self-regulatory control. As these fears waned, he envisioned acquiring mastery and greater efficacy, and taking matters into his own hands. He accused both parents of not adequately taking care of him. Defecating into his pants and stealing their money was an indirect message to them, a defiant accusation. It was concealed by him and ignored by them. I reframed Nick's narration to underscore his attempts at self-assertion, mastery, and control. In his response, "I wanted to learn things on my own," he continued the theme that I had underscored—striving for agency. Simultaneously, the rigidly organized, stereotypic view of his family, a parallel to his unidimensional self-perceptions, became more shaded.

The work on the toilet trauma model scene contributed to a major renovation of Nick's past. His stereotypic view of his parents and of himself began to shift. In his daily life, his relationship with Jeff stabilized. In the analysis, we branched out from the initial scene that depicted Nick and his mother to an elucidation of Nick's dilemma—longing for a father on whose strength he could rely and dreading the humiliation and disappointment that would come should he count on his father's support.

The material of the subsequent sessions centered on the father he wanted and also on remembering the mother who in spite of her limitations did get things done. For example, she made sure that all the children went to college. Childhood experience and fantasies, together with his reactive rage, suspicions, and expectation that he is in danger of being humiliated, were woven into a rich and complex tapestry. The work on Nick's dilemma continued. His father had accepted him but could not provide the strength he needed. To ally himself with his father meant that he would remain ambitionless as well as in constant danger of humiliation. His mother was terrifying to him, but she was a source of ambition. Nick hated his own ambitious strivings because they reminded him of his mother's destructiveness. Summarizing much of the previous material, I offered a trailing-edge interpretation, "Unless you can turn me from the father you wanted into the mother you feared, but who was ambitious, nothing much can happen." By that time sufficient prior work had enabled Nick to recognize that his work difficulties were a consequence of his rage at his own ambitiousness, which he felt was a legacy of his mother.

Initially in the analysis, Nick tried hard to be "a good boy." Although he was afraid to show how enraged he felt toward me for not being sufficiently attentive to him, this feeling came through in subtle ways. For example, he would tell me he feared that if he showed he was angry at me for not having his insurance form ready, I would not like him or take care of him. The model scene contained his sense of not being taken care of as a child and led to the broadening of Nick's self-experience. His sense of himself expanded from a restricted view as an uncontrolled, unrecognized, unwanted "soiler" to a recognition of himself as affectively resourceful, a more assertive person who could acknowledge concern for others. A consequence of this joint work on this model scene (as well as other model scenes that we constructed in the course of the analysis) was that the therapeutic process itself engaged Nick, the solitary soiler, in a collaborative production over a lengthy period of time.

His emotionally unresponsive family and the ambience of deadness this created compromised Nick's development from the vantage point of the self and the five motivational systems. His mother's periodic depressions and his father's benign aloofness prompted Nick to withdraw from attachments. He anticipated that attachments, no matter how much he desired them, would be unsatisfying at best and lead to humiliation at worst. As attachments and affiliations became increasingly strained, assertion and exploration became increasingly suffused with fear and shame. Self-expression and exploration became ever more private and confined to the realm of masturbation and fantasy. His affective life became increasingly disregulated as his social withdrawal increased. Beginning in early childhood, the need for regulation of physiological requirements was sacrificed in an imperative attempt to wrest emotional responsiveness from his parents. Sexuality was drawn into the service of self-enlivening, to cement attachments, and to provide an antidote for depleted feelings, boredom, and anxiety.

AFTERTHOUGHTS

The concept of "the broader context" is illustrated in the analyses of both Nick and David. For David, the broader context referred to his recognition of the extent to which he had been relegated to solitary self-regulation throughout his development. Furthermore, he began to grasp the implications of his repetitive experiences of over- and underarousal. His most familiar childhood state was his seething, hostile withdrawal. For Nick, the broader context contained his sense of alienation from familial relationships and his strivings for recognition and to be cared for. These themes converged for Nick. He felt pressured to "produce" to gain approval, but needed to defy to express resentment. In consequence, his productions were ill timed, which deprived him of the acceptance and caregiving he sought. Instead, he found the very humiliation he so dreaded. His most familiar childhood state was one of sullen withdrawal.

Detailing Nick's self-organization through the motivational systems illustrates the clinical applicability of the motivational systems theory, the complex interplay of his competing motivations, and the extent to which aversive motivations became dominant, overshadowing and restricting other needs. Reassessing Nick's self-organization after six years of analysis reflects the extent to which numerous difficulties in self-regulation had been concretized in his struggle with bowel control. Over time, producing in the analysis became increasingly more spontaneous. Affective swings and sexual impulsivity diminished so that neither his health, physiological regulation, attachments, nor his relationship with Jeff were compromised. Ambitious strivings, especially in the work area, were gradually less and less encumbered by his attempt to maintain a low profile to avoid humiliation. Simultaneously, ambitiousness, the legacy of his mother, stirred up his rage at her and at himself for wanting to be ambitious.

In presenting the analysis of Nick at a conference, I was told that I completely missed the role of anal sadism in his treatment. Such a line of interpretation, I believe, would neglect the interactive nature of Nick's problems with aggression and would re-create in the analysis the circumstances that led to his feeling that he cannot take care of himself: his difficulties in self-assertion, and his propensity to react "hysterically" through outbursts of rage.

Toward the end of his twelve-year analysis, I asked Nick if I may use some aspects of our work in a paper I was writing. He agreed and asked me what the paper would be about. I said that it would be about model scenes. He asked me to explain. "Oh," he said, "you mean how you toilet trained me?" Although we had not used this imagery in several years, his experience of our work on the model scene had evidently remained fresh in his mind. I asked Nick how I toilet trained him. He said, "I had never made the connection between what you take in and what you shit out. I kept pushing all these feelings down, and I couldn't shit out. What really helped me was that when I had trouble talking to you, the stance you took was that it will all be okay. I translated that to when I sat on the toilet. I used to sit all hunched over and tense. I just sat back and it really happened. It made a difference. That's how you toilet trained me."

In those years that I described, I noted that indeed he did speak more readily in the analysis. But I did not know that he had, on his own, made the connection to his actual toilet behavior. I had not literally investigated his "twisted shit" experience. In retrospect I am glad that I had left him in charge of his own bowel movements. On his own he connected our therapeutic interactions and his increasing ability and confidence in self-regulation of physiological requirements.

Nick also described the gradual diminishing of his rage reactions at salespeople and others. He said that he just doesn't feel that enraged any longer. Over the course of the years he reported run-ins with people with less and less frequency. He told me that our discussion about his getting so enraged because he does not feel recognized by these people, as he felt ignored within his family, was very helpful to him. I had described him as the "disciplinarian to the world, enforcing good manners, efficient behavior, and trying to clean up messes and messy behaviors." It was what he had wished his father would do to his mother, make her tidy up their house and herself. Needing to be recognized became less concrete, and he succeeded in finding ways of gaining and accepting recognition through his work, his efforts, and his ingenuity.

4

State Transformations in Psychoanalytic Treatment

In my discussion of David's provocative withdrawal and Nick's outbursts of rage, I focused on our interactions and their effect on the pervasive, current states of these patients. David's most familiar childhood state was a seething, hostile withdrawal. Nick's most familiar childhood state was one of sullen withdrawal. For both, these states lingered into adulthood with some variations. In addition, both described rage outbursts, which grew out of, and were reactive to, injuries, rebuffs, and experiences of abandonment. Both had felt rejected and ignored by their families. Attention to and exploration of their aversive reactions (rage and withdrawal) as these states appeared in the analytic relationship placed these reactions into the context of the analytic interaction, empathic failures, and selfobject ruptures. For both, self-reflection was increased to the extent to which they felt understood by me and became increasingly more understandable to themselves. Their reactivity to the slings and arrows of everyday life became less rigid and their self-cohesion was thereby increased.

My grasp of David's experience during and after his discovery of his uncle's pornography, and of Nick's experience during and after his school accidents, enabled us to place these experiences into the contexts from which the withdrawn, angry states evolved. Unlike the Ornsteins' vignette of the soldier who became orgasmic when he killed, and for whom the interviewer's empathy missed the mark, in these cases, immersing myself in the patient's experience promoted our joint construction of model scenes that captured those experiences. But it did more. It shed light on subtle triumphs and defeats, bodily states, and affective nuances that enriched our understanding of their current interpersonal difficulties. As I understood our analytic encounters, for both patients solitary self-regulation was drawn into the analytic interaction. It thus became less solitary as it became part of a new context. A process was set in motion whereby alterations of the sense of self contributed to the transformation of rigid, dominating aversive states. As David and Nick relived aspects of painful past experiences in the treatment, the lopsided imbalance between solitary self- and interactive regulation shifted toward expectations of reciprocity. For example, for David, the dominance of aversive motivations and solitary sexual excitement decreased as other motivations, such as attachment, assertion, exploration, and regulation of physiological requirements gained in prominence. For both patients, seeking sexual excitement lost its compulsive, driven quality.

Although therapeutic action is not limited to the role of transformations of self-states, this dimension of therapeutic action is of particular relevance in the treatment of pathology that derives from developmental misregulation of antagonism and withdrawal. This chapter considers transformation and self-states in more detail.

THE TRANSFORMATIONAL MODEL

A transformational model recognizes that in the interaction between child and environment, and patient and analyst, each one affects the other, so that from one point in time to the next neither the child nor the environment, neither the patient nor the analyst, remains the same. Since each has influenced the other, each shifts the other and each is shifted or transformed. Analyst and patient potentially reorganize themselves and each other from one point in time to the next (see Sameroff 1983 and Sameroff and Chandler 1976 for a detailed discussion of the transformational model). Transformations are neither immutable nor permanent since there is an ever-present dialectic between repetition and transformation. In this discussion, however, I emphasize transformations, and consider repetition and its dialectic later.

Even though transformations may not be permanent, they do affect subsequent interactions. Thus, for example, early interaction patterns between the child and the environment, through which reacting aversively by antagonism and withdrawal is organized, can be subject to later transformations and reorganizations through the interactions of analyst and patient.

In the process of development, self-regulation and interactive regulation are concurrently organized in the infant–caregiver dyad. Whether they are in balance or not, interactive regulation impacts and thereby transforms self-regulation, and alterations in self-regulation impact interactive regulation. Beatrice Beebe and I (1994) have proposed that this model applies to the child–caregiver and to the patient–analyst dyad. Early patterns of interaction between child and caregiver have been called representations of interactions that are generalized (RIGs) by Stern (1985). RIGs provide the basic building blocks for later symbolic elaboration of early interaction patterns. After the first year of life, with the advent of symbolic capacities, transformational and repetitive experiences continue to be jointly organized through self- and interactive regulations.

Transformations can be understood to be in a dialectic with repetitions. Each one functions as a check and a balance against the other. If repetition prevails, the present can become a rigid replica of the past. If transformations go to an extreme, a person's life can become chaotic.

Traditionally, analytic practice has emphasized that we must be alert to ways in which the past is being repeated, rather than remembered (Freud 1914a). Repetition, as in the compulsion to repeat, was accorded the status of a drive, part of the endowment of living matter (Waelder 1936), and placed in the service of ego mastery (A. Freud 1936), sense of guilt, and the need for punishment (Fenichel 1925, Freud 1924). In consequence, technical recommendations for psychoanalytic treatment have emphasized the necessity for analytic concern about the manner in which self-defeating patterns tend to be repeated and enacted in subtle variations and guises (Ferenczi 1919). Analysts search for such repetitions in both the transferences and in the patient's personal relationships.

The transformational model reminds us that transformations can be ever present in all behaviors, even in repetitive acts. We are alerted to the way in which patterns of behavior can include slight shifts and subtle transformations of the past, as well as the extent to which they are replicas of the past.

The dialectic between repetitions and transformations can be discerned in the analyst–patient interaction, as well as in the patient's dreams and associations. Observing this dialectic in a patient's development and experiences (the continuing processes of repetition and transformation), recognizes the significance of post-infancy events in a person's life. For example, for both David and Nick there were numerous precursors to their predominantly repetitive self-defeating patterns, but decisive experiences at ages 9 (David) and 5 (Nick) organized their repetitive nature. These experiences decisively transformed patterns of experience in the direction of greater rigidity and an increasing propensity to anger, either through erupting "hysterically" or behaving provocatively.

In the case of David, repetitions were noted in the similarity between his sexual fantasies and his provocative and self-defeating behavior toward his professors. He repeatedly placed himself in a vulnerable position where he could be criticized, found inadequate by "shooting myself in the leg," as he described it, through his procrastination. In presenting this material to me, he also attempted to engage me in enacting his sadomasochistic fantasies in the transference. I described the dilemma we faced when we discovered the similarity between his fantasies and his behavior in school and in treatment. In describing our dilemma, I repeated neither the stance of the sadistic object of his fantasies nor the familiar parental pattern of ignoring or rejecting him. I indicated to him that these were twin dangers that we now faced. I attempted to engage him in an interaction that was novel for him, thereby to harness his activity and cooperation. His customary passivity, withdrawal, and defiance could not be avoided since, as was true for Nick as well, passivity, despair, defiance, and hostility were, to him, familiar and enduring. Nick and David knew themselves because they had become accustomed to these repetitively experienced states.

Tilting toward repetition or transformation in making interpretations, although ideally based on the patient's material, may still rest on the analyst's bias.

> A young woman was considered to be extremely fragile by her family. As a child she often avoided unpleasant social and school events by claiming to have some physical symptom. Her family rewarded her by accepting these excuses. Later she developed a series of complaints that she did experience as physical. Although her family continually tried to dissuade her from participating in various events because of her fragility, in adolescence and young adulthood she forged ahead in spite of some physical discomfort. In the course of her therapy she developed an intense preoccupation with transient aches and pains in various parts of her body. Were these physical symptoms a repetition of her place in the center of her family? Or was she taking the focus away from her family and watching *herself* rather than continuing to be the object of their anxious attention? Was she taking a step toward, although not yet having arrived at, a more autonomous position?

Clinical material may be ambiguous and the analyst's clinical judgment will be drawn in. Whichever direction the analyst tilts can have a transforming effect on the patient's preoccupations and symptomatology. To be understood as repeating an old pattern in order to remain as the focus of her family is quite different from being described as struggling to take matters into her own hands and to free herself of her family's anxious eyes. However, there is a danger in the opposite direction as well. To be described as struggling to free herself while she feels tied to the constraints of her family may convey the analyst's failure to grasp the patient's painful experience. Clearly a clinical decision is required here, and in circumstances like this it is important that one or the other options are not closed off because the analyst holds to a theory that privileges repetition over transformation or vice versa.

Kohut (1966) discussed transformation, specifically with respect to the developmental line of archaic narcissism. He postulated unrestricted grandiosity and the child's expectation of perfection in the parents as characteristic of early childhood. However, he did not place object relations at the end of the developmental line as did Freud (1914b). Early in his theorizing, Kohut proposed two separate lines of development, one along the dimension of archaic narcissism to *object love*, the other from archaic narcissism to higher forms of narcissism. From its origins, early forms of narcissism were gradually transformed, in the course of favorable developmental circumstances, into "man's creativity, his ability to be empathic, his capacity to contemplate his own impermanence, his sense of humor, his wisdom" (p. 446). He conceptualized these transformations as a gradual, developmental process that was furthered by caregivers' phase-appropriate attunement with minute, tolerable disruptions. Analogously, the analyst's attention to disruptions and the ongoing undisrupted process of treatment provide the stuff that transformations are made of.

Whereas Kohut placed transformations into a broad trajectory of development, Sameroff and others described the minute transformations and repetitions that characterized the moment-by-moment infant–caregiver interaction. Kohut's proposal, geared toward analytic treatment and favorable developmental circumstances, adds a wide-angle view to Sameroff's close-ups. Together they offer a rich picture of the complexities of transformations in development and in the dialectic between transformation and repetition in the treatment process.

Recognition of this dialectic is of particular importance in the treatment of pathology in which aggression dominates. An analytic stance that privileges either repetition or transformation carries the danger of contributing to the patient's experience of feeling wounded, frustrated, and misunderstood, and then becoming (secondarily and reactively) enraged in the treatment.

STATES AND SELF-STATES

The term *self-state* draws on contributions from two sources: Stern's (1983, 1985) and Sander's (1983a,b) discussions of state transformation and the self-regulating other, and Kohut's (1980, 1984) discussion of self-states as they are depicted in self-state dreams.

"State" in the empirical infant literature (for example, Wolff 1991) refers to variations in sleep and wakefulness that occur as the infant passes between states of distress and crying to alert or quiet activity, to drowsiness and sleep, between wet discomfort and dry comfort, and between hunger and satiation. Different states affect how things are perceived, how those perceptions are integrated, and how such information is processed (Hofer 1990). These states of alertness, arousal, activity, and sleep are socially negotiated, a product of infant–caregiver regulation (Sander 1983a,b). Sander suggests that the earliest self is organized around the infant's recognition of recurrent, predictable transitions of state in particular interactive contexts. Sander thereby lays the groundwork for linking one's sense of self with one's affective-physiological state.

Stern (1985) uses the term *self-regulating other* within the context of mutual regulation. Although he acknowledges the role of the infant in this regulation, Stern emphasizes that it is the caregiver who regulates the infant's states of arousal, affect intensity, and security of attachment. "The infant is with an other who regulates the infant's own self experience" (p. 102). According to Stern, early state transformations accrue to both self-regulatory capacity and to the expectation that interactive regulation can facilitate or interfere with these transformations. In psychoanalytic theory state changes have generally been associated with drive satisfactions. For example, being fed when hungry has been assumed to lead to an infant's attachment, a libidinal cathexis of the hunger-drive–satisfying object.

Various clinicians and researchers (for example, Ainsworth et al. 1978, Bowlby 1969, Stern 1983) have proposed a contrasting view. First, if state changes are salient, whether through feeding, drying, or rocking, they accrue to the infant's attachment to the caregiver. Second, there are numerous infant–caregiver interactions that promote infant attachment that have nothing to do with state transformations (Stern 1983, 1985). These interactions are mutually regulated, reciprocal exchanges in which each partner influences the other on a moment-to-moment basis.

Stern (1983) described three categories of mutual regulation: (1) state sharing (for example, mutual cooing), (2) self–other complementarity (for example, a ball pushed back and forth between the infant and the caregiver), and (3) state transforming. He argued that the state transformations that occur during feeding, changing, and calming do not accrue to the attachment system unless they are accompanied by the first two: "The experience of being hungry, getting fed, and going blissfully to sleep does not, even when associated with a particular person, lead to subjective intimacy with the feeding person, unless accompanied by self-other complementing and state sharing" (p. 79). These experiences dramatically transform self-states and require the physical mediation of an other (Stern 1985). In the empirical infant literature, state transformations accrue to self-regulation and pertain to bodily, physiological, and affective changes in interaction with caregivers.

With the advent of symbolic capacities and increasing elaboration upon one's subjective experience, self-states in the child and adult include the domain of the self in a psychological sense. Post-infancy self-state transformations may increase a sense of control, mastery, and agency. But, in the case of traumatic self-state transformations, states of dissociation, devastation, or fragmentation may become dominant.

Analogies to Stern's categories of interactive regulation are found in adult treatment. Analogous to mother–infant state sharing is the analyst's attempt to grasp the patient's experience from a vantage point within the patient's frame of reference. Whereas this perspective may enable the analyst to better understand the patient's experience, this empathic mode of listening (Ornstein 1985) may simultaneously enable the patient to feel that his or her state is shared by another person. Thus, a previously solitary experience can be embedded in an interactive context, as illustrated in the way Nick described his experience of our exploration of his toilet trauma model scene.

Analogous to Stern's second category, mother–infant complementarity, is an adversarial quality to the analyst–patient exchange. The analyst pushes back to the patient something the patient has pushed toward him or her. In this back and forth between analyst and patient there is both recognition of each as separately organized with respect to the other, as well as an acknowledgment of a special attachment. In spite of standing on opposite sides of the tennis net, each is engaged with the other. Both are asserting themselves and both are participating in a joint venture. Telling David the "I'm dancing as fast as I can" story conveyed this adversarial quality. Analogous to Stern's third category of interactive regulation, mother–infant state transformation, is the interpretive sequence, illustrated in the treatment of Stan, discussed below.

In addition to Stern's discussion of self-states, the other source from which to understand self-states is Kohut's (1984) delineation of a kind of dream, the self-state dream. In this type of dream, imagery is undisguised or only minimally disguised in depicting the dreamer's sense of self. Kohut likened these dreams to Freud's (1920) discussion of dreams in traumatic neuroses in which a traumatic event is realistically depicted.

In dreams, self-states may be depicted as "an empty landscape, burned out forests, decaying neighborhoods . . . an airplane out of control that wildly flies higher and higher" (Kohut 1980, p. 508). These dreams reflect the aftermath of a devastation. They herald self-experiences such as aimlessness, depression, hypomania, fragmentation, despair, and hopelessness. For treatment purposes, it is the imminence of these states that requires recognition. As in Freud's (1920) traumatic neurosis dreams, obtaining associations to the landscape, forest or neighborhood, in an effort to uncover repressed contents is not useful. Such investigation obscures recognition of the state itself. The analyst's understanding and recognition of the state is a prerequisite to its transformation.

Self-states may or may not be directly available to consciousness and self-reflection. In psychoanalytic treatment, they are inferred from affects and moods, dream imagery, and psychopathology. Alternatively, a person's sense of well-being can be encompassed in a self-state. These indices of self-states may reach awareness and be accessible to self-reflection, introspection, observation, and empathic inquiry by an analyst.

Feeling different may accompany the analytic interventions that lead to the transforming experience.

As in the caregiver–infant dyad, transformations of states also accrues to self-regulation within the analyst–patient interaction. The issues at stake in self-state transformations touch on self-control, mastery, agency (including self-reflection and self-criticism), affect regulation, and self-determination over one's life and experience.

The terms *state* and *self-state* are used interchangeably and apply to infancy as well as adulthood. I prefer the term *self-state* to convey the intimate connection between an affect, one's state, and one's self-experience. Lichtenberg, Fosshage, and I (1992) and Schwaber (1998) have made similar proposals. Along with Stern, however, we distinguished affect, cognition, and arousal as dimensions of states. Furthermore, I do not confine the term to dream imagery as described by Kohut. Dreams provide a glimpse into a person's self-state but moods, symptoms, and transference manifestations reflect self-states as well. The focus on self-state transformations links a developmental construct with the analytic process. Self-states comprise input from affects and cognition as well as bodily and physiological sources. Throughout development these states are responsive to, interact with, and influence one's environment.

I use *self-state* to refer to the level of psychological organization at which (1) trauma leaves its scars, (2) creative endeavors accrue to self-restoration, and (3) psychoanalytic interpretations are transformative and exercise their therapeutic action. In this chapter, I focus on the last of these.

THE TREATMENT OF STAN: SELF-STATE TRANSFORMATION THROUGH INTERPRETATION

Self-state transformations occur in the course of analysis through a variety of interventions including the ongoing, predictable analyst–patient interactions, their disruption and repair, and heightened affect that may be organized by the analytic interactions (Beebe and Lachmann 1994, Lachmann and Beebe 1996a). Specifically, the variety and forms of interpretations can transform rigid self-states in the direction of increased flexibility, such as a wider affective range, an increased sense of agency, and a feeling of well-being.

In the discussion of the treatments of David and Nick, I focused on interactional patterns: the ongoing interactions of the analyst–patient relationship and attention to its disruptions and repair. Shared moments of heightened affect transformed David's and Nick's expectations of being ignored and abandoned, and their expectations of nonresponsivity. In the treatment of Stan, whom I saw for three sessions a week for three years, self-state transformations were brought about directly through interpretation in his psychoanalytic treatment. Here I recount a brief portion of his treatment as his self-state changed quite quickly through a sequence of interpretations.

Stan, an anxious, depressed, obsessional, and very articulate man in his late thirties, recounted the circumstances under which he first experienced painfully humiliating, intrusive, obsessional thoughts. In one instance he drove his car near his girlfriend's house and saw her little son playing in the street. He developed the worry that he had run over her son with his car. He felt compelled to check his rearview mirror repeatedly to see if the boy's body was lying in the street. In a second instance, when he first left his parental home to work in another city, he suddenly thought, "You're a homosexual!" In a third instance, while participating in the High Holy Day service at his synagogue the thought, "You're Christ!" intruded upon him. He offered several associations to the circumstances under which these thoughts occurred to him, including his relationship with his girlfriend and her child, his father, and his religion. I said to him that the three instances depicted problematic father–son relationships. In this interpretation I connected the disparate obsessional symptoms, which he had not done on his own. He experienced a profound sense of relief. Further exploration of the intrusive thoughts led us to view this father–son relationship as characterized by death, love, and a mystical union. Stan realized that his obsessional symptomatology had been aggravated as he noticed increasing signs of his father's decline and impending death.

In the course of the session just described, Stan's self-state transformation was dramatically evident. Following my interventions, his body appeared less tense, and he spoke in a more engaged, less depressed manner. From having felt despondent and worthless as the producer of what he considered to be "bizarre, psychotic, crazy" thoughts, he felt increasingly burdened as he became aware of his father's impending death and his troublesome relationship with him.

My interpretation was based on my understanding that Stan's intrusive obsessional thoughts (for example, his fear of running over his girlfriend's child) were not derived from a hostile wish toward the child as a competitor. Nor did I understand them to be primarily a reversal of a guilty wish toward his own father. Both of these dynamics may indeed have been operative. Such trailing-edge interpretations would have highlighted Stan's conflicted, ambivalent relationship with his father. In my leading-edge interpretation, I addressed the quality of Stan's vulnerability as well as his need to have his affection and longing for intimacy with his father recognized. That is, I interpreted his striving for his father's love, his anticipated loss of his father, and his disappointment that his father might never recognize how much effort Stan put into taking care of him. My interventions addressed the extent to which Stan felt that his life was linked, inextricably, to that of his father.

In the following session, further exploration of Stan's relationship with his father led to an amplification of aspects of this troubled relationship. He reported that the intrusive thoughts occurred when he experienced an exhilarated feeling of aliveness and momentary independence from his father. For example, they occurred during times when he was fully engaged in his work, feeling proud of a place of honor at his temple, or enjoying a walk on a sunny day. One effect of the obsessional thoughts was to immediately and radically alter his self-state from alive and happy to depressed. Stan felt that his intrusive thoughts provided him with a connection to his father. Through the obsessional thoughts, both he and his father shared comparable states of misery. Stan responded with relief. The content of the subsequent sessions shifted as Stan spoke about similarities between his father and me. In contrast to himself, he thought of his father and me as worthy and kind. He then described instances in which he felt inadequate and morally inferior to others.

The sequence of Stan's associations led from his relief that his affections for his father had been recognized to his acknowledgment of moral failings and feelings of guilt. Thus, through his own associations, he took up the issues that would have constituted the trailing-edge interpretation that I might have made. I assumed that he now felt safe enough to explore a variety of personal and professional situations in which he felt guilty for having been hostile, greedy, sacrilegious, and fraudulent.

In the analysis of Stan, interpretations contributed to his self-reorganization and brought about immediate transformations of his self-state. First, a shift occurred from fragmentation, confusion, and intimations of insanity to an increase of self-cohesion, even though as a "fraud." Depicting himself as a fraud represented an interim sense of himself, but did not represent the final resting place of his sense of decency. Second, a shift occurred from a sense of hopelessness and despair to an expectation of being able to understand his confused thoughts and feelings, and in having them understood by me. Stan now felt beset by understandable problems and conflicts. He experienced an active, inner struggle to live, whereas previously he had been ready to resign himself to sharing his father's decline. Third, a cognitive shift occurred from considering himself to be a victim of bizarre thoughts toward being capable of self-reflection and self-criticism. These shifts combined affective, cognitive, and bodily features and accrued to his self-regulatory capacity and his increasing expectation of successful interactive regulation. The transference issue that accompanied these explorations was: To what extent did his "fraudulence" provide the repetitive dialectic in these transformations? In this instance, being alert to this possibility was sufficient in enabling Stan to reveal and explore ways in which he had expected to "cheat" me, for example, by lying about his income.

His father's decline and Stan's own increasing vitality provided the content in which he felt torn between his affection for his father and the burden that this affection placed on him. At this stage of their lives, his parents were financially dependent on him. He anticipated with resentment that his life would have to become more limited as his father's need for attention and care increased. A background selfobject tie had become engaged quite rapidly in the course of his analysis, making possible the revelation and exploration of his shame and guilt-laden experiences. The selfobject tie provided a background sense of safety, a necessary connection to a responsive, accepting, and validating surround akin to his earlier relationship with his now failing father.

Psychoanalytic treatment provides one avenue for self-state transformation. However, not only in the context of the interactive regulations of psychoanalytic treatment but also through the restoration of selfobject ties in the world-at-large can expectations of a responsive environment shift the state of the self. Trauma, narcissistic injuries, and loss shift the sense of self along the dimension of intactness-fragmentation toward greater fragmentation and along the dimension of vitality-depletion toward increased depletion. Self-state transformations in the reverse directions, from fragmentation to intactness, and from depletion to vitality require an interactive process between analyst and patient as has been described in the various treatments presented. Through this process analyst and patient develop a reservoir of experience that bolsters a sense of efficacy and expectations of being understood and being understandable.

In the next five chapters, self-state transformations are considered from different angles—through trauma and through creativity. Depending on numerous factors, including the context in which they occur, transformations can go in either direction, not always in the direction of developmental advances. I shall consider transformation through massive deprivation and abuse, whereby reactive aggression is transformed into an extreme form of eruptive aggression. Finally, I will discuss the transformation of reactive aggression into more moderate forms of eruptive aggression as encountered in a clinical population.

5

State Transformations and Trauma

This chapter focuses on the need to react aversively by withdrawal. Although reacting antagonistically or by withdrawing can be characteristic of the same person, some variant of antagonism (for example, passive defiance) will frequently make an appearance alongside withdrawal. Exposure to trauma is a frequently implicated basis for chronic withdrawal and may set in motion the self-state transformations that eventuate in feelings of depletion, hopelessness, and malaise.

TRAUMA

Trauma is generally classified from the vantage point of an outside observer as being a consequence of either a shock or a strain (Sandler 1967). The prototypic shock trauma was a railroad accident. Its occurrence typically caught the riders unprepared and took them by surprise. The Chinese water torture illustrates a strain trauma. Having water drip on one's head is in itself not traumatic, but the cumulative effect of a constant drip, drip, drip constitutes a trauma. There is a third category of trauma, which is probably most common, that combines aspects of both of these. For example, persistent massive evocation of aversiveness early in life through brutality and emotional and physical abuse and deprivation and neglect combines elements of shock and strain.

In contrast to the previous chapter in which the transformations were brought about in psychoanalytic treatment states, and Stan moved toward a more flexible way of organizing his experience, in this chapter I discuss transformations through trauma that have increased the person's rigid organization of experience. I will focus on the impact of trauma in transforming a man who prior to his trauma tended to be somewhat withdrawn. Through a medical procedure that was traumatic for him, his aversive tendencies were transformed into a chronic state of hopelessness and helplessness.

When trauma is viewed from the vantage point of the experience of the victim, it can be defined with respect to the *effect* of a particular event or sequence of experiences. I propose that an event becomes traumatic when it ruptures a person's selfobject ties without an opportunity for self- or interactive repair, and simultaneously dramatically alters the person's self-state. The impact of a trauma can lead to a violation of expectations and a sense of betrayal that transforms flexible, transient self-states into increased rigidity, depression, and restriction of emotional responsivity. Such states can then become impervious to subsequent self-restorative efforts.

A classic illustration of the effects of a trauma leading to withdrawal occurs in Melville's *Moby Dick*. When the whale bit off Captain Ahab's leg, the captain became emotionally deadened, withdrawn to the point of extreme reclusivity, and monomaniacal in his determination to destroy the whale. He risked and eventually lost his life in this pursuit. Although clearly a physical trauma, having one's leg bitten off by a whale satisfies the definition of a psychic trauma as well.

Trauma originally referred to a physical wound. Freud translated its three defining physical elements into the psychological ideas of a violent shock, a wound, and consequences that affect the whole organism (Laplanche and Pontalis 1973). In the realm of psychological life, just what constitutes the essence of the "wound" inflicted by a trauma is conceptualized differently by various psychoanalytic theories. The wound inflicted on Captain Ahab can be considered a massive, life-threatening assault, a symbolic castration that evoked counterphobic defenses, a confirmation of a profound infantile fear of being devoured, or an assault on his bodily integrity and self-cohesion.

Melville scholars (for example, Sidney Kaplan 1990, personal communication, 1991) suggest that prior to the trauma, Ahab had been "an ordinary, stern, whaling captain with a strong philosophical-theodical bent." From Melville's book we also learn that Ahab had been married and had a son just prior to the voyage in which he lost his leg. Melville's depiction of Ahab coincides with the view that a powerful physical and psychical event could permanently debilitate a hitherto ordinary, relatively symptom-free person.

Attributing psychopathology to a specific event fell into disrepute when Freud rejected the seduction theory and theorized that unconscious fantasies determine the effects of a trauma (see Balint 1969). Within this view, the effect of recalled traumatic events is ascribed to the confirmation of preexisting unconscious wishes. That is, an event becomes a trauma when it gratifies a particular unconscious fantasy. Furthermore, the event that appears decisive in marking the beginning of psychopathology must have derived its power by synthesizing prior similar events.

Freud's trauma theory implies extraordinary subjective states of feeling overwhelmed, inundated, and helpless. For example, in the case of childhood trauma, the child's immature ego is unable to cope with overwhelming affects activated by a "seduction." Or, in the case of the railroad accident type of trauma, the person is accidentally subjected to massive excitation that overwhelms the nervous system.

Captain Ahab illustrates still another angle on the psychological effects of a trauma. For Melville and Captain Ahab, the whale was the instrument of God. Captain Ahab lost his leg not by accident, but through the whale's maliciousness, which represented to Ahab a betrayal by God, in whom he had placed his trust. Ahab's expectation of order and justice was shattered, and this betrayal by God was the source of the pathological consequences of the trauma. It transformed him, leaving him depressed, emotionally dead, and motivated by only one desire—revenge. He was reduced to a state of helplessness and went to great lengths to disavow this state. For example, Ahab was unmoved by the pleas for help of another whaling captain whose son had been lost at sea. Rather than search for the lost boy, Ahab continued his pursuit of the whale. Even Ahab's attachment to his own wife and son did not deter him from his single-minded, dangerous quest for retribution. His sense of betrayal was such that his humanness was destroyed.

Ahab's psychic trauma consisted of a betrayal of the expectation that he could rely on God and an ordered world. The betrayal of such trust is a universal psychic trauma (Erikson 1959). Such trust begins with a secure attachment relationship and under optimal circumstances is transformed as the person feels protected and shares in the power of an idealized other.

Three major perspectives on trauma can be found in the psycho-analytic literature. One view places gratification of unconscious wishes at the root of the pathology of traumatic events (for example, Dowling 1990). A second view emphasizes reality factors over fantasy. The im-pact of the event is assumed to define its psychological impact. This approach is illustrated in the well-intentioned assumption that all the children in a school will be in need of counseling after a tragedy has befallen one pupil. The third view emphasizes the violation of a bond of trust between the child and the "potentially traumatogenic objects" (Bacal and Newman 1990, p. 132). This third view has been detailed by Ferenczi (1933), Balint (1969), Miller (1981), and Kohut (1984). In this view, attention is shifted to how the bond of trust was traumatically shattered, what was experienced by the child, and how that experience was elabo-rated. Thus, mediating factors in trauma in addition to the gratification of unconscious fantasies must be specified.

In the first view the pathological effects of a trauma are a conse-quence of the gratification of unconscious wishes. For example, in treat-ing a patient who had been sexually molested, the analyst would follow a theory in which the confirmation of unconscious incestuous wishes is emphasized. Such unconscious wishes call forth defenses against sexual excitement and can be germane in the treatment process. But a patient's efforts to convince the analyst of the realness of the sexual molestation then may fail to get adequate consideration.

Simon (1991) goes a step further and criticizes the emphasis on fantasy where "fact has been misconstrued as fantasy, which occurred in the psychoanalytic understanding of sexual abuse" (p. 517). He holds that "psychoanalysis has failed to adequately understand the outcome of severe trauma by underestimating its devastating impact and the resources necessary for coping with the overwhelming consequences" (p. 517).

Balint (1969) concurred with Freud that most psychologically destructive traumas occur in early life. He departed from Freud when he proposed that for an event to become traumatic, it must be preceded by the establishment of a reliable, trusting relationship between child and parent. The trauma consists of the betrayal of the child's expectation of reliable responsivity. Kohut (1977, 1984) conceptualized the betrayal that constitutes a trauma as a rupture of the selfobject tie between the child and the parents. Such ruptures may be produced through massive disappointments, rebuffs, or even through minute but consistent failures in empathy. Balint's and Kohut's concepts of trauma are similar in that they emphasize a loss of a necessary tie, and a betrayal of expectations of being understood, accepted, and protected in a reliable, responsive world.

I assume that some people have the resources to restore themselves after a trauma and do not require specific professional help to do so. I further assume that traumatic shock or strain has not, in these cases, simultaneously utterly deprived them of the selfobject ties and attachments that could enable them to restore themselves to a well-functioning state.

In cases where therapy is sought, a massive disruption, a consequence of a trauma, has shattered a person's expectations of control, agency, and self-determination. Trauma may then occasion self-state transformations into helplessness, hopelessness, and despair. Furthermore, a trauma may simultaneously rupture selfobject ties so that despite efforts at self-restoration and self-regulation, the person cannot restore the tie on his or her own. For a trauma to limit the person's flexibility and repertoire of self-states, I propose that some selfobject ties have been ruptured and remain irreparable by the person on his or her own. In these instances treatment can provide the raw materials out of which stable selfobject ties can be organized.

A twofold perspective on trauma follows. An event or series of experiences becomes traumatic, requiring psychotherapeutic treatment, when (1) a person's selfobject ties are ruptured without opportunity for self or interactive repair, and (2) simultaneously, the person's self-state is dramatically altered. The advantage of this twofold perspective is that it focuses on the subjective effect of the trauma, rather than on the magnitude of the event as seen by an outside observer. I am not specifically distinguishing between shock and strain trauma, since these two often overlap. Rather, attention is directed to the effect of trauma and to the adaptive capacities and transformative resources that were unavailable to the person to address the trauma on his or her own.

Together, these two conditions—ruptures of selfobject ties and dramatic self-state alterations—make it likely that the person will react aversively through antagonism and/or withdrawal. In particular, the tendency to withdraw, in my view, will attain motivational dominance. In clinical practice these two dimensions are difficult to tease apart. Withdrawals can be angry, and hostility can serve to ensure further isolation and withdrawal.

EXPECTANCIES

In the course of earlier chapters, and in the case discussion of Ben, to follow, I have used terms such as *expectations of being understood* and *expectations of being understandable*, which are derived from the role of expectancies as they are organized in the course of development. Beginning in early life, expectancies are a powerful factor in organizing the interactions between caregiver and infant. Expectancies are defined as the recurrent, characteristic patterns that the infant recognizes, expects, and anticipates. Predictable patterns are set up as to how a relationship usually goes, as embodied in Stern's (1985) representations of interactions that are generalized (RIGs). RIGs may later accrue to expectations of interactive responsivity. Or RIGs may accrue to expectations of maternal, spatial intrusion, and thus withdrawal by the infant may follow. For example, an infant may expect that whenever he begins to play with his own fingers and put them into his mouth, his mother will remove them and intrude her own hands into his space. Such repetitive experiences can organize expectations of being intruded upon, overaroused, and inundated (Beebe and Lachmann 1988a,b, Beebe and Stern 1977, Lachmann and Beebe 1992, Stern 1977, 1985). Such expectations will also interfere with the child's self-regulation.

The term *expectations* can be extended and applied to conceptualizing trauma. That is, a traumatic event precipitously and insidiously violates expectations of living in a predictable world, and being reliably, positively responded to. The concept of violation or betrayal of expectations mediates between the traumatic event(s) and the state of the self that is immediately, dramatically transformed through the trauma. The concept of "violations of expectations" can also be applied to a range of phenomena—from pleasurable surprises to feared shocks and ordeals.

A single event such as having one's leg bitten off by a whale may be traumatic in and of itself (Beebe and Lachmann 1994, Pine 1981) or a single event may provide a synthesis or be used as a metaphor. It can braid together prior themes whereby fantasies amplify the affects evoked and contribute to the overall impact of the event.

Among the consequences of trauma, "affectlessness [and] giving up all hope of satisfactory human contacts" have been specifically described by Krystal (1976, p. 106). Interestingly, Henry Murray (1967) has portrayed Melville in just this way. Melville apparently ascribed to Captain Ahab a state similar to his own. To explain Ahab's state, however, Melville provided a traumatic origin, having his leg bitten off, a single event.

A single event may itself be decisive in transforming a person's self-state when the pretrauma personality can be characterized by relatively little evidence of neurotic symptomatology. The previously intact self-state is then transformed through the traumatic experience. The presumption is that, had the trauma not occurred, a comfortable life without psychotherapy would have been possible.

A single traumatic event may transform the self-state in either of two ways: (1) It is one of a class of similar events, the last straw, or the final shot, or a gathering together of the effects of the prior events into a telling blow. This conceptualization of trauma had long been favored in psychoanalysis. (2) It is a circumscribed event that has an immediate, massive impact on the self-state of a person who had, until then, been reasonably well functioning. I would add that only in broad strokes can one document that the pretrauma personality of a person was essentially well functioning and that the difficulties noted after a specific event are indeed the consequences of that experience.

THE TREATMENT OF BEN: THE SINGLE-EVENT TRAUMA

It is very difficult to support the contention that a person in therapy was so healthy that, had a specific event not occurred, he or she would have led a satisfying life, probably without the need for therapy. The treat-ment of Ben, whom I saw for one session per week, illustrates the effect of a single-event trauma and comes as close I can get to describing a man who became massively debilitated but had lived a reasonably comfort-able life prior to his trauma.

At the age of 60, Ben required heart surgery, a triple bypass. Prior to the surgery he did suffer mildly from some phobia about riding in airplanes, elevators, and subways. However, he was able to use elevators and airplanes when necessary for his business, and he was able to avoid subways in his day-to-day life. These symptoms had developed over a ten-year period prior to the surgery. During that same time period, at age 50, he started an affair with his secretary and soon afterward ended his marriage. Since all of his symptoms entailed a restriction of activities and movements, the link between these symptoms and his guilt about leaving his wife was apparent. He felt selfish for breaking up his mar-riage and said when I saw him ten years later, "It was not a bad marriage, it was just that my wife and I grew apart. There was no more feeling between us, though she was a perfectly fine person."

Ben was the only living son in a family that escaped from Europe prior to the outbreak of World War II. An older brother died in infancy of various unspecified defects. Ben believed that neither this tragedy, nor three other salient incidents he reported, had any adverse effect on his life. He reported that at age 7 he was thrown into a swimming pool to learn how to swim, and he nearly drowned. The second incident he recalled was lying to a teacher in elementary school. He claimed that he owned a dog and was subsequently spanked by his father for lying. His third recollection was from his teenage years. At a summer camp he was considered arrogant. To teach him a lesson, other campers blindfolded him, led him into the woods, and left him there. He emphasized that he found his way back easily, and that he returned to the camp the following year with no hard feelings. Although in hearing these accounts, one might view them as consisting of a series of narcissistic injuries and events that could have been experienced as traumatic, Ben reported them with an emphasis on his toughness.

Prior to the surgery Ben prided himself on his ability to triumph over challenges, exercise control over the circumstances of his life, and make difficult business decisions. He felt he could maintain a sense of competence and authority, and could rely on his capacity not only to survive but also to come out ahead. Most importantly, he always felt himself to be in control. Being reasonable and rational enabled him to maintain a normal life. Although he had not made this connection, I believe that to maintain these qualities was crucial to Ben. He could decisively distinguish himself from the brother who failed to survive.

The cardiac surgery was a medical success. Subsequently, however, he developed a depression, panic states, impotence, and a vast increase in the preexisting phobic symptomatology. The surgery resulted in his feeling vulnerable. He felt it resulted in his no longer having the strength and stamina on which he once prided himself. As a result of his psychological symptomatology, he no longer considered himself to be normal and rational, and he felt despairing about this "fall." To retain his prior self-control, he closed off his affective life even more rigidly.

Figure and background were now reversed for Ben. The scary experiences of the near drowning, being caught lying, and being humiliated by his campmates now became the affects that defined his daily expectations. His previous expectation of mastering and controlling unfavorable circumstances faded as he felt he could no longer rely upon himself. He had betrayed his ideals by leaving his wife for "selfish" reasons. Now he had been betrayed by his body and himself. At the core of his increased phobias was his loss of expectation of self-control.

Psychotherapy began two years after the surgery. After about six months the phobic symptoms stabilized. That is, the phobias did not increase in severity, nor did new symptoms appear, as was the case during the two years after the surgery. I understood the surgery to be a trauma that dramatically altered and rigidified his self-state. However, as we focused on the impact of the surgery on his depression and on his feelings of vulnerability, or rather his long-standing conviction of invulnerability, new symptoms did appear. He often cried "for no apparent cause." Exploration of the circumstances that prompted his tears indicated several common themes. For example, he cried when he read an account of the Yale–Harvard football game that Harvard lost. He had attended Harvard, which he considered a notable achievement. He had felt at one with Harvard, which, like himself, he considered a bastion of invincibility. Now even Harvard was no longer what it once was.

Previous to the surgery aversive reactions tended to be dominated by antagonism. Subsequently, they shifted further and further toward social withdrawal, and his consumption of alcohol increased. Through his surgery, he glimpsed his vulnerability and dreaded potential helplessness and incapacity. In various dream images he depicted his self-state as "the ceiling of my apartment falling," "equipment for a job not working," and "trying to make coffee in an ancient kitchen but the freeze-dried crystals had coagulated into rock-hard syrup." Ben initially combated the relevance of these images as self-descriptions with comments such as, "Well, you would know that better than I." Through rigid character defenses, based on a dread of following in the footsteps of the brother who died before he was born, Ben had attempted to maintain his hold on his reason and normality. The heart surgery shattered his carefully maintained distinction from his brother. He was terrified he would now become as "abnormal" as his brother had been depicted by his parents. Though we had spoken about the contents that evoked his moments of crying many times, it was not until he reported his crying while reading the account of the Harvard defeat that he could realize that he was crying for his own decline.

Responding to Ben's self-state dreams by articulating the various states that were depicted gradually enabled him to connect his fears, panics, and crying outbursts to the surgery and his reaction to it. These reactions became understandable to him in the light of the value he had previously placed on being in control of his world and himself. Prior to his surgery, the admiration he received for his competence and resource-fulness, especially for the independent manner in which he had made his own way, had been most gratifying. He had felt that competence and control over his life was expected of him by his parents. In turn, he expected that these qualities would remain available to him, serve him in good stead, and be valued by the world. Prior to the surgery, this had indeed been so. He felt as acknowledged for his talents and abilities by his friends and business associates as he had been by his parents. He felt that the successes he achieved reflected his capabilities. He could rely on a world in which he was in charge. The breakup of his marriage did introduce an ever-present quiet self-reproach. Gallbladder surgery two years before the heart bypass had left no psychological scars. However, the bypass surgery ruptured Ben's self-sustaining selfobject tie to his in-vulnerable body and the admiring world. Ben's strength and normality were no doubt a relief to his parents, and throughout his development they supported his stance of rational invulnerability and normality. Ben was now trapped in a body that did, and could again, betray him. He no longer felt himself to be invulnerable, and the world became dangerous. After two years of therapy, feeling better enough to suit his expectations, Ben ended his treatment.

The case of Ben illustrates the effect of a trauma on a man whose prior symptomatology was mild. He probably would not have sought psychotherapy but for the psychologically devastating effects of his sur-gery. The combination of the prior rigid but well-functioning character structure, his emphasis on self-control, and the loss of confidence in his own powers added up to an overwhelming sense of betrayal. He felt he had failed to retain his invulnerability. The surgery altered his self-state into one that congealed around his loss of power, competence, and control. His pride at his self-control was transformed into pervasive shame.

Ben's need to react aversively by withdrawal protected him against the shame associated with his failing powers and his sense of decline. He had been able to sustain his archaic grandiosity in spite of the narcissistic injuries he described in the three memories he reported at the beginning of his treatment. However, when confronted by the surgery, he withdrew in shame. In the course of the therapy, Ben's rigid insistence on his previous invulnerability and his currently shattered sense of self were gradually and modestly transformed. In our dialogue he very gradually became more self-reflective, even when these self-reflections depicted him as weaker than he had been willing to accept. He came to feel that if Harvard could lose a game, so could he.

AFTERTHOUGHTS

In reviewing Ben's early experience privately, I speculated about the impact of his being born *because* his brother failed to thrive. That is, I wondered if he was a replacement baby. He reported the disdain, ridicule, shame, and contempt that his parents expressed directly and snidely about that brother. An effect of that early exposure to the consistent devaluation of his dead brother was an inability to contemplate even the idea of his own vulnerability. What he recalled about his experiences attested to his determination to "tough it out" and not yield to feelings of inadequacy, weakness, and vulnerability. Part of this determination to be normal was his character style of not being aware of himself, being un–self-reflective. With this in mind, Ben could be said to have suffered an early strain trauma that eventuated in a character style that would have sustained a reasonably normal life, had his invulnerability not been challenged.

In the course of his therapy, Ben's ability to self-reflect increased to a degree. He became somewhat curious about himself. Specifically, he was stymied as to how a healthy person like himself could feel such depression and anxiety. The dream imagery of disintegration, which I thought of as dramatically evocative, initially meant little to him. Over time it captured his interest. However, the turning point in the treatment came with the discussion of the football game that Harvard lost. That touched him. That evoked his familiar self-state of despair and loss. That resonated with his shattered expectations of invulnerability.

I have discussed transformation with respect to self-states and expectancies. I think of these concepts as related, but as conceptually distinct dimensions of experience. Expectancies are affected directly by the therapeutic interaction. Through the process of treatment, expectations of being understood and being understandable can develop. Ben came to feel, slightly, that he could be understood, not only on the rational level on which he habitually related, but also on the level of metaphoric communications, which captured and contained his vulnerability. It was as though Ben drove through life with cruise control, and in the course of our sessions he occasionally slowed down to see where he was going and how he got there.

Transformation, as it refers to self-states and expectancies, impacts on the capacity for self-reflection. Fonagy's (1991, 1999) discussion of the capacity to mentalize is relevant here. In development, Fonagy holds, the child's ability to locate his or her mental state or affect in the "face" or the "mind" of a primary object leads to a sense of knowing one's own mental state and to recognizing the mental states of others. The child's failure to experience the parents as holding a sense of the child's presence, or the child's sense that the parents feel murderous rage toward the child, will impede or preclude the development of a mentalizing capacity. Lack of self-reflection and lack of self-awareness are consequences of these unfavorable developmental circumstances.

Ben's history resembles that of patients whose early experiences were marked by an inability to get a sense of their existence in the minds of their parents. Specifically, both of Ben's parents were intent on seeing Ben as the healthy, normal, strong, competent replacement for the brother who died.

As Ben recounted his experience, I became aware of the extent to which his dead brother had been obliterated in his family. Their attitude limited the extent to which Ben could become aware of himself. When self-reflection can lead to awareness of one's vulnerability, and such rec-ognition endangers one's acceptance and survival, then self-ignorance can be bliss. Ben's lack of self-awareness was, among numerous func-tions, an adaptive strategy. It shielded him from the risks he faced should he "take after" his brother or be seen by his parents as resembling his brother. From two sides, Ben's ability to reflect on his vulnerabilities had been compromised.

Ben was able to live up to his and his family's expectations of invul-nerability quite well until they were shattered by the cardiac surgery. In his treatment Ben came to view himself somewhat more modestly, in line with my view of him as a sturdy man who had been ill-prepared for the slings and arrows of everyday life. Most grievously, he had been be-trayed by the vulnerability of his own body. In his development, the flexibility that best characterizes self-regulation had been maintained by an avoidance of self-reflection and by his rigid adherence to his pursuit of normality and rationality.

Having made the argument that Ben illustrated a relatively healthy person, I must now backpedal just a little. Ben's surgery undermined the very essence of what he required in order to feel like an independent agent. It undermined the selfobject experience that he derived from his trust in the invulnerability of his body and mind. This feeling of invul-nerability was derived from the support of both of his parents. But, his self-reliance and self-satisfaction, especially with his ability to triumph over adversity, were qualities of his that had acquired a life of their own. He felt he was betrayed by himself, and there was no escape from that sense of betrayal.

The affective states that Ben complained about—depression, de-spair, and hopelessness—are frequently encountered transient states af-ter major surgery. For Ben they became chronic. Neither his divorce nor his gallbladder surgery had interfered with his ability to self-restore. The cardiac surgery did. It undermined the self that is crucial in self-restora-tion. His relationship with his former secretary, and now partner, could also not provide the interactive basis for his self-restoration. That rela-tionship was suffused with feelings of guilt. He still faulted himself for not having behaved honorably. And so, I must concede, the ceiling in the dream image of the ceiling falling in on an apartment had a few old cracks in it. Nevertheless, such ceilings can last a long time without buckling, depending on how much weight the upstairs neighbors place on it.

Like Ahab, Ben also became determined to redress the injury that had been inflicted on him. What became a murderous wish for revenge in Ahab became a despairing resignation for Ben. The cases of Stan and Ben illustrate that trauma and interpretation can change self-states. Unlike Ahab, in whom trauma led to a rageful reaction, Ben was determined to be normal, rational, as well as ambitious and assertive throughout his life. He did not become vengeful after his operation. Rather, he felt betrayed by his expectations of normalcy and rationality. He did not have the creative resources to overcome this assault to his pride, unlike Henrik Ibsen, whose response to an affront to his expectation of a mixture of moderate criticism and admiring responsivity led to a work of art.

6

State Transformations through Creativity

Ben's ability to restore himself was limited by his rigid adherence to the rational and normal. To Ben, metaphors already required a stretch toward irrationality that he found difficult. Not so for Henrik Ibsen. I move from the couch to the theater to discuss a function of the creative process. What is lost in not having an analytic dialogue will have to be replaced by a quilt of artistic productions, biographical reports, and autobiography.

I use Ibsen's recovery from the attacks by his critics of his play *Ghosts* (1881) to illustrate his capacity to create a triumphant victory from the rubble of a humiliating defeat. In writing *An Enemy of the People* (1882), Ibsen held his critics and detractors up to ridicule.

My discussion of relevant aspects of Ibsen's biography and plays will be anecdotal. I approach Ibsen as a playgoer rather than as an academic. Furthermore, this chapter is organized somewhat differently from the other chapters in this book. The biographical and autobiographical material that may account for the nature and quality of Ibsen's self-state transformation will appear at the end of this chapter, rather than at the start, as it might in a clinical account. That is, traditionally, case presentations begin with the person's history and development and then proceed to discuss the relevant dynamics derived therefrom. I have chosen the reverse sequence because it follows the style of Ibsen's plays. The key explanation comes at the end. I hope this organization provides a more dramatic conclusion to a chapter on creativity. End of disclaimers and explanations!

Freud (1893) credited an unnamed English writer for remarking that "the man who first flung a word of abuse at his enemy instead of a spear was the founder of civilization" (p. 36). This unnamed writer recognized the role of creativity in responding to an assault or physical or narcissistic injury by triumphing over an enemy by humiliating him. Although one can run away and live to fight another day, flight can be more risky for one's self-esteem. However, rather than literally fleeing, there are always variants of withdrawal that are far less obvious. Creative retaliation puts power into the hands of those who are physically weaker but intellectually stronger than their attackers.

Conversely, a person's creativity can be assessed by the ability to transcend the eggs and tomatoes thrown by critics. To be able to form a work of art out of the rubble left by such an attack is, of course, not the only way in which creative abilities can show themselves. But, it is one way (for other ways, see, for example, Freud 1910, Greenacre 1957, Maher 1993, B. Meyer 1967). Kohut (1966) considered the capacity to turn a humiliating rebuff into a creative triumph to be a developmental ideal, one of the transformations of archaic narcissism.

The response of the critics to *Ghosts* left Ibsen in a state of devastation and outrage. He reacted by quickly writing *An Enemy of the People* and thereby succeeded in transforming his depleted self-state creatively, on his own, utilizing his own resources.

To facilitate the discussion of Ibsen's creative self-state transformation, a synopsis of the plots of the play that resulted in his resounding rejection, *Ghosts*, and the play that constituted his retaliation and self-restoration, *An Enemy of the People*, follows.

IBSEN'S PLOTS

In *Ghosts*, Oswald Alving has returned home from Paris because he is terminally ill. In the course of the play he learns that he had inherited syphilis from his late father, Captain Alving. His mother, Mrs. Alving, had shielded her husband's reputation so that her son would not be disillusioned.

Pastor Manders and Mrs. Alving discuss the opening of an orphanage named for Captain Alving. Manders reminds Mrs. Alving that a year after her marriage, she complained to him about the Captain's dissolute ways. When she told Manders that it was him she really loved, Manders counseled her about her marital duties and sent her back to her husband. Manders now insists that the orphanage should not be insured, since that might reflect a lack of faith. Furthermore, Manders praises Engstrand, a deceitful man who is soliciting funds to open a home for sailors. Engstrand has tried to enlist his daughter, Regina, Mrs. Alving's maid, in this project, but she initially refuses.

Oswald Alving is attracted to Regina's liveliness. Mrs. Alving even considers letting Oswald marry Regina even though she is really the Captain's illegitimate daughter.

Engstrand sets fire to the orphanage, but convinces Manders that it was he who accidentally started it. Mrs. Alving reveals the secrets about the Captain to Oswald and Regina. Upon realizing that Oswald is her half-brother, Regina leaves to make her own way. Oswald, now quite ill, had obtained poison to end his life when his condition became unbearable. The time has come, and his mother agrees to bring him the poison.

In *An Enemy of the People*, Dr. Stockmann has made a great discovery: the water supply, which affects the town's healing Baths, is polluted. The pollutants come from waste spilled by a tannery owned by Morten Kiil, his father-in-law. The Baths were a tourist attraction and provided financial security for the town. Should Dr. Stockmann's discovery that they were polluted and a health hazard become known, the economic base of the town would be destroyed. The movie *Jaws* updated this same moral dilemma.

Stockmann believes that his discovery will be welcomed. However, his brother, the mayor, gradually turns public opinion against him. Withdrawing their suport of Stockmann's scientific findings, the press—editor Hovstad, subeditor Billing, and printer Aslaksen—argue that to publicize the findings would embarrass the town government, ruin the economy, and require a tax increase to defray the cost of moving the intake pipe.

Denied access to the press, Stockmann arranges to speak to the public at the home of his friend, Captain Horster. Denied permission to speak about the Baths, Stockmann lectures about the lies that are at the foundation of society. He does not blame prejudiced officials like his brother, the mayor, but rather the majority. Stockmann is called an enemy of the people. Subsequently his home is stoned, he is dispossessed by his landlord, and his daughter is fired from her teaching position. The mayor brings a letter dismissing Stockmann from the board of the Baths, thereby taking away his income. But if he were to retract his position, he might be reinstated.

Morton Kiil has bought up all the stock of the Baths with money that was to go to his daughter and grandchildren. Unless Stockmann retracts his position, those shares will be worthless. The mayor assumes that Stockmann's attack on the Baths was coordinated with Kiil to drive down the price of the stock. That story is picked up by Hovstad and Aslaksen, who want to cut themselves in on the profits from the stock. Stockmann throws everyone out. With only his wife, children, and Captain Horster at his side he decides to open a school to teach his own children and any poor boys in town who need an education.

In comparing the plots of *Ghosts* and *An Enemy of the People*, salient themes from Ibsen's past works reappear in the former but are displayed in an amplified form in the latter. In *An Enemy of the People* the themes of the tyranny of public opinion, the sinful legacy of father to child, and the strength inherent in one's solitary loyalty to the ideal of truth appear on an unadorned stage. The characters of the play recede into the background, leaving the enemies of Ibsen, those who had attacked his previous play, exposed under glaring spotlights.

TRANSFORMATION THROUGH CREATIVITY

Humiliating life experiences can provide the context for an artist's work. To some extent, the creative product is, in addition to contributions from other sources, a transformation by the artist of the effects of his own painful and triumphant past as well as a record of experiences of narcissistic injuries. In these circumstances the process of transformation requires self-regulated alterations, the capacity to alter one's self-state. Such transformations, in this instance in Ibsen's life, were motivated by his exposure to contempt, derision, and ridicule. To turn painful self-states into a sense of triumph requires transforming the narcissistic rage that is evoked (Kohut 1972) into some more manageable experience. A sense of having righted the wrong or avenged the slur or turned the tables on one's attackers can restore a sense of pride and lead to a sense of intactness.

Two types of transformation are noted when *Ghosts* and *An Enemy of the People* are contrasted. One transformation refers to the way in which themes from the first play are altered in the second play. The second type of transformation refers to Ibsen's self-state; the transformation of narcissistic rage is a response to criticisms and rejection of *Ghosts*. Thus, we can follow two parallel transformative processes, one in Ibsen the artist, as revealed in the content of the plays, the other in Ibsen the man, as he recovered from the assault of his critics.

In *Ghosts,* Ibsen depicted central themes that organized his past experience in their "purest, boldest" (M. Meyer 1986, p. 7) form. The extent of his self-disclosures left Ibsen in a particularly vulnerable position when he was attacked by critics and ignored by his audience. In *An Enemy of the People* Ibsen regrouped, and argued for an uncompromising stance through which the artist can defy social pressure and withstand ridicule and isolation. Utilizing biographical and autobiographical reports to construct a model scene for Ibsen, I will link an organizing theme of his life and his plays to the state he recaptured after his narcissistic injury.

CREATIVE TRANSFORMATION: FROM *GHOSTS* TO *AN ENEMY OF THE PEOPLE*

The negative response to *Ghosts* came from critics and public alike. Copies of his play remained unsold in the bookstores. When King Oscar II of Sweden told Ibsen that he should never have written that play, Ibsen responded, "Your majesty, I had to write *Ghosts*" (M. Meyer 1971, pp. 293–294). The play was called "filthy, putrid, naked loathsomeness, an open sewer" and Ibsen was called "an egoist and a bungler" (Watts 1964, p. 11). Ibsen's remark to King Oscar II must be taken quite literally. He had to write *Ghosts*. The themes of that play—father–son tensions, living a lie, the effects of learning the truth, inheritance, bankruptcy, and illegitimacy—had appeared in prior plays. However, in *Ghosts*, one of the themes, the sins of the father (the son inheriting syphilis from his father) is taken to an extreme of horror. In so doing, Ibsen addressed this compelling, burning, residual issue from his past and depicted it as a metaphor for his society as well. *Ghosts* thus combines a painful autobiographical statement, his disillusionment in his own father, with a devastating social critique. Personally, I believe he expressed his disillusionment at his father's legacy as well as his quest for an idealizable father of whom he could be proud.

Ghosts centers on the homecoming of Oswald Alving. His syphilis is getting worse and he has come home to die. His mother blames her own limitations as the cause of her husband's dissolute ways. In so doing, she wants to avoid her son's casting blame on his father for having inherited the disease. She depicts her husband as the victim of societal pressures so that her son might retain his idealized, compassionate view of him. By showing father, mother, and son caught in the vise of societal pressures and hypocrisy, Ibsen reiterated a leitmotif of his dramas. It was as though he continually tried to transform his own history, but his ambivalence toward his father prevented him from exonerating his parents.

Apparently Ibsen felt compelled to bare himself in a thinly disguised form. He gathered together his past injuries, infused with his rage, and created several despicable characters out of this mix. They embody the lies, hypocrisy, deception, and duplicity that he hated in society. In his uncompromising depiction of the sins of the father, the ghosts that demand placing duty and public appearance above self-expression and individual freedom, Ibsen expressed his long-held rage in its purest, boldest form.

In *Ghosts*, Ibsen revealed his vulnerability by thinly disguising his conflicted feelings, his longing for an idealizable father, and his sense of betrayal by the legacy his father left him. Presumably accompanying such self-exposure is the expectation of relief from some persisting inner pressures, and presumably there is an expectation that the self-revelatory work will be welcomed and admired by an audience. That is, through the creative transformations that constituted his dramatic writings, Ibsen attempted to expiate his psychic "syphilis," a long-standing sense of guilt and unacceptability. Had the reception of *Ghosts* met his usual expectation of just disturbing his audience, he might have felt satisfied. Instead, *Ghosts*, the play he had to write, the play in which his "inheritance" was most blatantly and unmitigatingly depicted, was resoundingly criticized. His self-revelations were confronted and shattered. If there was a moment when the capacity to transform shattered narcissism into artistic creativity was called for, this was it.

Ibsen was shocked by his sudden unpopularity, but within three months after *Ghosts* appeared he began work on *An Enemy of the People*. Though he had the ideas for the new play earlier, he rushed to complete it in a year. Thereby he broke the every-two-year tradition he had maintained in writing his other plays. *An Enemy of the People* became his response to the devastating reception that was given to *Ghosts*.

The themes woven together in *Ghosts* reappear in *An Enemy of the People*. The inherited sin of the father is now a tannery, owned by a wealthy patriarch, that pollutes the waters of the town. The potential victims are all the townspeople, and they must choose between health and moral integrity on one side, and deception, greed, and narrow self-interests on the other side. The battle lines are drawn.

In *An Enemy of the People*, Ibsen depicted himself as Dr. Stockmann, its whistle-blowing hero, a man who was totally decent and honest, but naive with respect to political wheeling and dealing. His goodness is contrasted with the narrow-mindedness of society. The authorities appear to be a rigid, unimaginative, self-serving, bureaucratic lot, banal at best and corrupt at worst.

Dr. Stockmann makes a discovery that results in his being pitted against the powers of society. The discovery is a metaphor for the precious recognition and appreciation to which Ibsen felt entitled but which the popular press denied him. In response, he mocked his detractors by exposing them as mean-spirited and unprincipled. Ibsen had believed in the capacity of the people to discriminate the true from the false and to exercise sound judgment. In *An Enemy of the People* he illustrates their inability to distinguish scientifically backed findings from self-serving rationalizations.

Dr. Stockmann values the support of the solid majority at the opening of the play. Naively, he believes that they will be swayed by truth and evidence. But by the time the curtain falls, he is heard to say that the most dangerous enemy of truth and freedom amongst us is the solid majority. "The majority is never right! . . . The minority is always right!" (Ibsen 1882, p. 473). By the end of the play, Stockmann can only trust his immediate family. Even their loyalty appears to be more out of devotion than conviction about the scientific accuracy and urgency of his findings. Aside from his family and an old friend, Stockmann's supporters may at best include some street urchins who have not yet been corrupted by public opinion.

Wounded by the shortsighted public, Ibsen asserted that the creative artist stands alone, a minority of one, to maintain his integrity and the purity of his vision. In *An Enemy of the People*, Ibsen speaks with one uncompromising voice. Stockmann loses all support and ends alone: "The strongest man in the world is the man who stands most alone" (Ibsen 1882, p. 506).

In *Ghosts* the two major protagonists, Ibsen and public opinion, are in the background. They are in conflict and this conflict shapes the motivations of the characters. But they always remain behind the scenes. Not so in *An Enemy of the People*. All gloves are off. Ibsen himself steps upon the stage and drags his enemy, public opinion, front and center with him. In doing so, he did risk producing a stagy setup in which the good, honest, and selfless Dr. Stockmann is pitted against the hypocritical, deceptive, and selfish townspeople. But Ibsen categorically rejected any triumph-of-good-over-evil solution, as indicated in the scene in which Stockmann's daughter refuses to translate an English book. She cannot believe its theme of advocating the subjugation of oneself to a higher authority as being preferable to self-determination.

The criticism leveled at Ibsen for his self-indulgence in writing *Ghosts* is treated with wry humor in *An Enemy of the People*. It is placed into the mouth of Dr. Stockmann's brother, the mayor. He attempts to act as an elder statesman, but, alas, lacks perspective and wisdom. He spouts self-aggrandizing platitudes. Ironically, he accuses Dr. Stockmann of compromising himself time after time without being aware of it: "You have a restless, combative, rebellious nature. And then you've this unfortunate passion for rushing into print upon every possible—and impossible—subject. The moment you get an idea you have to sit down and write a newspaper article or a whole pamphlet about it" (Ibsen 1882, pp. 431–432). This lecture had as little effect in silencing Dr. Stockmann as the criticism had on Ibsen.

Ibsen depicts Dr. Stockmann as paying a price for his naïveté; he is socially totally isolated. But he remains undaunted. Even at the final curtain, he still tries to restore his world, based on the principle that the truth will win the day. He announces: "I've made a great discovery!" His wife evidently has heard enough of his "great discoveries" and cannot really believe that, in effect, he has not learned anything from this whole misadventure. She says, "Not again!" Dr. Stockmann now utters the line that embodies Ibsen's defiance of the majority and defines the state in which he feels himself to be independent, invulnerable, and exquisitely self-contained. "The strongest man in the world is the man who stands most alone!" To this, Mrs. Stockmann can only smile, shake her head, and say, "Oh Tomas."

To Ibsen, the artist's strength lay in his undaunted capacity to maintain his vision in the face of opposition. He was engaged in a solitary enterprise. Ibsen's ideal for the creative artist required him to cleanse and decontaminate the whole community. He must disturb, be perpetually misunderstood, and walk alone. In comparing *Ghosts* and *An Enemy of the People*, salient themes from Ibsen's past works are found in an amplified form in *Ghosts*. Subsequently, in *An Enemy of the People*, the tyranny of public opinion, the sinful legacy of father to child, and the strength inherent in one's solitary loyalty to the ideal of truth appeared on an unadorned stage. From these transformations of themes and contents, I turn to the second type of transformation, that of self-states.

SOME BIOGRAPHICAL ROOTS FOR IBSEN'S SELF-STATE TRANSFORMATION

Initially, Ibsen took the critical onslaught against *Ghosts* calmly (M. Meyer 1986) and compared it to the furor that had greeted his other plays. As with prior plays, he expected to disturb but not alienate his audience. He anticipated the rejection by the right-wing press. But, when Arne Garborg, a novelist who had just published *The Freethinker*, dismissed *Ghosts* as "the most unpleasant book we have had in a long time" (M. Meyer 1986, p. 7), Ibsen's expectations were betrayed. He then depicted Garborg as a double-crossing newspaper editor in *An Enemy of the People*. The defection of the liberal press left Ibsen with only a small coterie of supporters.

Traumatic, painful, or humiliating life experiences sometimes provide the context for the artist's transformation of the effects of narcissistic injuries. In this instance, transformation requires a capacity to alter one's self-state, when, for example, the person is exposed to contempt, derision, or ridicule.

Ghosts and its troubled reception in some ways recapitulates an important incident from the puppet shows Ibsen produced in his youth. As the puppeteer, Ibsen remained on the sidelines; the shows were popular. Perhaps he drew on the popular reception he received for those puppet shows as encouragement to pursue the brazen plot of *Ghosts* in which, like a puppeteer, he stays in the background. If, indeed, he hoped to refind the success he had enjoyed in his youth, and to harness his knack for appealing to an audience with a personal, painful variant of his puppet show plots, he failed. Ironically, the reaction of the critics repeated an attack by some ruffians. They upset one of the performances by cutting the strings of the puppets.

As reported by M. Meyer (1967), an elderly lady, Benedike Paulsen, had seen these puppet shows when she was a little girl in 1841 or 1842. She recalled how angry Henrik became when Ole Paulsen and Peder Lund Pederson disrupted his show and cut the strings of the puppets. Although Ole was much bigger than Henrik, Henrik was tough and he pounced on Ole. Peder went to help Ole, and Henrik was about to be outnumbered two to one when the voice of Henrik's father rang out. He came to help his son and dispersed Ole and Peder. Ibsen quickly repaired the puppets and drew a large crowd for his next gala performance. The quick recovery and response to the vandals in his youth was later repeated by Ibsen in his quick response to the critics of *Ghosts*.

The vandalization of his puppet show proved to be a rare moment when Ibsen's father, by then massively devalued, suddenly emerged to support his son. The vignette not only preserved a picture of Ibsen, fearlessly responding to his attackers, alone, against a far stronger foe, but also contained a moment when he felt support from his father. His ambivalence now becomes more understandable. His "inheritance" did not only include his father's sins but contained a touch of support as well.

The puppet show incident occurred when Ibsen was about 11. When he was about 7 his father's bankruptcy and decline began. The puppet show incident may have been associated with recollections of the prebankruptcy, idealized father of Ibsen's childhood. His solitary triumph coupled with the memory of his father's support may have provided the strength that enabled Ibsen and Dr. Stockmann to stand alone.

Ibsen tried to expiate the hatred he harbored toward his father in *Ghosts*. If he only wanted to pillorize those hypocrites who shunned him in his hometown in his youth and who abandoned his father, he succeeded. But if he simultaneously expected to retain the appreciative audience of his puppet plays, he failed. If he expected to right the wrongs done to him and his father, he rained criticism upon himself instead. The peace that he sought, that had been wished for him by his father, did not come.

After Ibsen's disappointing reception of *Ghosts*, his self-state could be characterized as enraged by new disappointments, as well as by the revival and retention of the old hurts and disillusionments. He sought refuge through the transformation of this painful state to one that may also have been an enduring legacy of his childhood, a state devoid of impingements from others and free of the disappointment he felt in his father. Akin to a puppeteer, he longed to be above the squabbles of the mundane world, without concern for social status, economics, or prestige.

I have been working backward, from Ibsen's adult years as a dramatist to his preteen years as a puppeteer. I now draw on two memories from his earliest years to illustrate the centrality of the proposed self-state transformations and its relation to Ibsen's creativity.

At the age of 53, which is when he wrote *Ghosts*, Ibsen made his only autobiographical notes. In them he recalled two incidents that must have occurred before he was 4 years old, according to M. Meyer (1967), who was familiar with their locale. The earliest memory concerned the tower window of the church across the street from Ibsen's house. It remained of special importance to Ibsen throughout his life.

> My nursemaid carried me . . . up into the tower and let me sit alone in the open window . . . held from behind by her. . . . I remember clearly how impressed I was at being able to see the crowns of people's hats; I looked down into our own rooms, saw the window frames, saw the curtains, saw my mother standing down there in one of the windows. . . . But then there was a hubbub, . . . and the maid pulled me hurriedly away and ran down with me. . . . afterwards they often told me how my mother caught sight of me in the window of the tower, had shrieked, had fainted . . . and later, having got me back, had wept and kissed and petted me. As a boy I

never afterwards crossed the square without looking up at the window in the tower. I felt that that window belonged to me. . . . I have kept only one other memory from those early years. As a christening gift I had been given a large silver coin with a man's head on it. The nursemaid taught me that the man on the coin was King Fredrik Rex, and once I tried to bowl it along the floor, with the unfortunate result that the coin rolled down into a crack. I think my parents interpreted this as an unlucky omen, it being a christening gift. The floor was taken up and they searched and dug around assiduously but King Fredrik Rex never saw the light of day again. For a long time afterwards I could not help regarding myself as a wicked felon, and when I saw the town constable emerge from the town hall and make his way towards our door, I ran as fast as I could into the nursery and hid myself beneath the bed. [M. Meyer 1967, pp. 23–24]

It is always risky, when discussing an artist, to draw inferences about his life from his creative output. However, these autobiographical reports do provide an additional source of information that may be legitimately used to draw parallels between Ibsen the artist and his art. These two early memories recalled by Ibsen can be used to construct a model scene: a little boy, alone, is beset by powerful emotions, sees the world from a bird's-eye view, and is excited at viewing familiar details and familiar people in familiar settings, but from a new perspective. A surprising, precipitous descent from such a height follows, leaving behind a longing to reexperience those precious, solitary moments. The little boy discovers that he can have a powerful, disturbing effect on others—his mother faints. Furthermore, the litle boy uses a coin for exploratory purposes, and, as a result, the floor is dug up. Worse, still, a sense of bad luck is unleashed. He had to manage not only states of exhilaration on his own, but also his guilt and a mysterious sense of having done something wrong.

Was Ibsen's "good nursemaid" instrumental in setting him up for these two situations and then unable to help calm him after their distressing outcomes? Ibsen did not report the presence of any other available adult, either to reflect his joy at having seen the world from on high or to calm and soothe him after his loss.

The search for a missing coin presents a mystery. How did it disappear? Where is it? The disappearing coin contributed to the centrality of solitary self-experience. From an experience of playfulness he was suddenly transported to a state of loss and an inexplicable sense of guilt. He felt like a felon and hid when the constable approached his house. The loss of the coin ushered in a transformation from a positive, playful, exploratory, self-absorbed state to a secret state, marked by guilt and personal blame for wrongdoing. He did not find solace for his loss. On his own, he bore his guilt, as well as the surprising discovery of the enormous, disturbing impact he can have on others.

The coin memory also signaled another transformation in the direction of having to regulate painful states on his own without the support of others. In the memory Ibsen implied that his parents were more concerned with the fate of the lost coin than with the state of the coin loser. The model scene was constructed to organize Ibsen's experience as a solitary, impactful onlooker. His tower window provided sanctuary and protection. Self-regulation was achieved by removing himself from ordinary life. Thus, after his rebuff in response to *Ghosts*, Ibsen returned to his church tower window and in *An Enemy of the People* disturbed the world around him.

The critics of *Ghosts* proclaimed that he had gone too far, but to Ibsen the loss of his audience, his "minority," may have appeared as mysterious as the loss of the silver coin. However, unlike his childhood loss, he now had resources with which to transform his state. As a child he had lived with a sense of guilt and shame for some time. Now he was able to harness his talents to reverse the state that followed the loss of his audience and readers. Akin to his effective response to the vandals who cut the strings of his puppets, Ibsen responded rapidly. He came down from the church tower and placed himself into the center of the action of his next play, *An Enemy of the People*. Just as he "had" to write *Ghosts*, he had to dispel the ghosts of his past lest they reoccupy his affective life.

His prior pattern of creative transformations of narcissistic injuries enabled him to transcend this deeply felt blow.

For Ibsen, the states that required repair were characterized by loss of respect from his community, profound disappointment and disillusionment, and outrage at societal hypocrisy and the betrayal by his friends. He had specific preconditions for such reparation and placed his strength on his confidence to maintain his vision in the face of opposition. This was necessarily a solitary enterprise. Speaking through Dr. Stockmann, Ibsen asserted that the artist accepts isolation as a consequence of his superior and unique vision of the world, the view from the church tower. He refound his childhood grandiosity and creatively restored himself to his preferred position: alone, and uncompromisingly morally superior to others.

Creative work is one avenue toward transforming one's self-state. The subjective discomfort of painful self-states can provide an impetus for finding the means by which such states can be altered. Such transformations are a form of self-righting and self-regulation. However, a level of creativity and talent comparable to Ibsen is not a requirement for such transformations. Such creativity is only one means of transforming one's self-state. But even when one's means are more modest, the range and freedom of the self-regulatory capacity can be enhanced, internal reorganization can occur, and the state of the self can shift toward greater cohesion and toward a richer affective repertoire.

In response to the attacks on his work, Ibsen got more than angry. Presumably there was a change in self-state through the reactivation of his experience as a puppeteer, which he dealt with creatively. If he experienced narcissistic rage, he was energized rather than depleted by it, a possibility that we may also encounter in clinical practice.

7

The Transformation of Reactive Aggression into Eruptive Aggression

I believe in a cruel god, who has created me in his own image and whom, in wrath, I name. From vileness of some germ or atom, I have been born vile. I am evil because I am a man. I feel the primeval slime within me. Yes! This is my creed!
—translation by Mauro Calamandrei

So sings Iago in Verdi's opera *Otello*. This "credo" ("I believe") was added by Verdi and his librettist, Boito, to Shakespeare's *Othello*. Shakespeare's Iago reveals his evil nature through the actions of the play, but Verdi's Iago faces the audience and proclaims himself to be born evil. Iago is further provided with several motives for his villainy by Shakespeare. He claims that Othello cuckolded him with his wife, and he resents Othello for passing him over to appoint Cassio to be his lieutenant. Thus, Iago's evil could be understood to have been motivated by narcissistic injuries, humiliations that were intolerable blows to his pride. Were these Iago's reactions to failures on Othello's part to mirror his archaic grandiosity? Do these motives explain the extent of Iago's villainy? Or do we see Iago as the embodiment of man's evil nature?

Shakespeare brilliantly positioned Iago's treachery just beyond understandable human motivations akin to the allegorical character of Vice as found in medieval plays (A. Lachmann 1999). We, in the audience, want to understand evil and look for motivations that we can recognize. But is there evil that defies such recognition? Are there Iagos, people whose "intrinsic design" demands an extreme of destructiveness toward others? Here the question of innate and reactive aggression resurfaces.

When investigating the extremes of destructive behavior, our empathy for the perpetrators, for the Iagos, can easily fail us. We may be able to extend our empathic grasp beyond "murderous wishes," and even to the extreme of killing out of revenge, or for personal gain or self-protection. But to understand destroying another person, killing with pleasure, and to use Anna Freud's (1972) term, "for no obvious reason," challenges the theory of reactive aggression. It requires advancing a hypothesis that can explain how an inborn propensity to react aversively can be transformed into an aggressive act that appears unmotivated with respect to the extreme of violence that it expresses. To develop such a hypothesis, I turn to an investigation of an extreme of violence as exemplified by several serial killers.

If we place experiences of early, massive, or traumatic activation of aversive motivations on a continuum, an extreme in the quality and quantity of emotional, physical, and sexual abuse would be found in the life histories of many men who became serial killers. In this group of violent adults we find manifestations of, and an extreme form of, apparently unmotivated or driven, destructive aggression.

Serial killers are men who have killed three or more strangers for no obvious reason. Even the usual surface motives for murder, such as monetary gain, revenge, or sexual jealousy, are not basic to this group of killers. Their behavior appears to illustrate an uncurbed impulse to kill. Typically, these killers prey on weak, vulnerable, defenseless people and those whose absence is not likely to be noticed for some time. The most frequent victims are young children, runaways, prostitutes, and men and women in isolated places. The killer may have stalked his victims or encountered them by chance.

It was by chance that I encountered the serial-killer literature. My wife, Annette Lachmann, has been an avid reader of gothic novels. Serial-killer fiction is a prime example of current gothic literature. For the past several years she has been teaching a course entitled "The Serial Killer in Fact and Fiction" at the New School in New York. We have collaborated on several papers on the motivations and the evil self of the serial killer (A. Lachmann and F. Lachmann 1994, 1997). The study of this literature is as close as I have come to an encounter with a serial killer.

Although the disadvantages of using secondary sources outweigh their advantages in formulating a psychoanalytic view of the motivations and development of a serial killer, the main advantage is that the information gathered by reporters, law enforcement personnel, and family members of the killers is unlikely to be tilted toward a specific psychoanalytic theory. No doubt the reporters and interviewers whose material I used have their own slants. But the accounts tended to be factual and straightforward.

A major disadvantage of secondary sources is that the kinds of questions a psychoanalyst might have asked these killers were not asked. There is no account of the process of the interviews. Nonverbal, postural, affective, and gestural responses are rarely included. In the interviews, the killers' responses sound to me as though they have been coached or advised by lawyers, or have picked up psychological explanations for their killings from popular literature. It is difficult to assess the genuineness of their self-reflections.

Brief developmental histories of four serial killers follow. These accounts highlight individual differences that characterize this group of men. However, in the similarities in their histories, I believe, lie clues to the pathways along which reactive aggression is transformed into eruptions of killings.

THUMBNAIL SKETCHES OF SERIAL KILLERS

Henry Lee Lucas, according to Newton (1992) and Norris (1988), began a killing spree in his thirties. By the time he was 53 years old, he had been arrested for murder, rape, and kidnapping, and was sentenced to death. He confessed to a series of slayings and to dumping the bodies along a highway.

Lucas was the youngest son in a dysfunctional family. His father had been a severe alcoholic who lost both legs in an accident. His mother, a prostitute, beat Lucas and killed his pet animals. When he attended primary school, she dressed him as a girl and kept him in girls' clothing. Lucas had one significant, caring, nurturing contact during those early years, an elementary school teacher. She cut his curls, dressed him in pants, and fed him during school lunchtimes.

Both Lucas and his father were subjected to watching his mother have sex with other men. His earliest memory was of his mother finishing up with a customer, then pulling out a shotgun and shooting the man in the leg. Lucas observed the man's blood spatter all over the room. Even with this background, horrendous as it sounds, it is not self-evident that Lucas would end up as a derelict, and be responsible for making the American police aware of serial murders (Wilson 1990).

As a teenager, Lucas was cruel to animals, and he had sex with their corpses. Imprisoned for various minor offenses, he was finally apprehended for the murders he committed. Lucas became fascinated with police procedures and their techniques in pursuing investigations and developing leads. This helped him to predict the moves of the police and to evade them. He knew how to be a murderer, and, according to his own account, in prison he learned how to be a career criminal.

When at age 38 Lucas was recommended for parole, he warned the prison officials not to release him because he would kill again. Because of prison overcrowding, he was released. True to his word, shortly upon his release, he began the killing spree that lasted fifteen years.

No doubt, Lucas's violent childhood and chronic drug and alcohol abuse contributed to his homicidal frenzies. When interviewed, he stated that he could not feel sexually satisfied with a living person and that he killed in order to be sexually potent. To me, this statement is suspect. It illustrates the possibility of Lucas's prior exposure to psychological formulations about necrophilia. These disclosures are often made after considerable exposure to interviews and psychological explanations. However, many other serial killers have also described their greater comfort relating to dead rather than living creatures.

Unlike Henry Lee Lucas, Randall Woodfield, according to Newton (1992) and Rule (1987), was the handsome, athletic boy-next-door type who cruised the highways of the Northwest in search of prey. His list of victims grew to a total of at least forty-four murders. His crimes began with robberies and rapidly escalated to sexual assaults on women. In these assaults, Woodfield gave scripts to his victims. For example, he ordered one woman to say that he was a better lover than her boyfriend. Eventually he shot a woman who did not comply with his orders. She had laughed, thinking his threat was a joke because he wore a ludicrous-looking disguise, a fake beard.

Woodfield's crimes continued and included the sexual abuse of two girls, aged 8 and 10, and the killing of a mother and her 14-year-old daughter. Lab tests revealed that he had sodomized the girl after he shot her to death. Through the description of a woman whom he had permitted to escape, he was apprehended, convicted, and sentenced to life plus 165 years in prison.

Randall Woodfield was born to apparently functional, educated, upper-middle-class parents. His hard-working father wanted to give his family all the advantages that he had missed. His mother, a homemaker, admired her son because he was handsome and walked earlier than other babies. His two older sisters doted on him. He was socially graceful, well mannered, and popular. However, there were some problems that Woodfield described when interviewed as an adult. He felt women dominated his home. He resented his sisters for being given privileges because they were older. When his mother, the disciplinarian of the children, punished him, he felt humiliated. He wanted to please his mother but found that he could not meet the unrealistic goals she set for him.

Signs of sexual deviance began to appear in junior high school. Woodfield began to expose himself. When he was caught he was neither punished nor referred for treatment. The police did not want to hurt his chances for a sports career by bringing charges against him. In college, Woodfield was drafted by a professional football team. Through indecent exposure, he destroyed his promising sports career. The girls Woodfield dated found him sexy, at first, but empty, and they quickly became bored with him.

The discrepancy between Woodfield's outward appearance and his conventional family and his self-state of deadness is striking. As in the case of Iago, do Woodfield's presumed narcissistic injuries, that is, the domination he felt by the women in his family and his feeling of inadequacy in relation to his mother's expectations, provide understandable motives for his killing sprees? Or, as with Iago, are we ultimately left with a mystery?

As Woodfield increased the frenzy of his killing, and the police were getting closer to discovering the identity of the killer, a tentative psychological profile was drawn by a police investigator *prior* to his apprehension: "He may act like a monster, but he looks like the guy next door. There are probably a lot of people who know him well, who think he's a great guy. People who are going to be struck dumb when we catch him" (Rule 1987, p. 123).

As is quite typical of serial killers, Theodore (Ted) Bundy, as depicted in accounts by Newton (1992), Rule (1989) and Sears (1991), led two lives: one was admirable and respectable, the other was shrouded in secrecy. He was an intelligent, handsome, and well-liked young man, a law student, Republican party worker, and volunteer counselor in a rape victim clinic. Bundy represented himself at his trial, and the presiding judge told him, with regret, even after sentencing him to death, that he would have liked to have Bundy try cases in his court. He thought that he was bright and would have been a good lawyer (Sears 1991). Bundy had murdered more than twenty-one young women. Like Woodfield, Bundy also looked like the all-American boy.

Bundy was born in a group home for unwed mothers. He was left there for three months and then raised by his grandparents as their adopted son. His mother was called his "sister." She claimed that Bundy's father was a student who deserted her, but there was some suspicion that Bundy's mother had been the victim of incest and that his grandfather was the real father. According to Moes (1991) the grandfather was intolerant, tyrannical, volatile, sadistic to animals, and the possessor of a large pornography collection. However, he doted on young Ted. Bundy's grandmother suffered from depression that required several series of electroshock treatments. His mother was an emotionally blocked, prudish, obedient, and church-going woman.

As a teenager, Bundy frequently brushed against the law. He was suspected of auto theft and burglary, but the court records were destroyed. In college, he stole television sets, textbooks, and ski boots from stores. It pleased him that, once again, he was not caught.

In his early twenties, Bundy very much wanted a serious relationship with a woman. However, he felt ashamed of his background and believed he would have nothing to offer the kind of woman he wanted. He then met the daughter of a wealthy family who was everything he desired. She was strikingly beautiful with long dark hair parted down the middle. He was infatuated, but she lost interest in him because he had no plans or prospects for the future. Upset over her elusiveness, Bundy allowed his college grades to slip. When she finally broke off with him, he was devastated.

Shortly after the breakup, Bundy found another girlfriend who was quite different from his first love. She was small, vulnerable, and shy, and she clung to him. She later described Bundy as having been preoccupied with sex and violence, and fascinated with bondage and sodomy. She agreed to act out some of his sexual fantasies with him. While still involved with her, he contacted his first love to get back with her. Neither woman knew about the other.

When Bundy tried to rekindle his first love, he was more self-assured and articulate. He courted her successfully with expensive gifts and luxurious dinners. Two months later, he ended their relationship. She was shocked and hurt. He had succeeded in wooing her and winning her trust, only, precipitously, to abandon her. She concluded that Bundy's courtship had been deliberately planned, to be in a position where he could make her fall in love with him, just to reject her, as she had rejected him. Presumably the pattern of seduction and establishment of trust, followed by betrayal, which Bundy enacted here, was derived from his early experience of abandonment, deception, and his mother's emotional elusiveness.

While Bundy was in law school he began to prowl at night, observing women undressing through open windows. However, he soon turned from watching women undress to forcing them to undress. His first murder of a tall, willowy 15-year-old girl followed. She was found with her jeans slit up the back seam from the crotch to the waist. She had been sodomized, strangled, and her throat cut. From then on, Bundy's early victims all bore a striking physical resemblance to his first love.

One day, a tall 18-year-old girl, with long hair parted down the middle, was approached in a shopping mall by a man who pretended to be a police officer. He told her that a robbery had just taken place, coaxed her into his car, and started to drive. Suddenly, he clamped handcuffs on one of her wrists and attempted to cuff the other when she managed to pull away. He tried to hit her but she escaped and hailed a passing motorist. She was one of the few women who succeeded in escaping from certain death and she later identified Bundy as her assailant.

As is evident from these three summaries, the early lives of these killers were quite varied. Henry Lucas's early life is typical of a group of serial killers whose early experiences were marked by extreme physical and sexual abuse. His killing of animals at a young age constituted an early signal that something was wrong. As we will see, these signals are clear in retrospect but, in the cases of serial killers, they were invariably ignored. Randall Woodfield also sent signals in his early life that something was wrong. His repetitive exhibitionistic acts, at least in retrospect, could be understood as desperate bids for attention that were ignored. Bundy's thefts and his bouts of voyeurism as a student also contained an exhibitionistic aspect. In each case, signals that something was wrong were sent to families and law enforcement personnel. In the cases of Woodfield and Bundy, these signals were disregarded in order to maintain a facade of middle-class conventional decency.

A family history like that of Lucas, replete with extreme violence, provides easy formulations as to why such a severely abused child should become an abuser. But Bundy and Woodfield came from the other extreme of this range. There was no history of physical violence in Woodfield's background. Bundy's "grandfather" was reported to have spanked Bundy on occasion. However, both of these men grew up in a family atmosphere of deception and emotional deprivation. Their histories lend themselves to psychodynamic formulations and explanation. However, such explanations never sound convincing to me because they apply to many people whose behavior is light-years away from committing serial murders. For example, to explain Bundy's killings as revenge, derived from the resemblance of his victims to his first girlfriend who rejected him, although possibly accurate, is woefully superficial and incomplete.

THE STORY OF ARTHUR SHAWCROSS

To amplify the perspective that can encompass the transformation of reactive to eruptive aggression, Arthur Shawcross's life is described in greater detail. Shawcross is typical of those serial killers for whom simple explanations of turning passively endured abuse experiences into active abuse or oedipal and preoedipal dynamics cannot adequately account for the enormity of the crimes.

Shawcross's biographer, Jack Olsen (1993), interviewed members of his family, his teachers, neighbors, law enforcement officials, psychiatrists, and one of his intended victims, and he consulted transcripts of his case. His book, *Misbegotten Son,* is my main source of information about Shawcross, and the following summary is based on inferences derived from Olsen's book.

Arthur Shawcross was the oldest of three children. He grew up in a two-parent home in northern Maine in which his mother was the dominant figure. She spoke in the "short vocal style of an Adirondack lumber boss" (Olsen 1993, p. 45). She was said to have been a fastidious housekeeper who ruled her home with a strong arm. Shawcross's father was a quiet and passive man who earned a steady income as a county road worker.

As a child, Shawcross was intimidated by his mother and put his father down for allowing his mother to take command. When he was 9, his mother discovered that her husband was a bigamist with a wife and child in Australia. Thereafter, the mother became even more domineering and abusive toward her husband. Shawcross recalled this relationship when he was already in prison for his killings: "From that point mother never let father be the man of the house" (p. 165). When Shawcross's father watched television, his mother would refer to the young women in the programs he was watching as "whores." She presented a clear dichotomous picture to Shawcross: young women were whores and older women were respectable motherly types. Shawcross would get angry with his mother for belittling his father and angry with his father for being so withdrawn.

In retrospect, Shawcross wrote, "Dad hung his head in shame. He couldn't look you in the eye and say it was not so! Mom took over and made life hell in that house. Dad can't even watch TV without Mom cursing or throwing something at him. Even when he worked he could have done better for himself, but now he started working in a gravel pit. I am ashamed of my father and now I am ashamed of myself" (Olsen 1993, p. 189). The predominant impression gained about Shawcross's early family life was that seething anger, followed by withdrawal and shame, saturated the atmosphere.

Although the tensions within the family were distressing, there was, nevertheless, a comfortable aspect to their lives. The Shawcross family enjoyed a modest level of prosperity and lived in an almost idyllic country setting. The entire family—Arthur, his younger sister by two years and younger brother, cousins, aunts, and uncles—attended church together and were involved in stockcar races, boat races, and other outings. Arthur tended to keep to himself, exacerbating his sense of isolation in a context in which the rest of the family was a close-knit community. However, early photos of Arthur already show him with a blank, affectless look; something seems wrong.

Shawcross's cousins remember him as a clinging child who craved attention and wanted a great deal of physical comfort and love. The cousins believed that he was increasingly rejected by his mother after her other children were born. At a young age, Arthur spent a great deal of time with his paternal grandmother. She was said to have loved him, and he did chores for her that he would not do at home. The time spent with the grandmother may have been the period when the other children arrived and his mother lost interest in him.

The neglect took its toll. By the age of 5 or 6, Arthur Shawcross suffered from frequent nightmares and enuresis. In the first and second grade in school he had scored A's and B's, but on later IQ tests he scored below normal. Antisocial behavior patterns began in first and second grades and subsequently became more and more pronounced. He resented younger children and seemed to enjoy making them cry through sadistic bullying, provoking them to feel pain, rage, and fear. His increasing propensity to provoke young children may have reflected his increasing emotional deadness, since, at the same time, he retreated more and more into a private fantasy world.

Shawcross's isolation drove him to create imaginary friends with whom he conversed, a boy his own age, and a younger blond-haired girl like his sister. This behavior gave others the impression that he was talking to himself. Called "Oddy" by classmates, he was the butt of daily jokes and cruelties. When bigger boys abused him in school, he screamed, went home, and tormented his sister and baby brother. Unsuccessfully, he tried to make friends at school by doing favors, distributing candy or coins, items that he had stolen from his mother or his teacher.

Speaking of these daydreams in his adult years, he recalled how much he loved his little sister and that he imagined having sex with her. By the age of 10 or 12 he would run away from home, and on one occasion hid under his house to watch neighbors search for him.

Denial of the seriousness of Arthur's destructive behavior was characteristic of his parents' response. By the time he entered third grade, Shawcross's grades went down and his aberrant behavior in school increased. Nightmares and bedwetting continued. His parents were contacted, but the school authorities found them to be indifferent to their son's deterioration. Instead, the parents blamed the school for Arthur's problems. Their indifference to his school problems may have reflected their general indifference toward him.

Shawcross's craving for attention continued; his delinquent behavior escalated. Beginning at age 9 or 10, he stole from shops and grocery stores and bragged about his thefts. He continued to tease and bully other children relentlessly. The school nurse observed that he once came on the school bus with an iron bar and menaced other children. At times he carried a .22-caliber rifle. More and more frequently, Shawcross retreated to the woods near his home and withdrew into daydreams. He gave up having friends and came home only to eat and sleep.

Matters only got worse over the years. In his early adolescence and mid-teen years, Shawcross was still enuretic, had nightmares, and made weird noises. One cousin recalled: "He took everything literally. If you told him the cow jumped over the moon, he looked up. Any nasty comment about his intelligence, he'd flip. He beat my brother Ron on the head with a block" (Olsen 1993, p. 196). When another girl said to him, "Don't act stupid," he took a baseball bat, waited for her to pass by, and hit her across the shins. He then grabbed an axe and threatened to chop her head off. Fortunately, her boyfriend rescued her. Instead of recognizing the seriousness of this behavior and being alarmed, Shawcross's parents condoned his violence through their passivity.

At about this time Shawcross started to torment and kill animals. His behavior was noticed by townspeople, who speculated that perhaps Shawcross's mother had crossed the line into child abuse, and that she had helped to create a tormentor. There was apparently no response to Shawcross's acts of violence against animals, these early signs that something was wrong. The suspicion that his mother may have crossed the line was later investigated by questioning Shawcross under hypnosis. However, no evidence of physical abuse was uncovered.

At 17 Shawcross dropped out of school and held a series of odd jobs. According to the neighbors who recalled him, his main interests were stealing, setting fires, looking into neighboring windows, and watching his sister undress.

Nevertheless, Shawcross undertook some attempt at stability when he married at the age of 19. During this time he held one job longer than any other—an apprentice butcher at a meat market. Thus, his fascination with killing animals persisted but in a less obvious way. With his wife he was mostly uncommunicative, secretive, and moody, and he warded off her attempts to get closer to him. However, she noted his troubled relationship with his mother. After speaking with his mother for only a few minutes on the phone, he would storm out of the house. His wife said that she did not dare ask where he was going or what he was up to. With the dearth of communication that characterized the marriage, and the fact that it was never consummated, it was no wonder that it soon ended.

In his twenties Shawcross married a second time, a woman with a 4-year-old son and a 2-year-old daughter. His second wife found him to be a good listener. She described him as fascinated by her children and playing with them enthusiastically, almost as if he were a kid himself. She referred to him as a "neat freak" who demanded freshly ironed white shirts every morning, even though he worked at the city dump at that time. She remembered him as a quiet, live-in companion, who neither drank nor used drugs, was undemanding about sex and slow to reach climax, and seemed to prefer to lie in her arms and be comforted. But to her dismay, he often disappeared after dinner and stayed out long after midnight.

Increasingly, Shawcross was drawn to children, invited them to go fishing, roughhoused with them, and ended up abusing them. He grabbed one 6-year-old and spanked him, and dumped another child into a burning barrel of trash. A 10-year-old boy, Jack Blake, whom he befriended and took fishing, became his first murder victim.

When Jack Blake's family reported him missing, the police were slow to respond. The crime of kidnapping was rare in that part of New York State so the police did not believe Jack was kidnapped but rather that he had run off somewhere. Furthermore, the members of the Blake family were not considered law-abiding and respectable citizens, so their complaint was not taken seriously. Later, when a little girl disappeared, the police acted more quickly. Shawcross's second victim, Karen Hill, came from a respectable family.

After the second child was reported missing, there was a massive search for both victims in which Shawcross joined. After spending the night searching for the missing children, he enjoyed chatting with the

police about these crimes. It is not unusual for a serial killer to participate in the search for his victims and keep abreast of police activity.

Not too long afterward, Shawcross was arrested and convicted of
the rape and murder of Jack Blake and Karen Hill. Because of the lack of
cooperation of police officers with the instructions of the chief investigator, the case was jeopardized and a confession had to be obtained through
a plea bargain, reducing Shawcross's sentence from life imprisonment to
twenty-five years. He was released on parole after fifteen years. Upon his
release, the parole board had trouble finding a place for Shawcross to
live. As a convicted child killer he was hounded out of two communi-
ties. He ended up in Rochester, New York, where he began a pattern of
serial killing of prostitutes and dumping their bodies into the river.

While he carried on this violent secret life, Shawcross had another
life in which he was married to his third wife, Rose, and unbeknownst to
her, had a girlfriend, Clara Neil. He had also become a familiar figure in
the red-light district, and prostitutes willingly got into his car. Shawcross
was a killer who did not plan his crimes but ended up murdering his
victim when his control was threatened. When Shawcross's pickup was
impatient or jittery, he would feel threatened and invariably would kill
her. As his killings progressed, his savagery increased. His later killings
appeared to have been more planned. He began to revisit the bodies and
mutilate the remains, and he resorted to cannibalism. From examination of the details of the bodies found, the FBI surmised that Shawcross
enjoyed the hunt, the murder, and his postmortem activities.

The pattern of playing with the police, as Shawcross did after the
murders of Jack Blake and Karen Hill, continued. He left a signature to
his killings, which involved leaving the bodies in a buttocks-up position. After his capture, he also admitted that he had tried to throw the
police off by killing a black woman, someone very different from the
type of woman he had been serially killing.

The women Shawcross killed were said to have physically resembled
his mother. They were short and thin and had brownish hair. In fact
they were all small, young drug addicts. Their physical statures were
also reminiscent of the two children he killed. Perhaps they reminded
him of his siblings as well. But they were "whorish." The women

Shawcross married and with whom he had relationships were older than he was, devoted to him, and took care of him in a maternal fashion. When a woman he picked up did not comply with his fantasy that she behave "whorish," she ceased to remain an object of hate for him and he let her go. Shawcross actually released one prostitute he was about to kill. She was a mother on welfare with four children. Apparently that touched him.

After several prostitutes had been found dead and mutilated, one prostitute was alerted by Shawcross's manner. She had been informed that a serial killer was in the vicinity, and she told Shawcross that she was nervous, had a knife, and knew how to use it. Later, she identified him as the man she had seen with one of the murdered women. She told the police that he was having erectile difficulties. He said to her, "Just play dead, bitch, and we'll get this over with in a few minutes." She was spared because she cooperated with him.

When the body of one prostitute was discovered, the police kept watch over the area. Shawcross was captured when he stood near the place where he had dumped his last victim.

EVIDENCE FOR A NEUROLOGICAL BASIS FOR VIOLENCE

It is difficult to pinpoint the basis of Shawcross's antisocial behavior. Dorothy Lewis (1999), who has interviewed numerous serial killers, is convinced that almost all violent criminals have grown up in homes where they were subjected to abuse and/or neglect. She found that many sustained brain injuries either through accidents or abuse, and manifested psychotic symptomatology such as paranoia. Lewis was the defense's only expert witness when Shawcross went on trial, having investigated the relationship between Shawcross's behavior and possible physical and neurological abnormalities. During his teenage years, Shawcross suffered numerous head injuries due to accidents, such as falling from a forty-foot ladder and at another time being hit by a discus throw. Lewis (as cited by Gladwell 1997) argued that these injuries could have produced some brain damage that would contribute to, if not account for, his aberrant behavior. Of course, the reverse can also be argued—that the accidents were a consequence of some difficulties in coordination and bodily control.

In her work with murderers, Lewis investigated evidence of childhood abuse, specifically that prolonged childhood abuse changes the anatomy of the brain. She argued that Shawcross's compulsion "to walk in absolutely straight lines even if it meant walking through puddles rather than walking around them," or tearing "his pants on a barbedwire fence instead of using a gate only a few feet away" (Gladwell 1997, p. 137) indicated the kind of abnormalities found on neurological examination. Nevertheless, at age 16 Shawcross appeared to be sufficiently well coordinated to participate in sports and to be proficient in wrestling. Yet, in this setting too, he was a sore loser and could not control his rage. Shawcross's coordination in sports would speak against any gross neurological foundation for his violent behavior, yet he simultaneously would erupt with rage when he lost in a sport.

Another avenue of investigation of neurological factors in violent behavior are the studies by Raine (1999) using positron emission tomography (PET) scans, which found differences in activation of the prefrontal cortex when the scans of twenty-two murderers were compared with the scans of twenty-two matched, non-murderer prisoners. In follow-up studies when the sample was increased to forty-one murderers and forty-one controls, additional structural differences were noted that distinguished the brains of the murderers from the non-murderer controls. Unusual functioning in subcortical regions (amygdala, hippocampus, and thalamus) led the researchers to speculate as to the implications of these abnormalities in the brain structures of the murderers. The implicated structures are involved in governing emotions, learning, and memory. "Their abnormal functioning may contribute to the failure to learn from experience that characterizes criminal and violent offenders" (p. 20). This "fearless theory" of violence also gains some support from these findings since "offenders have been found to have reduced autonomic arousal" (p. 20). Raine cautions that it is possible that "prefrontal dysfunction does not cause violence; instead, living a violent life (including substance abuse and fights) may cause the brain dysfunction observed" (p. 21). Furthermore, these results should not be interpreted to mean that antisocial behavior is located in a particular lobe of the brain, but rather that the role of the prefrontal cortex is part of a complex system involving many parts of the brain.

Raine then compared murderers from "good" (middle class) and "bad" (deprived) homes. Based on my description of Lucas and Woodfield, the former would qualify as having been raised in a bad home, the latter as having come from a good home. The murderers coming from bad homes showed relatively good prefrontal functioning, whereas the murderers coming from good homes showed a specific lack of prefrontal functioning. These findings suggest that environmental deprivation or structural abnormalities of the brain, or both, can eventuate in the killings that characterize the men at the extremes of eruptive violence. Of particular note in these findings is the caution with which these researchers approach the question of the relative contribution of environmental and biological factors in violent behavior. Raine is far more reserved about the contributions of biology and neurology to violence than are the analysts who insist that aggression is a basic, innate, human drive.

INFERENCES AND DISCUSSION

Young Arthur Shawcross's blank affectless look may have been an early indication of his disturbance in self-regulation of affect and arousal. His tormenting and killing of animals can be seen as an early signal of distress. He grew up with a never-satisfied craving for comfort and love. From his early childhood to his second wife's description of him as wanting to be held and comforted rather than sexually aroused, this craving persisted. To be calmed or soothed was more pressing than the pleasure of arousal. When he did permit himself to be sexually aroused later in life, his partner had to "play dead," perhaps so that her aliveness would not burden him. Apparently, he required simultaneous physical release and confirmation of his ultimate control and safety. It is always tempting to read additional understandable motivations into these eruptions of violence, such as revenge upon his mother, the woman he claimed emasculated him and his father. Of course, these are not either/or questions but rather a question of the relative contribution of various motivations: the need to regulate physiological arousal (states of deadness and aliveness), attachment (through control and domination), the need to react aversively through antagonism and withdrawal (revenge), and sexual excitement.

We are confronted with this question: Do we need to find an understandable motivation in acts of violence because the prospect of motiveless violence is untenable? To explain extremes of violence on the basis of severe self-regulatory disorders, perhaps buttressed among some people by neurological problems that interfere with affect processing and various aspects of emotional management, seems anticlimactic. At best we can say that there are certain preconditions that are typical of children who grow up to be serial killers, but these same conditions can be found in disturbed children who do not become serial killers.

Ressler and colleagues (1988) compiled a list of the most frequently encountered behavioral indicators in children who grew up to be serial killers. The list is headed by "daydreaming, compulsive masturbation, isolation, chronic lying, enuresis, rebelliousness, and nightmares" (p. 29). In his childhood, Shawcross ranked high on these symptoms, especially his long history of nightmares and enuresis. The prominence of these symptoms reinforces the presumption that he struggled with uncontrolled tension states and with his inability to regulate physiological requirements on his own. Attempts to self-calm led initially to periods of social withdrawal. He was unable both to tolerate connecting with others and to be alone.

Shawcross's invention of imaginary friends and his stealing, bribing, bullying, threatening, fire setting, and torturing and killing animals could be viewed as restorative fantasies and rituals. Like running away from home and hiding to watch his family search for him, by joining the search for the killer of the two children he had already murdered, he found a way in which to participate in the life around him while remaining concealed and safe. In his escalation of these acts of increasing violence, he tried but eventually failed to find tolerable social contacts and mastery over his own states. As Shawcross's capacity for affective connections withered, his drastic asocial behaviors increased. Here is another instance of the absence of an intervening observer. The absence of a responsive environment burdened Shawcross with increasing requirements for self-regulation for which he lacked the rudimentary resources.

Shawcross's attacks on children occurred when he was simultaneously playing with children "like a child." This play may or may not have been a premeditated prelude to the killings. The patterns of luring children (and others) into trusting him so that he could molest and kill them provided some analysts (for example, Bollas 1995, Miller 1990) to propose that the serial killer establishes a trusting relationship with the intended victim that is then dramatically, and traumatically, betrayed. The modus operandi of other serial killers fits a similar pattern, leading to a general formulation that the serial killings reverse the killer's experience of having felt murdered in childhood. Such explanations are useful dynamic considerations, but I believe they do not suffice to account for the horror of the killings.

A crucial problem for Arthur Shawcross appears to have been his inability to regulate physiological requirements, which translates into the regulation of bodily experiences such as affect, arousal, tension states, and alone states. Self-regulation of states of tension and mood then becomes a major challenge, requiring either withdrawal from others or domination of them. Shawcross and other serial killers master this challenge by taking their victims to a private world that they rule through total domination of a subdued, "dead" other. For Shawcross, as for the other serial killers discussed, this script hardly varied, and provided a source of regularity, repetition, and fundamental predictability to interactions.

ERUPTIVE AGGRESSION

The killing sprees of Lucas, Woodfield, Bundy, and Shawcross depict the extreme of destructiveness. To some extent these men killed and simultaneously led quite pedestrian lives. The typical reaction of neighbors of a serial killer, when he has been apprehended, is: "He was a quiet person who kept to himself a great deal. He was always polite." A frequent plea from the killer (for example, Lucas) is "Stop me or I will kill again."

Such descriptions highlight the extent to which the violence in the lives of these men occurs without a context. In this extreme form of destructiveness, which I have labeled "eruptive aggression," there is no self-reflection. At best, there is an after-the-fact, dry, affectless description of the killing with little regard for an explanation. When interviewed about his killing of a particular woman, Shawcross explained he was "just taking care of business." He feared that this woman might expose him, and so he strangled her. In these instances the un–self-controllable expression of aggression is most prominent.

Our capacity for empathy can link a variety of expressions of aggression. These may range from reactions of aggression that are easily understood to eruptions of rage and murderousness that can thus fall within our empathic grasp. The extent to which the Vietnam soldier who had an orgasm while killing Vietcong can be understood empathically probably varies from one person to another. His experience could be placed into a context of the pressure of war and the sanctioning of killing. However, I am placing the serial killer off the end of the range of eruptions of aggression. There is no context with which the killer is in touch and to which we can relate or can grasp empathically in order to understand the meaning of the behavior. The range from reactive to eruptive aggression is linked to the extent to which our empathy and introspection can provide entrée into the context of the person's outbursts. But I propose that the serial killer occupies a place past the end of that range and is off the spectrum of our empathy. He illustrates a variety of aggression that defies the formulations of reactive aggression, aggression that appears for no obvious reason at all (A. Freud 1972).

For Shawcross, eruptive aggression and withdrawal alternated. His pattern of killing presumably temporarily lifted his sense of deadness, while his social withdrawal offered some respite and sense of self-control. Early in his life, voyeurism served as a highly unstable compromise between two extremes: vicarious but active participation in social-sexual relations, and simultaneous safety while being concealed and withdrawn. The instability of this solution remained, as can be noted in Shawcross's escalation from voyeurism to pedophilia, and to his later revisits to the bodies of his victims and his sexually fondling them.

Shawcross's motivations can be viewed as reactions to narcissistic injuries and frustrations. As in the histories of serial killers such as Lucas, Woodfield, and Bundy, aversive motivations for Shawcross were reactions to gross neglect and lack of interest on the part of his parents. His early life consisted of a combination of shock and strain trauma. But does that view provide the motivations that account for his murders?

Like Shawcross, Woodfield and Lucas also stated that they felt dominated and even bullied by the women in their families. For each of the three men, to react aversively, through rage and withdrawal, became a dominant response that overshadowed other motivations and replaced them. That is, exploration, assertion, sensuality, sexuality, and attachments all gained expression through various forms of destructiveness. The early, massive, and pervasive arousal of aversive reactions is one predisposing condition that contributes to the transformation of reactive into eruptive aggression. The development of other motivations is then inhibited and aversive motivations may have to carry the entire motivational repertoire. Reactive aggression is thereby transformed so that it acquires a quality of a proactive, unmotivated, eruptive force.

Pine (1990) also addressed this question: How can aggression that appears reactive to physical restraint, denial of satisfaction, or narcissistic injury become proactive as a drive? Using studies by McDevitt (1980), Pine argued that the infant's developing cognitive capacities enable the infant to hold on to the idea of a frustrator long after the frustration has ceased. Thus, through advancing cognitive development and the capacity for object constancy, Pine holds, an aggressive drive is constructed.

In contrast, I am proposing that the drive-like appearance of aggression is a consequence not of average, expectable development, but of specific early traumatic circumstances whereby a process is set in motion through which reactive aggression is transformed into unprovoked violence or eruptive aggression. In these developmental circumstances, sexuality, as well as a perversion of assertion, exploration, attachment, and physiological regulation, can become merged and eventuate in destructiveness, murder, and serial killing.

THE TRANSFORMATION OF REACTIVE AGGRESSION: A SYNTHESIS

Following Kohut's (1971) proposal that sexual pathology and narcissistic rage are breakdown products of an enfeebled sense of self, Goldberg (1995) posited a structural failure of the self as a basis for sexual perversion. Goldberg argued that development at this rudimentary level of psychological organization is ordinarily accomplished through rhythms and regularity of mother–infant interactions. As I illustrated in the analyses of David and Nick, the quality of their interactive regulation led to problems in self-regulation, and to states of tension. For the serial killers, their massive interactive misregulation also led to states of emotional deadness. An unresponsive environment increases the sense of aloneness, frustration, and deprivation. In turn, the developing infant and child must exercise drastic efforts, alone, to self-regulate.

In the treatments of David and Nick, solitary regulation of tension states was noted within a context of essential parental care as well as gross lack of interest alternating with intrusiveness. Such early interactive disregulation was apparently massive for Shawcross. Attempts to self-regulate his chaotic and deadened inner life led to unprovoked violent outbursts as he tried to redress his inner disorganization and his sense of living in an unpredictable and un(self)controllable world. His attempts to counteract the threat of disintegration, or rather his sense of impending disintegration, led him to sexualize—to seek sexual, thrilling, enlivening experiences, to make himself feel firm, real, and stable through nonsexual behavior.

The role of early patterns of self and interactive regulation can be examined even more finely. Rather than formulating our hypotheses in terms of structures, which Beebe and I now consider too static, we have sought to conceptualize interactive processes. The phenomena that Kohut addressed with concepts such as "structural weakness" and "breakdown products" can be understood from a developmental perspective to refer to patterns and expectations that are organized in the caregiver–infant dyad. These patterns affect the regulation of affect and arousal, tension states, and alone states. The caregiver–infant regulation of these states, or the expectation that states of over- or underarousal must be regulated alone, can leave the infant, child, or adult chronically overaroused and difficult to soothe, deadened and difficult to enliven, and relying on frantic and dramatic means for self-regulation.

Development at the level of meeting needs for physiological requirements may become a problem in development in the absence of interactive regulation that aids in patterning self-regulation. These early disturbances in the dyadic organization of meeting physiological requirements are ordinarily organized through the rhythm and regularity of mother–infant interactions. Failures in the patterning of self-regulation in the context of interactive regulation may be another predisposing condition that contributes to the transformation of reactive into eruptive aggression.

For Shawcross, and for some, although not for other, serial killers, sexualization alone may not be sufficient to bring about a feeling of vitality and stability. Sexualization can be buttressed with repetitive violence to provide predictability and stability. In addition, sexualization can serve to counteract deadness and regulate tension states. Because the serial killer's task focuses on self-regulation, the people who are recruited to aid in this task, the killer's victims, are essentially interchangeable. They are not transference figures; that is, they are not stand-ins for significant people in the killer's life. The victims need only function like antidepressant pills. They can all look alike, so long as they do their job. Their lack of uniqueness, their anonymity, makes them suitable for serving the function of shoring up the stability of the sense of self. In fact, when a potential victim succeeds in distinguishing herself in some way, or in finding the killer's specific Achilles heel, the victim may no longer be suitable to function as the killer needs her to. In that case the serial killer may discard the pill, that is, the potential victim may be able to escape. Two of Shawcross's potential victims did escape—a woman with four children who was on welfare, and a prostitute who was suspicious of Shawcross but agreed to comply with his demand that she play dead during the sex act.

When selfobject experiences, in early as well as in continuing development, are marked, predominantly, by massive disruptions without opportunities for interactive repair, as in strain trauma (Chapter 5), the upshot can be massive disillusionment and expectations of being betrayed, exploited, and sadistically treated by other people. The inanimate, nonhuman world is then recruited to fulfill selfobject functions, for example, through drugs, alcohol, and the transformation of alive humans and animals into corpses.

In the absence of stable selfobject experiences and expectations that disruption can be repaired, the developing child is required not only to self-repair but often simultaneously to repair the "damaged" parent. Such a burden can lead to increased feelings of hopelessness and expectations that one's efforts to ameliorate the situation are bound to fail. To maintain vital ties to his parents, the child may then attempt to live in two realities. Shawcross took this path as laid out by his parents. He existed in two disconnected, even antithetical worlds. In one world, actions produced painful consequences. This was the world in which he could not control the humiliation he felt at the hands of his classmates and could not behave in conformance with social expectations. This was the world that was dominated by his mother and in which he tried desperately to spare Clara Neil, his last girlfriend, from becoming implicated in his killing spree.

In the other world, consequences were vague or nonexistent. This was the world of Shawcross's family, which tolerated his acts of violence. This was his world of prostitutes, as his mother described the women who appeared on television, and of his disappointing, bigamist father. This was a chaotic, unpredictable world. Shawcross lived alternately in this private amoral world, as well as with a public pretense of conventionality. I believe that living in these two antithetical realities prompted Shawcross, Woodfield, and other serial killers to send signals in their developing years that something was wrong.

Shawcross's and Lucas's early fascination with dead animals, like Woodfield's exhibitionism, were steps on a path to serial killings. To the extent that these constituted signals, in both instances the signals were ignored, and the behavior was condoned and even supported. Receiving a response to those signals may be a crucial deterrent to further escalation of destructiveness. Conversely, the failure to respond to these signals may be a long-standing pattern of nonresponsivity that propels the development of these children toward their eventual solution—eruptive violence. The response to these signals may serve to put a brake on an escalating pattern of destructiveness, or may be felt as a sign of recognition. However, such a response may require the recognition and acknowledgment that something is dreadfully wrong.

When reactive aggression is transformed into a propensity to erupt ragefully and violently, it is not a motivation or, for that matter, a drive that is implicated. Whereas reactive aggression can find a place in the community of motivations, the conditions that give rise to eruptive aggression are more diffuse. The person's ability to process affective experience had most likely been eroding for some time previously. Attachments to family and friends carry little weight, so that the person feels like a loner and increasingly becomes one.

Striking, in viewing the histories of serial killers, is the extent to which some variant of deadness characterizes the emotional life of these men. Using violence to buttress a failing ability to regulate arousal and affect constitutes attempts to transform the lack of affectivity, sense of deadness, or lifelessness, and gain some mastery or self-control over these states. The inability to self-calm or self-soothe is striking. Their childhood milieu was rich in opportunities for stimulating rage outbursts and social withdrawal. The organization of the other motivations, such as attachment, exploration, and sensual and sexual pleasure, was massively curtailed.

The formulations just offered do not apply to all serial killers. But I think the problems in self-regulation of affect and arousal are directly related to the absence of an experiential context out of which the person reacts. Such a context makes a person's experience amenable to empathy and introspection by an outsider. In the psychoanalytic treatments of patients, not serial killers, such as the patients I have been describing in this book, these regulatory problems were indeed profound.

SHAME AND VIOLENCE

So far I have discussed four factors that can predispose a person toward eruptive aggression: (1) developmental histories replete with experiences of abuse, deception, and neglect; (2) early failure to establish self-sooth-ing and affect-regulating capacities in dyadic interactions, or put differ-ently, early persistent dyadic misregulation that interferes in the devel-opment of self-cohesion and increases self-fragmentation; (3) living in two realities with sexualization as a drastic attempt to fulfill numerous nonsexual functions, and self-repair of states of deadness and fragmen-tation through sexualization, thus requiring additional reinforcement through violence; and (4) PET scan patterns in some cases, pointing to neurological abnormalities.

In addition, James Gilligan (1996) has pointed to another predis-posing factor in the development of a violent person. He has empha-sized the central role of shame (see also Morrison 1989) in the motiva-tion toward violence in armed robbers and murderers. He contends that the persistent motivation for crimes of violence is the person's response to being disrespected and humiliated, and to losing pride or self-respect. Gilligan states, "I have yet to see a serious act of violence that was not provoked by the experience of feeling shamed and humiliated, disre-spected and ridiculed, and that did not represent an attempt to prevent or undo this 'loss of face'—no matter how severe the punishment, even if it includes death" (p. 110). The murderers studied by Gilligan illus-trate the hot-blooded eruption of aggression, but yet within a context that, by a stretch of our empathy, we can understand.

Serial killings, like those of Arthur Shawcross, lie, I believe, be-yond our capacity for empathy. They are off the continuum. At one end of the continuum we can place the person who has the resources and ability to react aggressively with nuanced reactions. This is the end of the continuum that Kohut described where we readily grasp the context and motivations that organized the aggressive reaction. The other end of the continuum is characterized by "hot-blooded," violent eruptions of aggression, derived from a combination of the four factors I cited, and the absence of other resources that can help a person deal with rage and shame in its various forms. At the far end of this continuum stands Iago. Whether we can extend our empathy to include his level of destructive-ness is questionable. But beyond Iago, off this continuum, live the serial killers. We are hard pressed to find a context for their aggression that we can understand. Our difficulty in empathizing with this group of violent people, including their serial killing, probably parallels their experience in their developing years. They did not grow up in a context in which they experienced the empathy of others, an attempt to understand them from within their subjective world. Thus when we look at their killing sprees, we cannot find an affective context from which to understand them or into which we can place them. We are left without any way to engage with or empathize with their experience. Their destructiveness, rather than being reactive to an internal context constructed through past and current experience, is, I believe, primarily an attempt to alter a current and probably chronic or recurring self-state of affectlessness or deadness.

Shaming itself, according to Gilligan, is not a sufficient cause for violence. To the armed robbers and murderers he studied, nothing is more shameful than to feel ashamed. However, to redress the shame through violence only occurs when there are no nonviolent means available to the person to recover his pride and to ward off or diminish the feeling of shame and the loss of self-esteem.

Similar though not quite so extreme expressions of aggression and difficulties in dealing with feelings of shame are also found among the patients we see in treatment. In order to transform the chronic, eruptive expression of anger and transcend the propensity toward violence, other resources, such as verbal communication, self-reflection, flexibility, anticipation of consequences, frustration tolerance, withdrawal, empathy, humor, imagination, and creativity are needed by both therapist and patient. It becomes the task of the therapy, then, to develop these resources.

Although the need to react aversively through antagonism and/or withdrawal begins as a reactive system in the course of development, this reactive system can be transformed into rageful and destructive behavior that hardly requires any prior frustration or narcissistic injury as a trigger. Even though aggression is reactive under average expectable circumstances, under these specific adverse developmental conditions it can be transformed into chronic eruptive outbursts that emerge from a barely visible context or even from invisible triggers.

Those who assume that we are all born with a well of rage might argue that we are all capable of heinous acts, like serial killing, if we did not develop the capacity to control aggressive impulses, tolerate frustration, and thus delay gratification. What can a self psychological perspective, informed by the motivational systems, contribute toward understanding this phenomenon? What can a theory postulating a fundamental striving for self-integration provide in understanding this extreme of violence?

I have argued that when aggression is stimulated massively and early through abuse or deprivation and neglect, aversiveness can become the major avenue for expressing motivations derived from the other four motivational systems. For example, sexuality can find expression in necrophilia; physiological regulation, specifically, regulation of affect and arousal can be expressed or transformed through alternations of rage and withdrawal; attachment combined with sexual satisfaction emerges in cannibalism. The serial killer can express needs for exploration and assertion through sadistic domination and mutilation of the bodies of the victims. In these instances, the need to react aversively joins or recruits the other motivations.

Under specific developmental conditions reactive aversiveness is transformed into eruptive aggression. A variety of other nonaggressive motivations can then be expressed simultaneously with the aggressive act. Here lies a major difference between reactive and eruptive aggresion. In reactive aggression, other motivations are embedded in sufficiently satisfying experiences that these motivations retain a distinct place among the person's hierarchy of motivations. That is, they retain a connection to the context to which they are a reaction. In these instances, the person feels understood and recognized when the connection between the aggressive or withdrawing reaction and its context are interpretively and experientially reestablished.

Viewing the motivations for serial killings as perversions of aversiveness provides a more complex model that fits the multiple murders and subsequent mutilations committed by serial killers. This model includes and accommodates other motivations as subsets of aggressiveness. Killings are thus not reduced to one motivation. Murderers extend the range of eruptive aggression to the limits of empathy. But the study of serial killers illustrates an extreme form of violence that is past that range. Ironically, the state of the serial killer's self has undergone such extreme developmental transformations that an empathic link is not possible and simultaneously limits our ability to understand him any better.

In the population of patients ordinarily seen for psychoanalytic treatment, transformations of reactive aggression fall along a continuum. Milder forms of eruptive aggression can be seen with some frequency in analytic treatment. What is clinically important, however, is the extent to which a person feels reactively aggressive or considers himself to be intrinsically aggressive. The experience of aggressiveness, feeling aggressive and proud of it, can become an important dimension of one's self-state. It is to the milder forms of eruptive aggression and their transformation in analytic treatment that I now turn.

8

It's Better to Be Feared Than Pitied

Every few years members of the International Council for Psychoanalytic Self-Psychology have been meeting with members of the British Independent Group to compare ideas and to learn from each other. The dozen British attendees have included Pearl King, Malcolm Pines, Eric Raynor, Harold Stewart, and Bernard Barnett.

Thinking about the clinical material presented at the meetings of the two groups, I was struck by differences in style, particularly when speaking about aggressive motives on the part of patients. Interpretations that a patient was attempting to destroy or undermine the analysis had a familiar ring from my having read papers by Kleinian analysts. But when spoken by these British analysts, the words did not sound so accusatory or shaming as they had looked on the printed page. Especially when spoken with a British accent, such interpretations had a sardonic, chiding tone, rather than a condemning and dismissive quality. From the responses of the patients described, I gathered that they were neither devastated nor alienated by these interventions.

During one meeting in Chicago I began a dialogue with Bernard

Barnett, a member of the British group. Like me, he expressed interest in the treatment of the difficult patient. We decided that we would each describe our work with such a patient and comment, from our own perspectives, on the other's work. I saw this as an opportunity to discuss my difficulties with two patients, Julie and Clara, one of whom will be described in a later chapter. Each patient could serve to illustrate a negative therapeutic reaction, and for each, a negative transference dominated the treatment. From our joint meetings, I had the impression that these two treatment phenomena were a particular focus for interventions by members of the British Independent Group, who are masters of the trailing edge.

In my correspondence with Bernard Barnett I discussed only the treatment of Julie, but in our correspondence she was not given a name. Our correspondence spanned about a year and a half; it was enormously stimulating and useful to me personally. Segments of our letters follow. I believe that they provide a chronicle of particularly difficult treatment dilemmas and document a transformation in my way of working with a patient's aggression.

August 31

Dear Bernard,

In mulling over the packed weekend with you and the other independents, it seemed to me that, once again, we did not take full advantage of a golden opportunity. I think that we were too quick to try to formalize our similarities and differences. In so doing, I think we kept repeating surface descriptions and did not really get to the heart of common therapeutic dilemmas with our patients. I came away with the feeling that we were saying to each other, "If you would only do it my way, you would do much better treatment."

In the few minutes during which we spoke I sensed that, perhaps even from different vantage points, we encountered similar, formidable therapeutic problems. The patient you briefly described to me, the woman who kept reexperiencing her masochistic childhood relationship with her father, was very familiar to me from my practice. Framing an intervention one way or another may be helpful in one case, but it may make little difference in the treatment of another, even similar-appearing patient. Why clarification/explanation/interpretation makes little impact in some cases, I believe, is adequately explained neither by examining ruptures in the selfobject tie nor by positing unconscious aggression manifesting itself in a need to defeat the analyst through negative therapeutic reactions. It seemed to me that in the group discussions we each tended to address such issues by retreating into familiar answers. In our brief talk, I thought, we began to study this familiar question. I would be interested in a continued dialogue, by mail, with you. If you have the time and the interest, we could compare notes on cases, one of mine and one of yours.

Best wishes,

Frank

29th September

Dear Frank,

I was delighted to get your letter and I apologize for the delay in responding to you and your exciting ideas. First, the "Chicago Experience." I agree that it is similar therapeutic dilemmas that we, the two groups, have in common. Though I wonder whether the birth and growth of self psychology in Chicago, U.S.A. has a significant cultural-political context, in both the narrow and the wider sense, that we in the British Society do not share. Of course we, the Independents, have some of our own peculiar political-cultural roots. We, the "Middle Group," split off from two extremes of the British Society. Is what we share a kind of rebellion? A protest culture against extremism? (e.g., the excesses of ego psychology and Kleinianism, contemporary Freudian rigidity, etc.).

I will give you an outline of a case from my side of the Atlantic that I am struggling with. The main issue as I see it is the analysis of an orphan. Mr. A is 48 years old. He is emerging from a severe clinical depression, triggered by the ending of a self-destructive relationship with a young woman who seems to have used him to further her own advancement.

He is a highly talented businessman involved in ventures of millions of pounds, who, because of his mental state, has not worked for four years and has gradually lost his material wealth and business confidence. We quickly realized together how all his life he had adopted a victim role as a means of survival, but how in spite of this his capacity to look out for himself, his talent and aptitude, have seen him through one disastrous situation after another.

His experience of exploitation by psychiatrists, business partners, girlfriends etc. has a ring of truth as well as again considerable distortion as to his own part in the tale of woe. In short, his story begins with exploitative and indifferent figures who, he says, treated him from the beginning like a piece of furniture to be shown off occasionally but mostly ignored or farmed out to a succession of nannies, servants, tutors. Both parents died when he was eleven and he experienced his grandparents on both sides as even worse than his parents.

I am the fourth analyst he has seen as he was unable to engage with the other three. I have been seeing him three times weekly for three weeks. Session times are arranged in the afternoon because he feels he will miss early appointments, being unable to get up in the morning.

So far he seems to be communicating a fixed pattern—a personal story of business success, exploitation, and disaster that I described earlier. He is terrified of the couch and we sit together and I listen to this story, pointing out a few observations here and there, mainly observing and sharing with him recurring patterns in his life. In the last session he suddenly asked me some pointed questions and demanded answers to them. What was wrong with him? Why did I turn questions back on him as though I were a prosecuting barrister? What was going to happen in the future? Why did I comment on his previous life as "manic" activity?

Could we begin with a consideration of selfobject ruptures? So far I can think of him as a false self, and his very severe breakdown (hospitalization) as a bid for health. I have shared this with him. Much more to tell

of course but I will leave it there for your comments. Warm good wishes
to you and your wife.

Best wishes,

Bernard

_____

_____

November 15

Dear Bernard,

My delay in responding to your very interesting letter was not entirely
due to being lazy. I had in mind writing to you about a particular patient.
However, from week to week, I kept wondering whether or not she would
stay in treatment. Before embarking on the trans-Atlantic case discussion,
I wanted to be sure that she would stay—as sure as one can ever be of
that. But more of that later.

 The case you described raised many familiar and difficult problems for
me. I assume your question, whether an orphan can be analyzed, refers
to the nature of the transference that can be expected to develop, the
quality of attachment that can be expected in the aftermath of early losses.
In turn, that raises the question whether transferences must be object
related or whether the analyst can be experienced by the analysand as
serving functions but not be related to as an object. This distinction, as
you probably know, was addressed by Kohut when he coined the selfobject
concept. In these instances, the countertransference danger is that the
analyst somehow requires the patient to take his presence into account.
The patient, totally self-absorbed, treats the analyst as a mirror in that the
patient uses the analyst to experience a sense of cohesion and aliveness.
The analyst is experienced as providing for the patient a sense of the
patient as intact. This mirroring selfobject transference becomes established during the understanding phase of the analysis and may last for
years. From your description, it seems to me that you were doing exactly
that. You were listening to the patient's accounts of his experiences, tenta-

tively labeling them as exploitative, putting together patterns, and providing an ambience of safety. Kohut assumed that narcissistic pathology represented early arrested configurations that, when given an opportunity to develop, will become integrated into the rest of the personality. He did not believe that they defended against underlying aggression but that when confronted, reactive narcissistic rage was expressed. I apologize for the lecture, but once I get started I sometimes go on automatic!

The history of your patient is almost classical in terms of disturbances in his narcissistic equilibrium. That is, the emotionally unresponsive world in which he lived did not provide the "affirming echo" that is a prerequisite for his emotional development. The system of relying on and using cues derived from the emotional responses of others was useless to him. In your brief history, what struck me was the enormous resources this man must have had to have survived as well as he did. Given the losses and the quality of the caregivers who were available, he did remarkably well. I don't know how you would feel about telling him that, but I would. The question then becomes when did his talents and resources begin to fail him, and why.

The role of exploitative relationships is interesting in such a presentation. I do not think it has the same meaning as when exploitation is sexualized, when exploitation is seen as being loved and then becomes part of a repeated masochistic character structure. Is it possible that your patient cannot accept the idea that in his relationships or business decisions he might have made errors in judgment? That is, that he stays in exploitative relationships because of a grandiose fantasy, such as, "I cannot accept the idea of having made a mistake." Having grown up in circumstances in which he had to rely entirely on his own perceptions of people at too early an age, and being unable to validate his impressions by having them confirmed or disconfirmed by parental figures, he might well have developed an elevated sense of his judgment. He could not afford to doubt, or worse, to consider being in error. Perhaps the recognition that a particular situation is exploitative can come only after a period of tolerating trial and error about having shown trust or loyalty. His reaction, his sense of rage, may be related to feeling devastated. Here is where empathy comes in. If indeed these feelings are central, then it becomes

important to understand what it felt like for the patient to have the conviction that he was in trustworthy hands, shattered. Under these circumstances, for the patient to recognize the exploitation and to leave the ex-
ploiter entails a precipitous loss of self-esteem. When the patient feels
that this aspect of his experience has been recognized, it may become
easier for him to explore the complicated interplay through which ex-
ploitations are mutually organized, to recognize his role in shaping his
experience.

One more comment about the exploitation-masochism relationship.
What used to be considered the secondary gains—feeling needed, wanted,
important, when in such a relationship—are given more importance in
self psychology. As a matter of fact, when pathology is rampant, as it is in
your patient, the accent falls on understanding the functions of the pathology in terms of self-maintenance, self-regulation of affects, and self-
esteem restoration.

What I am writing to you may be well known to you. But what are the
clinical implications? My guess would be that you are probably treating
him very well but don't feel that it is deep enough. It is! I think this
touches on the question raised in our Chicago meeting. What can we
learn from each other? If your patient uses the treatment in the service of
self-maintenance, self-regulation, and self-esteem restoration, then listening, framing, and commenting on his associations are in the service of
conveying to him that he is understandable. Interpreting or making the
unconscious conscious may not work well because repression is not the
defense of choice. Your participation conveys a sense of organization and
cohesion to him. As in many analyses, it then also becomes important to
note the extent to which his life outside the analysis is becoming better
organized in spite of what goes on in relation to you.

My guess is that this treatment may not be characterized as an object-
related transference. Rather, your patient may be able to risk expressing
various transference reactions against the background of feeling safe
enough and secure enough with you to take these risks.

The patient I want to write to you about is someone who I think you
might understand and treat better than I do. Although born in Australia,
she was educated in England and lived there for a considerable time. In

addition, I think a theory of internalized (bad) objects might capture well the nub of the treatment difficulties I have in working with her.

The patient is a 46-year-old woman. I see her for three sessions a week, and she sits up. She has been anorexic, bulimic, and alcoholic. She has had a four-year classical analysis (not with me; I have seen her for only about half a year) and spent several weeks in an alcoholic detoxification center. According to her, the analysis did little good, but the detox helped, and she attends Alcoholics Anonymous meetings several times a week.

She is strikingly beautiful, brilliant, and with a wide range of interests and talents. She is divorced and has had a series of relationships, which have all followed similar patterns. Men flock to her. Those who are powerful and wealthy get through to her. Usually, after a brief courtship and sex, trouble begins. If their ardor wanes a bit, for example, when they don't call her for a day, or when they do call and their tone of voice is not loving, she becomes terrified about being abandoned and enraged about being mistreated. From that point on the relationship is in trouble and it is only a short time until the men back off and she becomes symptomatic. She develops stomach pains and sleep problems, and she chain smokes. During the phase when her lovers withdraw, she vacillates between picturing them as sadistic demons who are toying with her and depicting herself as severely damaged because she craves such constant attention. She is unable to accept that someone would withdraw from her, even temporarily. She does attempt to explain their cooling toward her as the normal fluctuations of relationships by reminding herself that these men have other obligations in their lives. For example, they have businesses, ex-wives, and children. This middle phase of her relationship with a man has taken center stage in the treatment to date. She focuses obsessively on the motivations of the men and on devising a strategy for herself. At times I find myself drawn into these ruminations. During a session she may rage against a man's unreliability and failure to take responsibility. I get pulled into raising the question of why she wants to be with or pursue such a man. In the following session she will rail against me for having supported her "paranoid" (her word) ruminations. If I question her perceptions (and in a sense defend the man), she becomes furious because if she had any self-respect, she would never pursue such a man. She then tells me that she does so only out of desperation. She assures me that none of her friends would put up with such a person for a minute. She accuses me of asking her to "just lie there and be immolated." When I caught on to the shifts, I described them to her and she said angrily, "I know that. I split." She then tells me how unsafe she feels with me and reiterates many times how I don't understand her. To some extent I believe she is right. Hence I turn to you.

A bit of background. Her father worked for the Australian government in a position that enabled her to grow up surrounded by people of wealth and prestige. With pain and outrage she told me that at age 2 she was sent to school—all day—and has painful memories of being sent out of the house, unable to return home until dark. Her whole school experience was marked by feelings of abandonment and exclusion, though academically she always did well. When she was about 5 her father left for a distant assignment for several years and her mother had some kind of a breakdown. The patient was sent to an aunt, Aunt Hope, who despised her and preferred her younger brother. Aunt Hope constantly criticized and berated her, and labeled her a worthless child. During this time she longed to be rescued by her idealized father or one of his colorful aides.

Being made fun of and criticized was a constant experience as she grew up. When it came time to attend college, she went abroad. Subsequently, as a young adult, she came to the United States and enrolled in a graduate program. To get through school, beset by anxieties, she got married, started to drink, and began analysis. Her marriage ended in divorce. Treatment for alcoholism brought on sobriety but shifted the need for a constant companion from the bottle to a man. No man was as reliable as the bottle, and that has been an issue ever since. She currently works on the staff of a large health-care facility. She hates her work, her field, and her co-workers.

At this point in her treatment, a new phase in her relationship with a man has emerged. When her latest boyfriend withdrew somewhat, she began to write letters to him. So far there have been three letters. This resulted in a warm phone call from him. But that, to me, is not the important part. What I find important is that when she reads the letters to me in the session, there is a marked shift in affect. She becomes calmer, more reasonable, and livelier. In these letters, five or six single-spaced pages in length, she describes the course of their relationship, her understanding of the problems that have come up, her role and contribution to the difficulty, and how she now understands their response to each other. These letters are eloquent, balanced, tactful, forthright, and reflect her at her best. It is a level of integration that is not evident in her personal relations. Nor is it evident in the sessions when she talks about these relationships. This is where we are. This is also the narrative of the treatment. In the sessions, I often feel like a cork on a stormy sea.

All the best,

Frank

Prior to receiving my next letter from Bernard, between the time I wrote to him on November 15 and received his reply five months later, while waiting for his response to my treatment questions, I carried on an imaginary dialogue with him. I speculated what a member of the British Independent Group might suggest. I thought about the joint meetings we had. Either out of heightened frustration or heightened empathy, I speculated about the level of rage that was expressed by my patient, toward others, herself, and me. When I heard the British Independent Group describe, in cultured English accents, analyses in which they offered interpretations that patients were spoiling and destroying their analyses with their rages, I wondered how that would sound if I were to say it. Very different, I thought, but yet I felt there was something captured by those formulations that I may have been missing. An article by Harold Stewart (1998), who had participated in the joint meetings, captured, for me, the alacrity with which murderousness is discussed in this group of analysts. Although the following letter was written some time after my imaginary dialogue, Stewart's description of his work with a silent, schizoid patient captured the flavor of his remarks at our joint meeting that I recalled. He wrote, "As the months passed, I felt increasingly furious and then murderous toward this patient, until eventually I found the situation intolerable. I then told him that I couldn't stand his silence, as it made me feel so murderous, and so, if he didn't speak within the next few days, I would stop the analysis. I added that he might then go to someone who might have a greater tolerance of his murderous silence than I had" (p. 504). Although I really did not feel murderous toward my patient, there was something about the word *murderous* that touched on the treatment problem I was facing. I wrote another letter to Bernard as follows:

July 5

Dear Bernard,

While awaiting your letter I carried on an imaginary dialogue with you, or rather with you as representing how I imagined a British Independent Group analyst might proceed in the case I described to you. My version of you may not at all coincide with your self-perception, but no matter. I hit upon this device because I felt (and my patient was very articulate in reminding me) that there was something missing in our work.

I don't know if I can yet articulate what I feel is missing in her treatment. But I think that added to her familial deprivations was her particularly influential cultural-social background. She was raised and educated in Australia and in Europe in a social setting in which rank, wealth, and status were extraordinarily important. I believe that these factors were devastatingly cruel in their impact for those who were socially not quite included and therefore excluded.

When my patient and I had been working together for a little more than a year, she was still as anxious, desperate, angry, and self-destructive as ever. Over this period of time the transference had been becoming more and more negative. We understood this as her seeing me as her inadequate mother who could offer her no direction.

She had felt abandoned by her mother who had a depressive breakdown when the patient's father was sent by his office to serve in a distant post. He was away for about two years. During that time, the patient, age

5, and her younger brother went to live with Aunt Hope, who loved the young boy and despised the patient. These years were hell for her and it was the mother's absence (she did not go with the father but apparently just withdrew) that defined the mother's inability to protect her daughter.

In the treatment we came to characterize the patient's inner world, her subjective experience, and her constant torments, self-attacks, and searing self-criticisms as "Aunt Hope." I was the inadequate mother who could offer her no protection from herself. In the way she ran her life, she reinforced her inner sense of badness. As a child she clearly longed for her father's return and in the analysis demanded that I "do something" to alter the current state of things in her life.

It was at that point that I began my dialogue with you. How would you look upon this? Her current relationships were still characterized by intense longings and attachments, vacillating with intense hatred and contempt. As I said, the transference turned more and more negative.

My sense of the language you use is that you are more likely to formulate interventions using terms like "murderous rage" rather than formulations like the ones I have used, for example, "having felt so neglected and abused, you felt like turning on your torturers" or "wishes to murder" or "rage in response to feeling annihilated." When I used these more toned-down formulations with my patient, it did not increase her feeling that I understood her. In fact, it increased her rage toward me and she accused me of having no idea of what she was about.

In my imaginary dialogue with you I decided that I had to describe her as a murderer whose only alternative to killing people off was to debase herself. So I began by telling her that I thought that if she had found in me a clone of her mother, it would be easy for her to walk away and find another analyst. But there are some things that she would be taking with her that feed the replay of the weak mother–scared and enraged child sequence.

What follows now is a summary of what I actually said to this patient over a period of time and in the course of many sessions: "To cling to your mother, and to feel that the only way to be taken care of is to force her to take care of you, enrages you. You feel humiliated and you want to kill her. Similarly, you want to kill your boyfriend and me for not providing you with the riches to which you feel entitled. But the idea of killing us off quickly turns into a suicidal despair on your part because you sense the familiar isolation that will ensue. Then to feel loved you have to accept crumbs. You can then feel safe but also self-contemptuous because you have demeaned yourself by settling for less than you believe is your due. To regain your self-esteem, you conjure up your father's image. You imagine him telling you that you are entitled to a better life, that you should not demean yourself by accepting such shabby treatment. You feel justified in your outrage and then you become a murderer again. You want to kill the crumb-givers and the balance is again shifted. It's either accept crumbs or kill the crumb-givers. There is no solution to this dilemma in that each side brings forth the other. It is all entwined with seeing the world as populated by people who are either weak and poor, or powerful, rich, potential caregivers but ultimate abandoners." All this I said to her over the course of several weeks, to dramatic effect. During these sessions her whole face lit up, she became excited, and there was a palpable shift in our relationship.

Since that time she has succeeded in holding on to a relationship with a man. Furthermore, she retook her state licensing exams in her area of specialization. She had failed them the previous year because she panicked, but she passed them this year. This was actually an enormous achievement for her. She despised the subject matter, hated to memorize scores of journal articles and papers, and felt superior to the others in her field and contempt for them. Nevertheless, she succeeded in exercising sufficient restraint to overcome her contempt for her field and its practitioners.

Passing the examination meant that she has an opportunity to get out of her financial "have-not" position. However, there was another ambivalently associated benefit for passing the tests. She now has no excuses and must work in her field. Fantasies of changing careers since she insisted she had no future in her field were no longer quite so tenable. When she told me that she passed the exams, she added, "It meant nothing to me."

We are now dealing with the following issues: the pain of social ostracism and rejection is profound. Even when she gives signals that she is not interested in a particular man or woman as a friend, she feels devastated when they don't continue to pursue her. She wants very much to replicate the aristocratic social circle that she believed she was a part of in her previous life. She was very much sought after by the sons of the rich and the powerful, but she received no guidance from her mother as to how to behave. Her mother felt the class difference between herself and her family on one side, and the "aristocracy" on the other side. Her mother never invited people to the house, fearing it was not good enough. Furthermore, her mother would fawn over the young daughters of the wealthy families and tell the patient to emulate them.

My patient felt that she should belong to, but was never a real part of, the upper-class group. This became increasingly an issue by the time she began her undergraduate studies. There her social life was characterized by striving to belong to a higher class and the constant dread that she would be found out and seen as not entitled, and that she would be exposed and dropped. Her strikingly beautiful appearance and, as one of her admirers described it, her "gargantuan intellect" provided her with both an entrée as well as a source of danger in the circles into which she tried to crash. She was too bright, too perceptive, too judgmental, too quick, too flirtatious, and too much of a threat to other women. She did not have to do anything to be perceived in this light. All she had to do was be there. She consistently felt she was on the outside, and taken aback by unprovoked slights and put-downs. This problem continues and even now she wants very much to be accepted by women, but they tend to drop her. She has men friends of long standing, with most of whom she has had brief affairs.

Well, that brings you up to date. As you may note, I don't feel quite as confused and helpless in the treatment as I have in the past. But there is no doubt that the whole atmosphere can change again in a second.

In your last letter you raised questions about her diagnosis. How borderline is she? I think quite. She is even aware of the extent to which she splits, and, in fact, asks me, "What do I do about it?" In a way, the frustrations of the analytic encounter are dwarfed by the enormous frustrations she experiences in her daily life. These frustrations are defined by the extent to which she feels that she wants what she feels entitled to. She sees that others get, without undue effort on their part, what she cannot seem to grasp. I am not so worried about suicide as I am about escalating rages that eventuate in her being nonfunctional. That is, she gets agitated, spends the night awake, falls asleep in the morning, misses work, or if she goes to work, is in constant danger of blowing up at people.

All the best,

Frank

9th December

Dear Frank,

I am of course pleased with your "imaginary dialogue" since this is better than no dialogue at all! As you say it is probably not so much with me as with an imagined representative of the "Brits" Independent group.

Now to your patient. I am very interested in her continuing anxiety. I see a year as a short time in the task of developing basic trust. After all, in her thought you will desert her as both mother and father did. Secondly, I wonder if you had played multiple roles in the transference, in the sense of Joe Sandler's role responsiveness? So you were at times the absent father, the critical Aunt Hope, as well as the inadequate mother. Would she or might she respond to interpretations in relation to a break? I have not got a picture yet of her direct or indirect response to interpretations, or, more generally, her capacity for insight.

I am very interested in the content and style of interpretations exemplified in your letter (e.g., "you felt like turning on your torturers"). One thing comes to mind straight away—my own style would be a more focused here-and-now intervention. I suppose something like "You feel me to be torturing you when I cancel this session and you need to see me."

The issue of your patient feeling understood or not is a complex one but I agree that at least both need to be on the same wavelength. For example, would you both agree that you are trying to explore together the unconscious determinants of her mood, behavior, etc.? Or is she simply more interested in gratification? I think I would be very careful before using an expression like "murderous rage." I think I would only do so if the patient had already been using language of the kind, e.g., "I could have killed him when he overtook me at the traffic light."

I have offered these comments only as minor clarifications so that we might stay on the same wavelength. I actually find the description of your work very impressive. It seems to me that much of what you say to her will indeed act as a brake on her self-destructive tendencies. One thought leads me to a more direct tackling of the patient's destructive narcissism since she seems to be a person impossible to please, at least for any length of time.

One point of difference between us again links to the here-and-now transference. You say, "If I articulate her boyfriend's strengths to her she gets angry," etc. I suppose I would probably take material such as this to be a displacement from her feelings toward me and I would share this with her, notwithstanding the likelihood that she would protest such an approach. What puzzles me is the discrepancy between her excellent intelligence and her grasp of the idea that you are not there to offer her guidelines, etc. I mean by this that I would be expecting her to actually comment sometimes along the lines, "I know you are not here to give me advice." Does she say such things?

Bad news about my patient. He terminated against my advice. He was increasingly persecuted by the sessions and always felt worse, more depressed and suicidal, after them. Was this a question of my style, technique, method being unsuitable for him? I don't know. I do know that he was most disparaging, contemptuous and destructive of all efforts to help him and I joined a long list of failures. Yet, I did not dislike him and felt very moved by his gifts, intelligence, talents, and charm. However, I was certainly defeated by malign aspects of him and his destructive narcissism.

I look forward to hearing from you, soon.

Bernard

May 11

Dear Bernard,

Since early this year, the treatment of the patient I have been discussing with you has been limping along. I expected her to stop at any moment and I waited in responding to your letter since I thought that the end was imminent even if there was an occasional productive session.

Two main themes captured her dissatisfaction with treatment: "I come here and recall my past and I hate it. I dread coming. I feel worse when I am here and worse when I leave." "Tell me what to do. Tell me my dynamics. I repeat the same relationships over and over. What went wrong in my relationship with Harry [a very wealthy man whom she saw for several months two years ago and who dropped her. She had described him as having the personality of white bread and felt demeaned by her association with him and contempt for him.]? I want someone to tell me what to do, how to act, how to behave with people. Then I can do it and not feel like a failure in every social situation or feel so terrified that I am afraid to go out and stay home smoking."

During the sessions of the past several months, we spoke about the extent to which her class, breeding, and status were unrecognized in her current circles and carried little clout.

What struck me was that she had totally discounted having passed her examinations. Being board certified gave her job security, which she persistently jeopardized by arriving late to work, for which she was placed on probation. During the past year she has sustained a difficult relationship with a new boyfriend that was fraught with verbal attacks and counterattacks, but there were also affectionate times.

In the transference I believe I was shifted among several roles. A prominent transference was of the benign but inadequate mother who could not protect her against the denigrating Aunt Hope and the dangerous but exciting father. Most of the time I was experienced not so much as a person but as an aspect of herself that was externalized and condemned. When I interpreted her criticism of me as depicting a devalued aspect of herself, at least that did not lead to a stalemate. It may have helped in the sense of Winnicott's "survival" of the analyst as the target of the patient's aggression. I tried to shift from this interpretation to her dread of damaging others. It seemed to me that her withdrawal from social situations and her extraordinary vigilance as to whether she has offended others had to do with anger at her father for not appreciating her and not providing her with the place at his side to which she felt entitled.

I agree with your emphasis on here-and-now interpretations. One that I believe may have been helpful, though she would not acknowledge it, was my description of how at this very moment she became enraged at me because she sensed I was not sufficiently harsh with her. I was "pussy-footing" around. I said to her that she feels she can only trust someone who hurts her. She responded, "I can take it. Tell me where I am neurotic." Our interchange at this point reminded me of the relationship between the masochist and the sadist: the masochist says to the sadist, "Beat me!" and the sadist responds, "I won't."

What made treatment difficult for me were rapid shifts from extreme narcissistic vulnerability and terror to arrogance and rage at being in such a devalued profession and in such an unsatisfactory treatment, to cool detachment with poise, charm, and wit.

After about three years of treatment, she decided to terminate. During the time I have been seeing her, I do believe that her life became somewhat calmer and more stabilized. She left me to work with a psychiatrist who has a reputation for giving advice and being very directive with his patients.

Best wishes,

Frank.

CONTRIBUTIONS FROM THE MOTIVATIONAL SYSTEMS

Early in the life of Julie, the patient about whom I corresponded with Bernard Barnett, aversiveness was triggered in circumstances where other motivations, such as attachment, assertion, sexuality, and physiological regulation, were compromised. Attachments were always imperiled and evoked the dread of abandonment and deprivation. Assertion and exploration were squelched and frustrated in her early school days. Her frequent changing of schools made the beginning of each school term nightmarish. As the new girl she was teased, picked on, and ostracized, and she remained friendless for long periods of time. Assertion became contaminated by aggression and was turned into contempt for others. Furthermore, later, to be self-assertive also contained despair. It meant that she had given up all hope of waiting for her idealized father to rescue her. Since it was essential for her to feel that she had power and was in charge, her beauty and sensuality provided the cement through which she could hold the interest of the powerful men she craved. Finally, fulfilling physiological requirements was sacrificed during postadolescence in favor of mood and affect regulation through anorexia and alcoholism. For Julie, reacting aversively by antagonism or withdrawal modulated painful affect states, anchored her sense of self, warded off searing feelings of humiliation, and asserted her presence in a world in which she anticipated hostility and indifference. In summary, in the course of her life, Julie became increasingly motivated to withdraw from intimate relationships in fear and to comfort herself through more reliable means under her control: alcohol, food, smoking, and sleeping, but most importantly, managing contacts between herself and others by being alternatively seductive and contemptuous. Maintaining the means of self-regulation in her own hands protected her against being abandoned. It also ultimately turned her outrage at being abandoned against herself. Although much of this material was addressed in her analysis, it was of modest benefit to her. Her retort was generally, "So what can I do about it?" I would ask her what it meant to her to be understood or described in this way. She would often then add other confirmatory memories and details. The most immediate benefit from such sessions was that she did not leave feeling angry and disappointed.

For example, Julie reported that her spiral of increasing rage and self-contempt was set in motion when she was about 25 years old. She felt severely disappointed when a love relationship she had counted on did not lead to marriage. She described this man as the combination of good looks and wealth that she yearned for. She blamed herself for the breakup. She was not of his social class. But, more important, she described how she expressed her insecurity by testing him and being provocative. In the twenty years that followed, aggressive eruptions encroached repeatedly and increasingly on her relationships. Based on her intellectual strengths, talents, and poise, she found ways to express her competence and curiosity through work. During these years she was successful in a variety of diverse careers that required considerable social skills and intellectual ability before settling into her current occupation. However, by the time I saw her, aversiveness through antagonism and withdrawal had become dominant in her life. As age and experience eroded her arrogance, she increasingly felt that she could only be successful if she attached herself to a powerful and assertive man. Then, vicariously she might enjoy the success that she increasingly felt was out of her reach. Her relationships were very precarious. It was during this time that she began treatment with me as I described in the letters.

SOME FURTHER THOUGHTS AND DETAILS

In the years prior to beginning her analysis with me, Julie typically verbally abused her lovers. Then they would either leave her or verbally or even physically abuse her. By the time I saw her these sadomasochistic patterns had toned down somewhat. However, over the years she sustained the abusive relationships. They carried her passion, not the toned-down relationships. In retrospect, I believe this was a problem in the treatment. Although I recognized it at the time, and we addressed it, the transference did not shift.

Even well into her treatment with me, Julie's uncontrolled contempt still erupted in her work relationships. Through her manner, which co-workers described to her as imperious and condescending, she provoked the staff and colleagues so that whenever possible they avoided working with her.

At work and with men, Julie was trapped between her demand

that she be rescued by a hero and her rageful contempt when she noted any signs of weakness in her potential rescuers. Signs of weakness were reminiscent of the feeble hands of her depressed, dysfunctional mother who would deliver her into the arms of her hated aunt. When she detected signs of indifference in others she felt devastated, inadequate, and then enraged. The indifference confirmed her aunt's denigration of her; namely, she was too worthless to be loved. Expressions of uncontrolled, fierce rage would then rapidly fluctuate between her and the flawed others.

As I described in my letters to Bernard, Julie oscillated between rageful contempt toward me and self-contempt. When a relationship with a man failed, she would become furious at herself for failing to maintain the relationship. For example, after her affair with Harry, a very wealthy man, ended, she met another man who was slightly less wealthy. She was angry at him for his inadequacy, at herself for not having been able to hold on to Harry, and at me for not telling her what she was doing wrong in that previous relationship. Although she had ended that relationship in a rage at his neglect of her, she now felt she failed to hold the man who could provide her with the lifestyle to which she felt entitled.

Julie's life experiences were filled with instances of narcissistic injuries, social rebuffs, exclusions, and neglect by people whose friendship she sought. For example, she described being greeted at a party by an acquaintance, "What are you doing here?" When I attempted to capture my understanding of her experience by recognizing her hurt feelings and her angry reaction, she was outraged. It was at these times that I attempted to place her outrage into a context that would make it understandable. Such interventions failed to enable her to feel understood, and increased her rage toward me as well. It was at that point that I offered her the view of herself as both trapped and murderously enraged. At the same time, I was ready to recognize her as adamant about being seen as feared rather than pitied. My efforts to place her experience into a context, and to make her more understandable to herself and to me, had the effect of depicting her as a victim of circumstances rather than an assertive, decisive provocateur. However, when I referred to her articulate vituperative eruptions as murderous rage, when in effect I acknowledged her wish to kill, she did feel better understood.

Julie's treatment with me was not a downhill spiral for the entire time. For the purposes of this discussion, however, I have emphasized the difficulties I encountered in working with her. Yet there were productive periods, especially during the sessions in which I spelled out the results of my fantasied dialogue, for example, such formulations as "accept crumbs or kill the crumb-givers." Then Julie's whole face lit up, she became excited, and there was a palpable shift in our relationship. In these interventions, I acknowledged her murderousness and her vulnerability to feeling shame. I neither demeaned her, destroyed her, nor fled from her. In so doing, I believe, I momentarily altered our interaction. I believe that this series of interpretations distinguished me from her weak mother, her sadistic aunt, and her idealized but abandoning father. Consequently, I believe she felt less enraged, less worthless, and less beholden to a rescuer. I felt less threatened, more hopeful, and more effective.

A second factor that contributed to Julie's increased self-assuredness over time was the evolving adversarial quality of our relationship (Lachmann 1986). When I spoke of her murderous rage and vituperative outbursts, I spoke from the vantage point of an observer who could recognize her as a potentially dangerous and powerful adversary. By not explaining her rage, she felt that I was accepting it. When she felt more to be feared than pitied, she felt better understood, with her pride restored. She thus felt less unequal and safer with me. She had been threatened and enraged by my earlier interpretations because they meant to her that I was weak and that I saw her as weak. She also worried that I was trying to be nice out of fear of her. That is, her rage dispelled one source of her shame.

At times, even prior to my correspondence with Bernard Barnett, there were instances when, although stymied, I was able to "decenter." In one session Julie had been obsessed with her financial exploitation by a previous lover. As this session was drawing to a close and she was still repeating her outrage at and fascination with this man, she turned to me and said, "I am like a deer, caught in the headlights of a car. You have to do something to help me out of this state." By this time we were both standing and she had her hand on the knob of my office door. I came up with, "If you think of yourself as a deer, and you think of him as a car, think of him as a car without a driver." She looked back over her shoulder and with a fleeting smile, left my office. When she returned the following day, she told me that she found my comment helpful and then said she had been thinking of him as a suit of armor without a knight inside. I felt very pleased with her creative transformations of my comment. The session went on, but eventually the topic of her fascination with this exploitative man returned. She recalled what it was like to dance with him. She described it as a transporting experience. I said to her, "Think of him as a tuxedo, without Fred Astaire." She laughed, and said, "Don't push it."

At the time I was working with Julie, I had also been seeing Clara, whose treatment is discussed in the next chapter. For both patients, I felt that their hostility and devaluation was not so much an attempt to destroy or undermine their analysis, but an indication that I was somehow on the wrong track. I believe Clara benefited from what I learned in my work with Julie.

Here was an instance in which placing contempt and eruptions of rage into a context adversely affected the treatment. I do not believe that the contexts we described as the spawning grounds for Julie's injuries and rage outbursts were irrelevant. For example, as the perpetual new girl at school she was constantly on the outs socially, mocked and teased by other children. Julie had not repressed these memories, but they had been dissociated from her propensity to speak contemptuously and become enraged at failures of people to live up to her requirements. In the context of those early experiences she felt humiliated and silently enraged. When I, in my comments or in my failure to understand her precisely as she wanted to be seen, reminded her of her vulnerability she became contemptuous and flared up in rage. When I understood her enraged reaction toward a boyfriend or acquaintance as deriving from her need to be recognized and treated in a particular way, she would become enraged at me. She was trapped by her anger but also cherished it as though it were her life raft. My comments did not sufficiently promote the transformation of eruptions of rage into more regulated reactions, and therefore they did not diminish Julie's propensity to become rageful and self-defeating. Furthermore, these contextualizing interventions did not enable Julie to draw on her considerable reservoir of adaptive resources. Instead, she oscillated between despair and self-contempt on one side and rage and hostility on the other.

In the case of Julie, a negatively toned weak mother and absent father transference was ever waiting in the wings. As a child, Julie longed for her father's return and believed that he would rescue her. In parallel fashion, she expected me to do something to alter her continual vacillations between despair and hopelessness on the one hand, and intense hatred and explosions of contempt on the other. When I failed to meet her expectations, when I did not rescue her, she became increasingly dissatisfied in her treatment. My attempts to grasp her humiliating experiences only led her to feel more hopeless in that she felt I was weak, like her mother. Simultaneously, she felt that I saw her as pathetic, which shattered her pride and enraged her further. A similar dilemma operated in my work with Clara.

9

The Empathy That Enrages

Patients let us know that aggressive experiences . . . feel real, much more real than do erotic experiences.

(Winnicott, "Aggression in Relation to
Emotional Development," 1950)

My treatment of Julie overlapped with the analysis of Clara. Although there were numerous similarities in the symptomatology of Julie and Clara, Clara was more overtly depressed and maintained an ongoing suicidal plan. Like Julie, she, too, felt ashamed of her vulnerability. Both became enraged when they sensed my empathy. Both presented me with a similar treatment problem: how to work simultaneously with their eruptive aversiveness and their phobia about having their vulnerability recognized.

In previous chapters I discussed transformation of aversive reactions, either through withdrawal or rageful flare-ups, by articulating and placing them in the past and current context of the analytic interaction. I now continue my examination of reactive aggression that has been transformed through a number of life experiences so that it has lost some if its reactivity. For Clara, eruptions of rage, contempt, and disdain were ever-present. However, she was aware of and ashamed of her potential destructiveness, and dreaded that she would enact her sadistic fantasies. Yet when I attempted to understand the circumstances in which her rage was organized in her developing years, she became even more enraged, hopeless, and suicidal.

THE TREATMENT OF CLARA

Clara made critical, devaluing comments about me and my treatment of her during more than six years of her eleven-year analysis. What was that like for me? Don't ask. As with Julie, a literal change in my analytic behavior was required to alter this pattern. I needed to be cautious about offering leading-edge interventions since these were heard as my attempt to negate, dispute, sanitize, or diminish the extent to which each patient valued her aggressiveness. When each patient felt that I no longer negated her aggressiveness, but accepted her in her entirety, not just in a "purer" version, each could maintain a sense of pride, vitality, and integrity.

There is a slippery slope implicit in the preceding paragraph. It concerns the distinction between when my interventions no longer negated her aggressiveness and when my interventions were no longer experienced as negating her aggressiveness. I used the former construction to highlight the necessity for a change in my stance. Both patients sensed my tilt in the direction of resonating with their vulnerability. For both, this signaled danger. They anticipated with fear that they would be lulled into accepting my version of the world as safe, and of people as trustworthy and reliable. Both felt in imminent danger of being caught off-guard. For both, anger provided protection and the only reliable shield against the dangers, in one case of self-betrayal (Clara), and in the other of exploitation and abandonment (Julie).

Both Julie and Clara were determined to hold on to their aggression, murderousness, contempt, or sadism. It provided vitalization, efficacy, and strength. Had I understood this earlier in the treatment of Julie, we might have gotten off to a better start. But Clara did benefit.

Clara, a 36-year-old divorced, professional woman, began her fourth attempt at psychoanalysis, three sessions per week, with a generally pessimistic feeling. Several years in three previous treatments had not succeeded in diminishing her depressive outlook on life, her inability to enjoy herself in any endeavor, or her sense that nothing she was involved in was worthwhile. She was chronically bitter and angry and held on to a suicidal plan as her best means of resolving her intolerable life. After the first month of treatment, she began her analytic hours with questions such as "How are you going to help me?" "How is this going to be any different?" "What good is this going to do?"

The way in which Clara organized her experience as she began treatment with me was based on her long-standing and pervasive pessimism: nothing makes any difference. When I reflected this to her, she responded that in her previous treatments she was called resistive. She was waiting to see when I would apply this label to her. Furthermore, she anticipated being accused of masochism, of being unwilling to help herself, and of being unwilling to make use of the treatment situation. She expected to be blamed for not improving. In fact, she said that if she were not blamed, it would only be because I was too nice, in fact pathologically nice, and had a problem with my aggression. In that case I would also be unable to help her, and she might as well leave.

I recognized how important these grim beliefs (Weiss and Sampson 1986) were to Clara. Furthermore, I acknowledged her insistence that she would not be helped, and that she could not change. I had to monitor myself carefully so as not to impose on her my wish that she be an easier patient. I was not always successful in doing so. I believe that maintaining my hopefulness enabled me to tolerate her pervasive contempt. I also had to monitor myself to keep myself from countering her pessimism by an increase in my therapeutic optimism. Had this occurred we would have grown increasingly out of touch with each other. I have always liked having one patient at a time (no more) who posed genuine challenges to me personally and to my psychoanalytic beliefs. After several months of exploration, we formulated a model scene based on a childhood experience.

THE HORSE MURDERER

Clara and her family lived on a farm in the Midwest. When she was 8 years old she was given a horse as a gift. Although she was told how to take care of it, she neglected to follow the instructions. She explained to me that in cold weather she fed the horse a mixture of grains that she had been told would be appropriate for the horse in the summer. In warm weather the horse could roam freely, but in the winter when the animal was more confined, this feed would make it too energetic. The horse became so frisky that it injured itself, became incapacitated, and had to be killed. On the day that the horse was to be killed, her parents told her that they were going to take her for a picnic. She knew that the horse was to be killed. She knew that the picnic was her parents' attempt to spare her the pain of having to be there when the horse was killed. Out of a sense of responsibility, guilt, and loyalty, she wanted to stay with her horse until the end. At the same time, she believed that her parents needed to feel that they were protective and caring of her. She gave in to her parents' need, betrayed her own ideals, and went on the picnic. When she returned and the horse was indeed gone, she felt ashamed.

This model scene—collaborating with her parents' need to appear "good" at the sacrifice of her integrity, and acquiescing to the picnic while her horse was killed—condensed numerous earlier dynamically similar experiences. It also provided the blueprint for the themes that organized Clara's experiences in adulthood, including the analytic relationship. To avoid further self-betrayal, to maintain self-respect, Clara could not allow anyone, ever again, to believe that they were doing anything for her or giving anything to her.

Clara's depressive, pessimistic states, her inflexibility, her resistive stance in the analysis, and the themes that organized her model scene, were explored and formulated as follows: "I must beware of people trying to make me feel good. If I permit them to do so, I run the risk of masking a painful but real event. A feeling of well-being could turn out to be self-deceptive. When others want me to feel good, or want to spare me pain, guilt, or anxiety, it is only out of their own self-interest. My self-respect and integrity demand that I not permit anyone to help me feel better. So long as I feel depressed, angry, guilty, and despairing, I know I have maintained my integrity." In fact, it became critical to Clara that she must never acknowledge that anyone could help her feel better. Only by feeling bad could she remain true to her horse.

The co-construction of the model scene and its interpretation became a heightened moment for me. She had contributed the narrative in a dialogue with my understanding of that experience. I could grasp her experience, based in part on her narrative, in part on the patterns of her past relationships (including her marriage), and in part on my experience of her in the treatment. All of a sudden I understood the nature of her battle with me and the dire necessity for her hostile opposition. However, my Pollyannaish formulations did not particularly impress her. I soon became aware that implicit in my formulation was my expectation that she would now feel understood by me. Then she would be able to view herself in this new perspective. She would feel freed from her constraint to be ever vigilant so that she would not repeat the self-betrayals of her past. My expectations evoked her distrust.

I accepted Clara's resistive stance as plausible and necessary. But this acceptance did not alter her dread of reexperiencing her self-betrayal. It did, however, provide her with some sense of efficacy. I believe that she was dimly aware of her impact on me. My acceptance of her also gave rise to an expectation of new possibilities with me, her new analyst, despite her worry that I might be too nice. I did note a shift in the unrelenting quality of her depressive state. She became cautiously hopeful in the face of this novel experience of acceptance. In addition, my not expecting her to acquiesce, to see herself through my eyes, may have diminished her dread of repeating her traumatic childhood experience in the treatment (A. Ornstein 1974, 1991). Nevertheless, numerous severe but temporary stalemates continued to occur. Acceptance of her need to feel hopeless prevented these stalemates from turning into impasses. At this point in the treatment, Clara continued to feel endangered if she did not resist. She dreaded allying herself with me lest she succumb and collaborate in a self-deception.

When Clara told me the story of the killing of her horse, I initially commented that she had been given the responsibility for caring for the horse, by herself, at a very young age. At that time I still thought that to place her experience into a context that would include her young age and the responsibilities that were expected of her would present her with the broader perspective in which she could view herself and her experiences in a new way. She became enraged and said that I was trying to find an excuse for her. She heard my comment as my inability to accept her as a killer. She felt that I needed her to be innocent of any crime. Her perception of me coincided with her experience in her family. When she or her siblings had an angry thought, they were required to sit in a specific chair in the living room until they said that they did not feel angry any longer. Then they were permitted to get off the chair and rejoin the family. Even understanding this connection, however, did not diminish her rage toward me.

Clara required me to accept her as a killer. Anything less indicated to her that I was unable to tolerate her murderousness. I learned from her later that the horse was not the only animal that died due to her neglect. Previously, several small pets had also perished from malnutrition. Thus, these experiences led her to demand that her destructiveness be considered undeniable and intrinsic to her self-definition. She required me to recognize and accept her as bad and angry. I understood this as a demand that I "join" her, based on her dread that she would feel isolated, alone on the chair, in her depressed and enraged state. Not having to exclude her darker side in relation to me, as she was required to do in her family, solidified her sense of herself. My initial acceptance of her as resistive and hopeless was expanded to include her murderousness. Acceptance of her darker side enabled her to feel lighter in that she felt her vitality was no longer so precariously tied to her rage and murderousness. My acceptance of her seemed to open the possibility for her establishing and sustaining a mirroring selfobject transference.

When I accepted Clara's conviction that she killed her horse, I did not endorse her theory of her innate aggression or her conviction that she is basically bad. Rather we explored the multitude of meanings of being bad and angry. To be seen as aggressive and to feel that I see her as aggressive meant to her that, in contrast to her experience in her family, she did not have to pretend that she had no aggressive thought in her head. It indicated to her that I could tolerate the extent of her anger, and I did not have to flee from her, as she feared.

In becoming enraged at my attempt to place her experience into a broader context, Clara re-created with me what would have resulted in her being confined to the chair in her family. At that point in her analysis, we had a somewhat legalistic negotiation. I told her that I would accept her as a "killer," but that I would not agree to accept her as bad. I told her of the danger that I foresaw. I would not confirm her sense of badness so long as she linked it to being aggressive. If that link remained, being bad would also remain as a major source of self-restoration.

This portion of the analysis focused on Clara's conviction that she was a killer. Through this conviction she derived a sense of vitality and strength. In contrast, feeling like an abandoned victim who had to betray herself to retain acceptance within her family evoked intense shame at her continuing self-betrayal.

In the course of Clara's early life, expressions of self-assertion and anger led to the loss of selfobject ties to both parents. Following Kohut, we might formulate that her propensity to react ragefully in her family, in analysis, and elsewhere, was a consequence of her readily fragmented sense of self. Her tenuous connection to her family, her unsupportive milieu, her enfeebled sense of self and vulnerable selfobject ties, would be understood to lead to eruptions of anger. But clinically, and with respect to her self-experience, the reverse was true. It was my attempt to provide support for her vulnerable self that enraged her and ruptured the selfobject tie. The crucial affirmation required was in regard to her being guilty of neglect and murder rather than innocent by virtue of youth, weakness, and emotional neglect.

In my attempt to place Clara's experience into a broader context, I inadvertently and indirectly placed her back into her aggression-denying, self-betrayal–demanding family. The selfobject tie was ruptured when I did not grasp the importance of her being accepted by me as angry. Therefore, she became angry. When I could accept her as a killer, she could be angry in my office without being sentenced to the chair.

THE CHAIR AND THE COUCH

My "chair" turned out to be a piece of furniture with multiple symbolic implications. During all of the preceding discussions, for about six years of the analysis, Clara sat on a chair during her analytic sessions. She adamantly refused to lie on the couch. During these years, on occasion, we investigated the meaning of her refusal. Eventually, she told me that the chair on which I sat was too close to the place on the couch where her head would be if she were to lie down. Her head would then be too close to my crotch. I was stupid, she said, not to be aware of the danger that I was courting. She could easily bite off my penis from her position on the couch. I told her that I was willing to take that risk since I felt confident in my ability to protect myself. She still insisted that I was naive, but now sat herself at the foot of the couch as far from my chair as she could sit. After several months, and several tests, she did lie down on the couch. During this period of the treatment I interpreted our dilemma: I could either be guilty of naïveté in asking her to use the couch, or of fear of her by not asking her to use it. Privately, I did not feel worried, but I knew if I betrayed my cool, she would escalate her threats.

When Clara began to use the couch, she usually removed her shoes before entering my office and left them in the waiting room. This action had a domino effect. A new patient followed Clara one day and he thought that I required my patients to leave their shoes in the waiting room. Then, not only he, but also the patients of my colleagues who share my office suite took off their shoes and left them in the waiting room. Within a few days the waiting room was filled with shoes.

When I asked Clara about leaving her shoes in the waiting room, she explained that she felt more comfortable with her shoes off. Then she admitted that she worried that her feet smelled. Could I tolerate her with her smelly feet and her "old, ugly, disgusting body"? I realized that through this ritual she was revealing what she felt most ashamed of. I realized that beneath this overtly provocative behavior was a silent question, which I articulated: Do I find her sexually repulsive? I added that the only response to this question that she would believe would be a resounding yes. We were both aware of her conviction that nobody could find her sexually appealing. Questioning this conviction would only prove to her that I was thoroughly untrustworthy. She agreed and said that she felt I understood her, because now I understood the traps she had set.

Clara tested me in a variety of ways in the course of her treatment. Sometimes they were unspoken tests, for example: Would I distance myself from her or leave her out of fear or disgust? Could I stand her physical presence close to me? At other times the tests were in the form of questions such as, "Yesterday I said something very important, do you know what it was?" In response, I would at times draw a blank, and at other times guess wrong. There were times when I did remember what she needed me to remember (for example, a dream image, a name, an anniversary of an event) or when I guessed correctly. Such moments made us both feel good.

We came to understand these tests as complicated attempts to determine whether her experience of feeling connected to me during a previous session was also felt by me. Did I reciprocate her feeling that we were on the same wavelength? However, the tests were more specifically designed to prove to herself that a shared intimacy with me had been spurious. My not knowing, which was frequent, reassured her that she had not betrayed herself by moving closer to me. The closeness she sought was a refinding of a beloved housekeeper who left her, and the closeness she feared was repetition of this same attachment–desertion sequence that had been traumatic in her early life.

The theme of my knowing or sensing, but not articulating, what I know occupied a central role in Clara's analysis. From birth until age 3, Clara enjoyed a warm relationship with a lively, adventuresome, intuitive, young housekeeper. She preferred the housekeeper to her "pretentious" mother. The housekeeper left when Clara's sister was born, ushering in a period of loneliness and loss. The housekeeper returned briefly when Clara was $4^1/_2$ years old, but stayed only a few months before she left again. Clara had thought that the housekeeper had come back to her to stay. On her departure she was deeply disappointed and attributed her leaving to some inadequacy or badness of her own. The housekeeper's emotional responsivity when she was present and her final departure laid the groundwork for Clara's increasing state of pessimism and despair. Clara's longing to refind the experience she had with the house-keeper and her dread of opening herself to disappointment and a reex-perience of her loss organized the mirroring selfobject and representa-tional dimensions of the transference.

ONGOING REGULATIONS

The relationship between Clara and me can be described with respect to the ongoing regulations that organized the analysis. Here was the di-lemma: Clara's critical, contemptuous, confrontational, pessimistic stance, interwoven with hints of suicide, was responded to by me with privately held feelings of irritation, impatience, withdrawal, and rejection. I also admired her uncompromising integrity, and valued the learning experi-ence with which the profound differences between Clara and me chal-lenged me. I never revealed these feelings to her directly. To do so would have been assimilated by Clara into her conviction that she was deeply flawed and irredeemably destructive. On the other hand, she would never have believed my positive feelings during these years of her analysis, although I don't doubt that she sensed them.

Most crucial in our ongoing interactions was the manner in which we each found ways to accommodate the limitations of our own self-regulation. For Clara, the self-regulatory issue was to shore up her self-protection so that she would not be abandoned or become too engaged or trusting and in danger of another self-betrayal. For me the self-regu-latory task was to manage my irritability and self-esteem in the face of her assaults. This dilemma was never directly interpreted.

I noted a striking contrast between my experience of the dilemma in Clara's and David's treatments. In David's treatment, our dilemma cen-tered on the connection between his self-regulating sexual fantasies and their expression in his self-destructive behavior in his classes. Convey-ing my understanding of this dilemma to him expressed my concern for the precarious way in which he regulated his states of depression. The dilemma in the analysis of Clara pitted us on opposing sides. What I needed for my comfort and what she needed for her safety were at odds.

I believed that in keeping this adversarial aspect of our dilemma in the background, she would not feel forced to make her involvement in the treatment explicit. We both had to understand, privately, for several years of the treatment, that acknowledgment of the extent of her involvement by either of us threatened her with intimations of having participated in another self-betrayal. In those circumstances, I believe, she would have become self-conscious and then defensive about the extent to which she had become connected to me. Late in her analysis, an adversarial dimension played an important therapeutic role, as I discuss in the next chapter.

Disruptions and repair of a mirroring selfobject transference hinged on my inferring, guessing, deductively knowing, and intuitively understanding her feeling states, and images from dreams and other experiences, for a period of several months, without her associations. More active collaboration with me carried the danger of participating in another self-betrayal. To work with Clara, I needed to alter my usual exploratory analytic stance.

To ask Clara to associate freely and to tell me her thoughts made her feel endangered and enraged, to a point where she was unable to function in her daily life (she was employed as a manager in a small business). However, to treat her without her participation, without her associations, would lead me to feel endangered, enraged, and unable to function in the analysis. She wanted to repeat with me the kind of experience that she had, at least in spurts, with the housekeeper, to feel intuitively understood. I acknowledged that such intuitive understanding had been an oasis in her early life.

When I felt that our connection had become attenuated, and Clara was silent, I experimented by musing aloud about my sense of frustration and puzzlement at not being able to reach her. These musings were both self-regulatory efforts as well as attempts to reach her. I speculated about her states, such as anxiety or anger. I told her that I sensed her pleasure in tantalizing me, and her desperation about refinding the lost housekeeper. I asked her about my musing aloud, and she expressed delight. She said it made her feel important. This ongoing regulation provided both of us with a glimpse of a more overtly shared bond.

In negotiating the dilemma of Clara's treatment (what I needed from her to feel comfortable, what she needed from me to feel safe), I had to alter my own self-regulatory style. In the course of these sessions, Clara diagnosed me as suffering from "terminal hopefulness." I had to monitor and sometimes dampen my enthusiasm and optimism, as well as my expectation that I would actually help her. When my self-control slipped and I revealed any hope, or when I would just misunderstand her, she would become enraged and sarcastic, and would develop head-aches. If I could tolerate her rage, we were back in business. In exploring this issue with Clara, I learned that I created problems for her when I expressed hope or implied that we were working well together. Of course, she knew that I would not be seeing her if I had no hope at all. At the same time, she needed me to have hope, since she had so little for herself. When I made these feelings public, I directly threatened her with possible repetitions of self-betraying experiences similar to those in her family. Thus, she was wary of cooperating with any direct expression of hope.

By about the sixth year of Clara's analysis, I had become more experienced in understanding her overt provocativeness in terms of the fears and wishes that were concealed beneath it. I was also no longer required to recognize her persistent testing behavior as her way of enlivening herself by being aggressive. We reached a point in her analysis when acknowledging her capacity for rage and her potential danger to me were in the forefront of our discussions.

Clara demanded my close attention to her states and feelings and that I monitor my states and feelings closely as well. I don't think she entered the analysis with this demand fully formed. It was certainly a theme in her life, but one of several. In interaction with me, this demand crystallized as her expectation and coincided with my expectations of myself in relation to her.

To the extent that I welcomed Clara's challenges, I did not find her tests and provocativeness to be destructive. When I felt her questions to be threatening to me, I came to understand that she had punctured my wish to be optimally attuned. Irritation and annoyance were my responses to having felt wounded and unappreciated. I did not use my experience of Clara as an indication of her unconscious aggression toward me or her destructiveness toward the analysis. Nor did I provide Clara with the knowledge of what it felt like to be the target of her tests. On the contrary, she was quite used to being described as hostile, accused of provocativeness, and told that she was an angry person, or, as she had been described in her prior analyses, masochistic and unwilling to help herself.

Had I used my personal experience and my reaction to Clara, the treatment would certainly be tilted in a direction diametrically opposite to her sense of me as being pathologically nice. It would have made me familiar and exactly as she had expected—cold and wanting to maintain my distance from her. Her anxiety and distrust of my niceness and, indirectly, of her own, would have deprived her of a potentially new view of herself, and therefore a new experience through the analysis.

In describing the treatment of Clara, I have sought to illustrate the benefit of focusing on the quality of the self-experience that she attempted to maintain. Furthermore, I have speculated about the danger of a therapeutic approach that assumes what feels good to the analyst will be beneficial to the patient. This danger extends from a narrow view of empathy to a privileging of the analyst's subjectivity as providing an insight into the patient's motivations.

My views on translating my experience with Clara into either assumptions about her unconscious intentions or generalizations about her effect on others will be expressed in the next chapter. Had I felt that she was hostile and wanted to destroy the treatment and me, and told her as much, I would have been providing her with a most familiar experience. Our interaction would have been for her like all the others in her life that reinforced her hopelessness and depression. In Chapter 11 I discuss the analyst–patient interaction as a system that is changed or transformed by perturbations, disturbances that alter the repetitiveness of a system. Viewing Clara as hostile or as an angry woman would maintain the system intact. In addition, it would have circumvented the meaning and experience for her of a pathologically nice person like me who suffers from terminal hopefulness accepting her, a murderess.

ENACTMENTS AND TRANSFORMATIONS IN THE SNOW

During a session in the eighth year of her analysis, Clara suffered from a chest cold. I noticed her cough and that she made a point of swallowing her phlegm. I commented about that, and she said she was afraid to cough it up because it would disgust me. Further inquiry revealed that what she really wanted to do was to smear the phlegm on me. I told her that I would smear it right back on her. We spent the session with her telling me that she wanted to smear phlegm, then urine, and later feces on me. I told her that I would smear it back on her. And so it went. The session that followed was scheduled at a time different from her usual hour. It occurred after my cleaning service had just cleaned and straightened my office. My office looked unusually tidy. Clara entered my office and said, "Your mother has been here and cleaned everything up." "No," I said, "my mother wouldn't do that. It was your mother." She had enjoyed the "smearing session" and wanted to blame me for bringing it to a close. She did so, not with the angry edge that characterized her earlier complaints about me, but with a lighter touch.

The extent of Clara's difficulty in managing her destructive rages persisted, although in a somewhat more muted tone. She described her anxiety about being alone with a neighbor's child. She feared that inadvertently she might do something, or neglect to do something, that could harm the child. In fact, so afraid was she that she might harm the child that she required the presence of another person when she was with her. At the end of the session, she said to me, "What would you do if I refused to get off the couch, if I just stayed here" (and by implication prevented the next patient from having a session)? I said, "I don't know" and insistently she repeated her challenge. Having now had a moment to reflect, I said, "I would interpret that you don't want to leave me." She shot up from the couch, looked around my office and said, "I feel like pulling all your books off the shelves and throwing them on the floor." I thought of a toddler about to have a tantrum. I thought of the preceding session and that she had masked her need to feel connected to me by behaving provocatively. I imagined that she needed to feel some sense of safety in finding a containing environment, like being embraced by a parent. I said to her, "I would interpret that as your wanting me to hold you." With a slight smile and a sideward glance she walked out of the office. By this time in the analysis sufficient trust had developed that I was able to address her vulnerability and need for intimacy without arousing her fear that she was placing herself at risk.

Several months later, Clara came to my office on a beautiful day after a snowfall. As she was about to lie down on the couch, she said, "I want to go to the park." I said, "Sure, what would you like to do in the park?" Clara lay down.

Clara: Make snow angels.
I said: How do you do that?
Clara: You lie on your back and move your arms up and down, and then you get up carefully and the impression made in the snow will look like an angel.
I said: Great, then we can make snow lamps.
Clara: How do you do that?
I said: You make snowballs and place them in a circle on the ground. Then you keep making snowballs and place them on top, in decreasing numbers, so that you make an igloo. Before you close it up you put a lit candle inside, and then put the last snowball on top. The heat of the candle melts the snow a little but the cold air immediately freezes it up again. And you have a glowing snow lamp.
Clara: That sounds beautiful. Then we could have a snowball fight.

Still lying on the couch as I sat in my chair close behind her, Clara proceeded to have an imaginary snowball fight with me. She told me that she was picking up snow and throwing it at me; I threw it back at her. She told me that she happened to pick up a piece of ice, put snow around it, and threw it at me. I threw it right back at her. "What happens if you get snow under your coat?" she asked. "Oh, you say, 'Are you all right?' and quickly throw some more snow." And so it went and when the session was almost over, she asked me, "How do you end a snowball fight?" I told her, "We have hot chocolate." "Ah," she said with a twinkle in her voice, "I thought we could do something sexual."

The session was a memorable one for both of us. Clara recalled it at the end of her analysis with a touch of regret. She was sorry that she did not avail herself of more opportunities to have fun with me. I thought of this session as a continuation, if not culmination, of the transformation of her murderousness and her dread of being destructive. In our snowball fight we constructed a new context for her murderousness. We built a play space in which she could enact her aggressive fantasies without endangering herself or me. It bore a certain resemblance to Gerald Stechler's day-care center (Chapter 2) in that I participated and interactively regulated the play.

Our snowball session began by our presenting apparently competing construction in the snow. However, Clara realized that I had also given her something that she could use in her play with her neighbor's daughter. We then moved into "puberty" play, where we could be tricky, more aggressive in our competition, and yet not harmful to each other. To the extent that aggression and assertion had been contaminated in her development, and to the extent that contaminated aggression had colored her sexuality, she had begun to differentiate among these motivations. Then, having spent an afternoon in a puberty-like snowball fight, she could move toward the adolescent-like sexuality with which she ended this session.

There are clearly any number of interventions that could have been offered in response to Clara's provocativeness. In the ones I described, I attempted, eventually, to place her provocations into a more playful context. Playing may have been sorely absent in her developing years, and my playing with her could be seen as an attempt to provide her with an experience that was missing in her childhood. However, that was not my purpose. Rather, I was co-constructing a current context for her provocativeness, which, in her developing years and in its raw form, had led her to doubt her ability to contain her destructiveness.

In spite of her overt resistiveness, provocativeness, and the myriad of complaints Clara expressed about me and my treatment of her, her attendance was impeccable. Even in her hostility, she was consistently responsive to me. Alterations in the schedule of our appointments were disorganizing for her, which revealed the viability of the selfobject tie that had been established. However, not until the eleventh year of the analysis did she overtly acknowledge the importance of the treatment to her. Such acknowledgment was only possible when her shame and humiliation about feeling so vulnerable had diminished. Then she could accept and work with my inquiry about her fantasy of biting off my penis, or harming her neighbor's child. We placed the fantasy of biting off my penis into the context of her conflicted relationship with her father. He had wanted her to be the son he had always wanted and even nicknamed her Rocky. Prominent in her fantasies was the theme of turning the rough quality that her father encouraged in her against him. We placed the dread of harming her neighbor's daughter into the context of her loss of the housekeeper to her sister.

I have deliberately offered few details about Clara's relationships with her mother, father, and siblings. These relationships emerged in the dynamic issues, and their interpretation occupied the forefront of the analysis at various times. My emphasis in this chapter has been on the therapeutic processes that created the context—in part familiar, in part novel—in which her murderousness melted as snow does on a sunny day.

Placing her experiences into the context of our relationship no longer threatened her or enraged her. She began to make herself understandable to other people, rather than to feel hurt and enraged when she felt misunderstood or slighted. In the closing stage of the analysis, she sold the house in which she and her (divorced) husband had lived. It had become dilapidated through more than a decade of neglect. She hired an architect and designed a new house for herself, which, she discovered with delight, turned out to be even more beautiful than she anticipated. The parallels to herself were obvious to both of us.

In the eleventh year of Clara's analysis, termination was possible. At that time we discussed what we had accomplished and what had not been sufficiently achieved. Clara said she always felt, no matter where I went off, that I took her seriously. But she regretted that she did not take advantage of more opportunities to have fun with me. On leaving she gave me a present, a card in which she had written, "I love you for all the things you gave me. I hate you for all the things you did not give me." I could not have asked for any clearer affirmation of our work.

10

A Requiem for Countertransference

When I present papers at conferences in which I discuss my clinical work, such as the treatments of the patients I described in this book, I am invariably questioned about my countertransference. In the case of David, I was asked, didn't he provoke me? In the treatment of Nick, why did I simply accept his "twisted shit" without addressing the hostility it contained? In the treatments of Julie and Clara, did I not feel abused and devalued by them? Why did I not use my reaction of feeling stymied and helpless by their insistence on my failure to treat them adequately? I should have apprised them of their effect on me. And what about Julie's beauty, did it leave me cold? What was my reaction to Ben's patronizing tone, and to Stan's exaggerated admiration of me? What about my countertransference? What about my aggression, or my sexual feelings? Where were they, and by implication, where was I in these analyses?

The concept of countertransference was indisputably useful in the development of psychoanalysis, although its use has certainly had a checkered career. Overall, it did provide a much-needed corrective to the one-direction influence implied in a singular focus on the transference of the patient. Even when countertransference was limited to the analyst's neurosis as triggered by the patient's transference neurosis, it introduced a bidirectional perspective into psychoanalytic treatment

As for my countertransferences, I certainly had feelings and various reactions in the course of Julie's and Clara's treatment, and, in fact, in the treatment of every patient I have seen. For example, in the treatment of Clara, as I described in the previous chapter, I heard her transferences to me, as well as my transferences to her (my so-called countertransferences) as having been co-constructed in our therapeutic interactions.

Recall that "co-constructed" means that each participant contributes to the interaction, though not similarly or equally. Co-construction of the analytic interaction can be extended to consider analyst and patient as constituting a system. In these circumstances, the terms *transference* and *countertransference* are absorbed into a system, a recognition of the bidirectionality and reciprocal influence inherent in the interaction between analyst and patient. Each participant brings unique ways of organizing experience to this interaction. Each contributes transferences—influences from the past interlaced with reactions to current experience. However, whereas I believe that the term *transference* continues to do justice to the unique, idiosyncratic contributions of each partner, analyst and patient, the term *countertransference* has become superfluous. It's time that it is laid to rest.

Before I propose systems theory as the alternative to countertransference, join me in an excursion in which I describe the mischief created by the manner in which countertransference has been applied in clinical psychoanalysis.

THE CATCH-22 OF COUNTERTRANSFERENCE

Adherents of the theory that the analyst's countertransference yields not just clues but "insider information" about the transference of the patient place analysts who do not subscribe to this view into a no-win situation. If an analyst does not use his or her countertransference in this prescribed way, it is tantamount to a confession to being emotionally absent from the treatment. Given this Catch-22, the questions I am asked contain a number of questionable assumptions: (1) There are universal expectable reactions, variants of anger, which, if not experienced by an analyst in certain circumstances, indicate that these feelings have been denied or suppressed by the analyst. (2) There is important information about the patient's interpersonal experiences to be mined from the analyst's feelings as they emerge in the course of a session. For example, Kernberg (1975) stated that he "recognizes in the countertransference the hidden intention of the patient's behavior" (p. 247). (3) These feelings and reactions of the analyst signal important aspects of the patient's transferences and should be made part of the analytic dialogue. For the analyst to withhold these reactions, for example, in the cases of Julie and Clara, feelings of being attacked and devalued, makes the analytic relationship inauthentic and deprives the patient of valuable input from the analyst.

All of these assumptions are plausible, to use the term Merton Gill (1982) applied to the transference distortions of patients. But plausible does not mean that they contain universal truths, or even that they are true until proven otherwise. There is a further implication that all good analysts share similar expectations, namely, the expectations that patients must respond to them and respect them as separate, reasonable, well-intentioned objects. The failure of a patient to do so is linked to the patient's pathology. Such expectations are particularly unjustified in treatments in which a patient needs to establish a selfobject transference as a condition for the treatment to become viable. Recognition of the dimensions of the transference, both selfobject and representational (illustrated, for example, in the analysis of Nick), aids in understanding whether a patient's overt devaluation represents emerging developmental strivings, something new co-constructed by this analyst and patient, or a repetition of familiar, past, problematic configurations. An analyst who entertains the possibility of this distinctions can co-create a vastly different therapeutic ambience compared to one in which a patient's devaluations are assumed to have one implication only, as resistive or as defensive projections. The distinction between leading-edge and trailing-edge interpretations is apt here. Entertaining both possibilities places the analyst in a better position to hear the complexities of the patient's transference. It can decrease the likelihood of the analyst's interventions solidifying a defensive, self-protective stance in a patient who is already in dread of retraumatization (A. Ornstein 1974), that is, a dread of re-experiencing in the present the selfobject ruptures of his or her past.

In Chapter 1, in comparing Gail Reed's case with psychoanalysis from a self psychological perspective, I suggested that a patient's non-compliance with an analyst's specific requirements for participation in treatment can be viewed in terms other than resistance. For Clara, non-compliance meant self-respect, and compliance with me was tantamount to self-betrayal. But her more compelling need was the engagement of a mirroring selfobject tie. She had derived selfobject experiences through her relationship with her beloved housekeeper. The tie was shattered when the housekeeper left. In her analysis, the engagement of this selfobject tie oscillated in the foreground with her dread of repeating in the representational dimension her compliant relationship with her parents. This two-dimensional view of transference permits grasping the complexities of Clara's transferences without foreclosing either aspect of it. However, if the only version of transference that an analyst works with is an object-related repetition of a past (oedipal) conflict, or of a past interpersonal relationship, the analyst can easily assume that his or her countertransference points toward one of these repetitions. In these circumstances, selfobject needs that emerge in the patient–analyst interaction are likely to be missed and assimilated into the analyst's object relations theory. When the only tool you have is a hammer, you are likely to treat every problem you encounter as a nail. This is an ever-present danger in working with difficult-to-treat patients, and these are the very patients who evoke in the analyst the more difficult-to-tolerate transferences that are often labeled by them as countertransferences.

COUNTERTRANSFERENCE AS AN EXPRESSION OF THE ANALYST'S AGGRESSION

Since its introduction into clinical discussions, the place accorded to countertransference has increased enormously. Like a balloon, countertransference has been blown up to encompass biases and prejudices of the analyst, used by adherents of one psychoanalytic school to discredit the treatments conducted by adherents of another school, and has eclipsed the place given to transference in postmodern psychoanalysis. The shift in emphasis by analysts from attention to transference to attention to countertransference manifestations has prompted Judith Teicholz (1999) to comment on the extraordinary place given to countertransference and to the subjectivity of the analyst as compared to the patient in present-day psychoanalytic discourse. The privileged place the patient once occupied in the analytic dyad has shrunk.

In the traditional view of countertransference, the analyst was required to recognize and deal with his or her personal, private reactions to the patient. These reactions included expectations, fantasies, and ways in which the analyst felt drawn into behaving with the patient that went beyond, or were outside, the traditional role of the analyst as interpreter of the patient's free associations. Outside these boundaries, the analyst was in danger of becoming a responder to the patient's wishes for gratification. This conceptualization of countertransference meant that the analyst was asked to exercise considerable self-control over countertransference reactions and avoid enactment. For good treatment to proceed, the patient and the patient's transferences must remain the focus of the analysis. From this perspective, a discussion between Anna Ornstein (1998a,b) and Stephen Mitchell (1998a,b) is illuminating. Their debate contains several of the issues that I have discussed and thus provides another slant on the analyst's use of countertransference. Since this debate took place in the context of a panel on aggression, it is not surprising that their discussions of countertransference revolve around the role of the analyst's aggression. Their dialogue clearly depicts their differing positions, specifically, the distinction between self psychological and relational theories on the place of countertransference in treatment.

Ornstein's patient suffered from paralyzing anxieties and social phobias, made continual derogatory self-references, and had made a serious suicide attempt. He sought therapy because of the difficulties he encountered in living with his lover and her son. He was acutely sensitive to any slight from her and would, in response, erupt in rage, damage their home, and become physically abusive to her. As he recounted this material, Ornstein became aware that she was resisting her patient's "efforts 'to take his side' in these incidents" (1998a, p. 60). She became aware that to control her reactions made her appear "stilted" and sound "wooden" (p. 60). These interactions became a focus of analytic attention, and eventually the patient became aware of his inability to "moderate his imperative need to retaliate" (p. 61) when he felt slighted. His awareness led to self-recriminatory confessions that precipitated a countertransference crisis. Ornstein stated that she had "difficulty accepting [her patient's] feeling about himself that he was an unalterably evil person." She found herself "either minimizing his negative self image or quickly 'explaining' its source" (p. 61). These responses made the patient feel that his analyst was "intolerant of [his] evil, revenge-seeking aspects." He felt that she did not accept him as he was.

The analyst–patient interchange described by Ornstein struck a familiar note with respect to my experience with Julie and Clara. In each of these cases the central therapeutic dilemma was, Would the patient's aggression be accepted by me as such? A similar case was reported by Gruenthal (1993). After having successfully interpreted her patient's "negativism and passive rebelliousness as (continuing) evidence of his angry struggle for masculine self-definition . . . his fantasies became more explicitly violent. . . . He burst out, 'You can't seem to see that I *am* a nasty prick'" (p. 336). This patient also felt that his analyst's explanations were "diluting his anger," "explaining it away," and "whitewashing him" (pp. 336–337).

With Julie, Clara, and with Ornstein's patient, dramatic, noninterpretive, enactment-like interventions saved the day. My acceptance of Clara's murderousness and later introduction of play and humor were transformative in her analysis. Ornstein's patient had decided to discontinue treatment over a vacation period. Her telephone call to invite him back convinced him that, contrary to his expectations, she was *not* glad to be rid of him. In these instances a departure from traditional analytic routine, an intervention that went beyond the usual verbal discourse, was crucial. Words were not enough.

In the course of the analysis, Ornstein had enabled her patient to gain some control over his rage tantrums in response to slights from his girlfriend. However, his girlfriend's inability to read his mind touched off his uncontrollable rage outbursts. Ornstein described these as if "he were sitting on a conveyer belt, heading toward the kind of behavior he knew to be destructive to [his relationship with his girlfriend] but that he felt helpless to stop" (1998a, p. 62). "Did you know," he responded, "how much I hated my lover's son and how frequently I found myself having the fantasy that he would be killed in an accident so that I could have my lover all to myself?" (p. 61).

Mitchell (1998b) took as the point of departure for his discussion of Ornstein's case her patient's reports of his hostility toward his girlfriend and her son. Mitchell assumed that this patient wants "unconditional acceptance" (p. 93) from his analyst, a term that Ornstein neither used nor implied in her article. He further assumed that this patient knows he is a bully and is abusive, and that he knows that his analyst must know he is a bully. To work on this issue, Mitchell proposed investigating the patient's awareness of the impact he has on others, including the analyst. Thus, argued Mitchell, the patient's conflictual struggles with different aspects of himself would be brought into the analytic situation. From Mitchell's perspective, it is therapeutically essential to enable the patient to find a place for his own hostility and destructiveness. He faults Ornstein's position of maintaining a "sustained empathic attitude in the analytic situation," and "for precluding a fuller expression of the destructive self which is structurally present but diverted" (p. 98). In essence, Mitchell holds Ornstein's theory, and her failure to use the countertransference he imagined he would have felt, as responsible for what he believed had not been addressed in this analysis.

Ornstein's "conveyer belt" metaphor was viewed by Mitchell as furthering the patient's efforts to disown his aggression. As I argue later, the conveyer belt image captures the experience of aggression erupting forth, with little or no control over it. Aggression has taken charge, and the person hangs on for dear life. We are left with the question: How do we determine whether the conveyer belt metaphor was an imaginative way of capturing the patient's attention and experience, or an exoneration of responsibility for his murderous fantasies and eruptions of rage?

Ornstein (1998b) responded to Mitchell that the metaphor expressed the helplessness she understood her patient to feel in relation to his narcissistic vulnerability. She believed that it was this narcissistic vulnerability that prompted him to react with destructive rage. Here lies the heart of the fundamental difference between these two analysts. To Ornstein the issue was not one of accepting one's destructiveness. In fact, this patient already accepted it and hated himself for it. Rather, she believed that her patient felt himself to be shamefully destructive. She considers shame as underlying the propensity to act ragefully. Therefore, she anticipated that analysis of the profound feelings of shame that beset her patient would alter his propensity to react with rage. Mitchell viewed the patient's aggression as underlying his shame. Enabling this patient to accept or "own" his aggression, and to become aware of its effects, would address the surface shame experience.

The contrasting views of Anna Ornstein and Stephen Mitchell point to yet another controversy: For treatment to be successful is it necessary that a patient express rage toward the analyst in the transference? If rage is seen as an inherent property of the individual, then the well of rage must be tapped and drained in the treatment. However, if a patient's expression of rage is seen as co-constructed then it may or may not gain expression in the treatment. I believe that the safety of the analytic setting may enable some patients to express rage toward figures outside the treatment setting and not toward the analyst. To interpret such expressions as displacements and assume that the rage is really meant for the analyst can destroy the patient's experience of safety and feeling understood. However, when rage is directed toward the analyst, the therapeutic interaction, as well as the patient's vulnerability to expressions of rage, would be explored to identify what the patient experienced in the interaction that triggered the rage. Some patients will express rage both in their lives and in their treatment, some in neither, and some in one or the other. Rather than viewing these different styles through a lens of theory, the meanings and implications of these differences are best explored with recognition of the uniqueness of each patient.

Where does countertransference reside in these two disparate conceptualizations? Does Ornstein's need to be nice, empathize with her patient's shame, and avoid confronting her patient's aggression constitute her countertransference? On the other hand, does Mitchell's engagement with the patient's aggression and thus, his avoidance of the more poignant experience of shame, constitute his countertransference?

In his understanding of Ornstein's treatment, Mitchell imagines that he might feel that the patient is provocative. He uses his personal reaction as an indication of the patient's aggression. Based on his reaction, Mitchell stated that he would apprise the patient of these impressions. In contrast, Ornstein struggled to disentangle herself from her personal reaction to the patient. Her struggle to do so is her response, and carries the authenticity of her participation. I believe that Mitchell, Ornstein, and I agree that a patient may want or need to have the analyst accept him as aggressive. Such recognition can be crucial for the treatment, and the failure to provide it can produce a near-fatal disruption of the treatment relationship. However, if aggression is not seen as a universal attribute that we must accept or own, then the analyst's task is to discriminate what one owns from what one has held on to out of fear of separation, guilt, or as a contaminant with assertion. If, as I have been arguing, aggression is seen as a propensity to react, aggression can come to acquire and provide self-affirmation and a sense of vitality. Then, indeed, acknowledging the person's ownership of his or her rage is crucial.

Teicholz (1999) conceptualized the distinction between Mitchell and Kohut with respect to the role of the analyst's authenticity as follows. Mitchell emphasizes engaging the patient interpersonally to mobilize relational patterns in the transference and thereby to help the patient move beyond them. In contrast, Kohut places "greater emphasis on the analyst's affective resonance with, communication of, empathic understanding of the patient's experience" (p. 60).

Ornstein's treatment is clearly in the tradition of Kohut. Can mobilizing relational patterns be compared with resonating affectively? Even if this comparison was empirically possible, how can Mitchell's version of mobilizing be compared to Ornstein's version of resonating? Clearly, neither of these analysts would espouse a "one-size-fits-all" approach in treatment—either only resonating by one analyst or only mobilizing by the other. This is the kind of cul-de-sac toward which discussions of countertransference tend to lead. Our personal commitment to one approach or another is not so much the problem. Rather, it is the shift in focus, away from substantive issues toward the analyst's personality, that accompanies such debates. Unfortunately they become, "I'm right and you're wrong" discussions. This is the kind of analytic mischief that comes when careful examinations of mobilizing and resonating are reduced to futile discussions of countertransference.

In my treatment of David, my "we'll have to talk as fast as we can" intervention mobilized his reactions toward me, specifically subtle suspicions and sensitivities that had not previously emerged. Our subsequent exploration led to a resonance that was new in our interactions. In my treatment of Julie, my vituperative rage intervention could be classified as both a mobilization and a resonance. Whereas these terms describe broad therapeutic approaches, in a specific instance the tilts toward one or another become more subtle. From the standpoint of clinical psychoanalysis, in practice, both have a place. A question that emerges is, Wherein lies therapeutic action? Is it in the resonating aspects of mobilizing a patient's resources?

In discussing the role of motivations to assert and explore (Chapter 3), I discussed the therapeutic and developmental readiness for engaging in adversarial relationships. Mobilizing a patient's resources points in the direction of placing the analyst in a somewhat adversarial position vis-à-vis the patient, for better or worse. However, I believe it is for worse when the analyst is committed to this, and only this, stance.

There are two further issues relevant to a discussion of countertransference that are raised by the Ornstein-Mitchell exchange. First, Ornstein considered her subjective reaction to her patient to be her private affair. She recognized his impact on the treatment, but did not assume that her reaction was pulled forth by the patient, or that the patient would benefit from being informed of her reaction. The impact a patient makes on a particular analyst may be characteristic of the patient's relationships in the larger social context, or indicative of a specific treatment impasse, or may reflect a highly idiosyncratic response of an analyst to a particular patient. Differentiating among these possibilities is an important consideration for analysts. How useful is it for the patient to be involved in the process of teasing apart the analyst's reaction? The complexity and sensitivity of this discrimination process argues for a careful, cautious assessment, and weighs against any rash, even if tactful, confrontation of the patient.

Second are the issues of style and authenticity. Ornstein cannot treat patients in the manner proposed by Mitchell, nor is the reverse likely. Yet, both are being authentic.

The first issue raises legitimate theoretical and clinical problems that are worth debating. The second issue can quickly turn into ad hominem attacks. Too often these issues are conflated. I did attempt to maintain the distinction between these two issues in my discussion of Reed's case in Chapter 1. Attention to profound differences in theory and, more to the point, their effect on clinical practice are, I believe, a legitimate subject for analytic debate.

In Kohut's eyes, if the patient has already established a mirroring selfobject transference, then the analyst's intrusion of his or her subjectivity into the analysis, for example, through apprising a patient of his impact on the analyst, repeats the very experiences that solidified the patient's narcissistic withdrawal or antagonism. On the other hand, if a patient is repeating a problematic aspect of a past relationship with an unreliable parent, attempts to test out the reliability of the analyst as an idealizable figure may be most salient. In this instance the analyst's failure to recognize the patient's attempt to test the waters repeats the very experiences of past disappointments that left the patient in need of powerful people to whom to cling. These twin dangers, often papered over in discussion of countertransference, speak to the therapeutic value of viewing transference as comprising both a selfobject dimension and a representational dimension in a constant foreground–background relationship to each other. Reducing psychoanalytic discussion to the narrow level of countertransference and restricted to object-related transferences can only lead to a dead end, a no-win standoff.

ANOTHER REQUIEM: PROJECTIVE IDENTIFICATION

And now for another hobgoblin, projective identification. Analysts who place countertransference at the center of the therapeutic process often recruit projective identification for a similar purpose. In the words of Steiner (1994),

> We have come to use "countertransference" to refer to the totality of the analyst's reactions in the relationship with the patient. The recognition of the importance of projective identification in creating these reactions led naturally to the idea that countertransferece is an important source of information about the state of mind of the patient. The analyst can try to observe his own reactions to the patient and to the totality of the situation in the session and to use them to understand what the patient is projecting. [p. 16]

That is, the patient projects and the analyst reacts and observes these reactions as information about the patient.

Projective identification began life as Melanie Klein's description of a phantasy of infants and patients that Joseph (1987) subsequently considered to be interlocked with "omnipotence [and] the splitting and the resultant anxieties that go along with it" (p. 139). Over the years, various analysts have reshaped this mechanism by suggesting different paths that this phantasy can follow.

Projective identification always begins with the patient projecting some negatively colored or painful affect or content on the analyst. Then different clinicians take different routes. According to Klein (1975), the analyst transforms the projection and the patient then identifies with the transformed projection. According to Kernberg (1975), the patient, having projected aggression, tries to control the analyst through a dependent attachment on the analyst, who is now endowed with the patient's aggression. According to Ogden (1982), the patient rids himself of unwanted aspects of the self and deposits these unwanted parts of the self into another person. Then the projector exerts pressure on that person to experience him- or herself and behave in a way that conforms to the unconscious fantasy of the projector. Finally, the patient identifies with the projection.

In treatment, the analyst believes that a particular experienced affect or visceral state belongs to the patient. At that point in the analyst's experience of that state, an identification with it has already occurred. Thus, the analyst has identified with the patient's projection and interprets those feelings, the analyst's self-experience, to the patient as the patient's projections. In this version, projective identification and countertransference, or the analyst's experience of the patient and transference to the patient, become confounded. There is thus some confusion in the literature about whether projective identification refers to a fantasy of the patient that an empathic analyst can pick up, or to a process whereby unconscious mental contents are transported from one person to another. I have no problem understanding the former definition, but it is the latter definition of projective identification that seems to be winning out. It is this version of projective identification that is illustrated in clinical reports, for example, by Sands (1997). She described an analysis in which she experienced a physical sensation, a visceral "pull" that resembled a conflict, a "pull" from the patient's childhood. Sands explained this "mysterious" (p. 653) occurrence, "Together we unconsciously created a physical experience of 'pull' in me so that I could better grasp his lifelong experience of feeling 'pulled'" (pp. 653–654). In a discussion of this case, Stolorow and colleagues (1998) responded that projective identification "allows analysts to disown unwanted aspects of their own affectivity, attributing them to unconscious projective mechanisms originating in the mind of the patient, in effect, the theory of projective identification does to the patient exactly what the theory says the patient is doing to the clinician" (p. 724). I agree.

In projective identification the patient is held responsible for pulling the analyst into unanticipated and unplanned directions. Certainly any person, including an analyst, can be pulled, enticed, seduced, or otherwise drawn into various roles or enactments by a patient. But this may reflect either the analyst's flexibility to relate to the patient in various imaginative ways, or the analyst's lack of a backbone. The term *projective identification* buries both of these possibilities in a common grave, and explains therapeutic action (or inaction) through a mystical union between patient and analyst.

In my view, the final product, the analyst's experience as a participant in the treatment of a patient, is a relatively seamless amalgam. It is a co-construction of the patient's expectations, "pulls," wishes, fears, and several contributions of the analyst. These are an understanding of the patient, reactions to being with the patient, attempts by the analyst to observe and understand his or her self-experience, and the analyst's own "pulls," wishes, and fears. The analyst–patient interaction is multiply determined, organized, or co-constructed, as I have illustrated in the various case discussions. To assume that one's experience of being with a patient can be understood as having identified with a mental content, feelings, or disavowed states that the patient has projected may at times be perceptive. However, it may also prove to be an overly simplistic organization of the treatment situation.

Engaging in a variety of role enactments with a patient is an ever-present aspect of treatment. In fact, such enactments may or may not ever be interpreted. In case presentations, when a courageous analyst describes some unusual interaction, a parameter in Eissler's (1953) terms, or an enactment, invariably someone adds the comment, "Of course, later this will have to be analyzed." Truth be told, in real life analysis, later rarely comes. Too much occurs within any analysis for analyst and patient to revisit every enactment, or, for that matter, many enactments. The failure to do so at the moment of occurrence is often a source of embarrassment to the presenting analyst, who then covers the alleged countertransferential slip-up by clinging to the model that, of course, everything will be, and needs to be, subjected to analytic scrutiny and verbalization. The model is thereby left intact, but, I believe it too should be challenged.

In my discussion of the treatments of Nick, Julie, and Clara, I proposed that the spontaneity of an enactment can be lost when words are piled on top of a unique improvisational moment. The obsessional thinking that can masquerade for analytic diligence can deprive enactments of their unique transformative role in the psychoanalytic process. Treatment in which an analyst successfully avoids being pulled into any enactments with the patient can lack playfulness, passion, and poignancy. Worse still, these treatments may never get off the ground.

In the treatment of David, I felt his "pull" toward establishing a sadomasochistic engagement. In fact, I silently commented to this effect after our first session. To some extent he no doubt pulled for this and to some extent the pull I felt was co-constructed through my usual reserve and in response to his manner and style. A subtle pull no doubt infiltrated into the treatment. I believe that had I pointed this pull out to him, as he later told me he expected me to do, his more active defiance would have been alerted and we would indeed have co-constructed a sadomasochistic relationship. More to the point, in its expressed, verbalized form, the treatment would have become dry and distant. Similarly, in the analysis of Nick there were pulls on his part to cast me as the mother with the enema, and to "purge" him. In both instances, these pulls were co-constructed in our interactive context. They shaded the treatment without obscuring it. To view these circumstances as a product of the patient's projection and my identification with the patient's projection, I believe, fails to do justice to the complexity and ingenuity of the motivations involved by both participants.

I agree with Gill (1994) that in many of its current uses, projective identification has become an interactive rather than a one-way influence concept. However, even from this view, the interaction does not seem to begin until after the patient has projected. The patient's projection is not seen as having been co-constructed.

Implicit in projective identification is the belief that the analyst's experience vis-à-vis the patient constitutes an identification with the projection of what the patient is disavowing. I find it ironic that the very same analysts who are so persuasive about recognizing the analyst's subjectivity in the analytic dyad also depict the analyst as a tuning fork, resonating to the vibrations of the patient. And even when this analyst becomes aware of his or her subjectivity, the feelings brought into awareness are not owned by the analyst but attributed to the patient and the patient's influences. A sensitive analyst may certainly become aware of what a patient is disavowing, but the awareness of that experience is also co-constructed. It is influenced by the patient. The interaction between the patient's specific input and the patient's reaction to the analyst, on the one side, and the analyst's input and reaction to the patient, on the other side, are a more complex matter than is implied by the model of a tuning fork.

According to Gill (1994), in projective identification the patient may hope to find in the analyst a good example, someone who will be able to deal with the attributions of the patient in a mature way. For example, the analyst may be expected to provide a model that will help the patient deal with unjust accusations. In this instance, the motivation implied in projective identification is not to divest oneself of unpleasant affects but to master them. The attribution of varying states, affects, motives, desires, or intentions to another person is a common occurrence in analysis. It is really not so different from a patient's need to idealize, seduce, frighten, devalue, or anger the analyst. All of these transferences involve attempts to express, master, free oneself from, integrate, repeat, and transform experiences that have been stirred up both in the analysis as well as in the outside-of-analysis life of the patient. An attempt to test both the analyst (Weiss and Sampson 1986) and the safety of the analytic relationship may also be inherent in these transferences.

Why not topple projective identification from its perch and consider it just another fantasy of a patient? Then we can divest it of its theoretical baggage and assumptions. I am not proposing that we retain projective identification as a phantasy in the sense that Melanie Klein (1975) used it, as in "The 'vampire-like sucking' [and] the scooping out of the breast develop in the infant's phantasy into making his way into the breast and further into the mother's body" (p. 69). Rather, I am proposing that projective identification assumes a place in analysis alongside Schafer's (1972) proposal that various defenses are best viewed as fantasies of the patient. In Schafer's view, the defense of introjection becomes a fantasy of taking something into one's body, identification refers to changing how one conceives of oneself, and projection entails the fantasy of expelling a content of one's body and localizing it within the boundaries of someone else. In this usage, projective identification appears as a fantasy of being merged with, inside of, absorbed by, or implicitly validated by another person. It shares aspects of "oneness fantasies" (Lachmann and Beebe 1989, Silverman et al. 1982). These are fantasies of a wished-for state of bliss that adults may have, or may imagine others have, about their childhood. These are fantasies of being part of or encompassed, merged, enclosed, and protected by a nurturing powerful figure. When the analyst feels malevolent, confused, or depriving, and attributes the source of these feelings to the patient's projections, the patient can feel that analyst and patient are united, or "at one with" each other (Schafer, as cited in Ogden 1979, p. 357), irrespective of the projected content under consideration.

In assuming projective identification, the analyst's meta-communication to the patient can be stated as "You and I share the same affect state." As a plausible assumption, projective identification entails not just divesting oneself of an unpleasant affect, but a desire to share an affect state, and to communicate this to another person. Projective identification can plausibly be understood as a fantasy of a patient not to rid him- or herself of a painful state, but to find a "state sharer." This assumption can equally well account for the vignette described by Sands without invoking a transportation metaphor of mental contents from one partner finding its way into the mind and body of the other. Both Sands (1997) and her patient found a term, *pull*, that derived from vastly different experiences for each, but which could provide a bridge that gave them, after much struggle to connect in the treatment, an affective connection, a sense of working together. Analyst and patient then shared a similar state, feeling pulled. Such state sharing may indeed be enormously beneficial to a patient in the course of an analysis as strivings for shared affective states. The motivation then would be to dispel aloneness, abandonment, and isolation. Anger or other negative affects that are usually assumed to be projected would then be seen as reactive to these affect states.

My argument with countertransference has much in common with Schwaber's (1992) description of her retreat from a particular patient in the course of his analysis. Schwaber held that to attribute to countertransference her not hearing the patient would ascribe to the patient a need to replay an old scenario, but more important would get her off the hook. Without recourse to countertransference, recognition of the co-construction of the analytic process places an analyst under considerable psychological pressure. As Gill (1994) pointed out, "An analyst who is ever alert to his (or her) participation in the process may be under as much, if not more, stress than the patient" (p. 103).

Though I critiqued countertransference and projective identification and argued for their elimination from our arsenal, I have also argued for a place in analysis for humor, play, spontaneity, improvisations and, in sum, enactments. But most important, I have argued for a vision of clinical psychoanalysis in which analysts attempt not only to enter, empathically, the subjectivity of patients to grasp the leading edge of their strivings, but also to enter, empathically, the subjectivity of other psychoanalysts to grasp the leading edge of their theory. In outlining my analytic stance, I have spelled out the analyst's responsibilities, as well as provided some relief from these pressures by opening the windows of the consulting room to the balmy breezes of spontaneity and humor.

11

A Systems View

Four vignettes from the analysis of Clara provide entrée into the alternative I am proposing to countertransference and projective identification as defining dimensions of the analytic relationship. This alternative, as I will soon discuss, is a systems theory perspective.

Each of the following vignettes is characterized by a disruption in the analyst–patient interaction and its repair. In these discussions I continue to place the dynamic content and the relevance of Clara's developmental experiences in the background, as I did in the discussion of her analysis in previous chapters. I focus mainly on the process and our interactions.

1. Clara complains about my talking or my being silent, about my not recalling what she thought I ought to remember, or my referring to something that she is no longer interested in discussing. Her complaints mirror my concern that I am not treating her as well as I would like. When I fail to respond to her with the exact tone, affect, or content that she expects, she feels abandoned and enraged. When she complains that I appear too active, too concerned, too inter-

ested, or too enmeshed in trying to ameliorate the cause of her complaints, she feels that I cannot tolerate her anger. I sense the cycle of anger, my attempt to respond, and her increased anger that we are co-constructing. I try to cool it a bit. When I then appear less active, she complains that I am too passive and incapable of helping her. In this process, our already tentative connection has been disrupted. When I sense that we are out of touch, I describe these sequences of distress and attempts at repair by recognizing the context in which she felt distress. This context contains the extent to which she felt obliged to recognize her parents' attempts to have her see them as good parents and the extent to which she felt endangered by being pulled into another self-betrayal, for their benefit. In retrospect I became more aware of the danger to Clara in appearing cooperative or compliant. At the time, I was aware that my attempt to be a "good-enough" analyst contributed to the obstacles in our interactions. I did not disclose this in my comment to her. Rather, as she responds to my descriptions with increased distress, I acknowledge the pattern of engagement and disruption, and thereby maintain an unspoken engagement with her. Clara is then able to reengage more directly. As I will describe below, this new engagement, this reengagement, contained elements that had not been previously present. A process of transformation had occurred.

2. Clara feels despairing and experiences me as too hopeful. She becomes enraged and mistrustful. I acknowledge that my appearance of hopefulness has been too jarring for her. In my comment I implicitly acknowledge my hopefulness, do not challenge her hopelessness, and describe the affective mismatch that has occurred. She continues to feel hopeless and feels she has an analyst who may never understand the extent of her hopelessness. I understand, silently, that she cannot respond to my acknowledgment, and I describe our interaction to her. As in the previous vignette, I do not immediately link her distrust of my hopefulness to her fear of self-betrayal and anger at her family. That is, I do not yet connect her anger at my hopefulness as reminiscent of her experience in her family when they fostered a pretense about the fate of her horse. I

believe that my not making this connection explicit enabled her to make it subsequently on her own. Not verbalizing the link between her current experience with me and her dread of reexperiencing scenes from her childhood, for example, being confined to the chair from which she could only get up if she promised that she did not feel angry any longer, indicated to her that I could tolerate her despair. Specifically, I did not have to explain away her hopelessness, I did not require her to pretend, and I did not flee from her. I learned that by not verbalizing the historical basis for her transference reaction of despair at my perceived hopefulness, I enabled her to retain a connection with a hopeful analyst who could tolerate her despair.

3. Clara experiences states of rage or longing that she does not reveal. Intuitively I correctly recognize her state. A clue, to me, that she felt enraged was a particular calm and quiet expression in her face. As I thought about these interactions in retrospect, I believed Clara needed continual reassurance from me that I would not make assumptions about her, based on superficial appearances. She had to make sure that her ever-present rage and despair were not glossed over and forgotten by me. In the context of these interactions, Clara felt immensely gratified and more hopeful about our work. We both experienced a heightened positive moment. Her state changed from despair to mildly hopeful anticipation. She wonder whether she was *really* acceptable to me, or whether she had betrayed herself. I worried silently whether I could be so perceptive again. My silent worry dampened my heightened affect and our connection remained intact.

4. Clara feels hopeless about her life and suicidal, and she threatens to quit the treatment. I accept these feelings and do not flee or try to talk her out of them. She feels understood and cared for. A complex interactive system is organized. I am able to match her distress, but at a level of intensity just under hers. I am able to stay with her in her distress state. Privately, I am able to manage my distress state without drawing attention to it. I am moved by her despair, accept the discomfort that this produces in me, and maintain contact with her. Clara accepts the level and quality of my participation. She can

accept our connection, probably recognizes my difficulty in maintaining it with her in her depressed state, breathes a sigh of relief, and appears to become more alive. The emotional abandonment that she continually anticipates has not occurred. But, more important, the affective tone of our interactions has gradually shifted while our connection remained intact. Clara's fear of complying with my expectations and betraying her integrity has been placed into the context of the analysis. Gradually she felt safe enough to maintain her integrity without reverting to an angry, depressed, rigid withdrawal.

Clara's pessimism, and her determination to hold on to it, presented formidable obstacles to me and our therapeutic relationship. Her specific fears and her "hope phobia" dictated a narrow range of responsivity for both of us. My interventions, including leading-edge interpretations and empathic contextualizing comments, aroused her anger and reinforced her distrust of me. Whenever I accepted her rituals (for example, taking her shoes off) and tolerated "disgusting" aspects of her and her self-denigrating and sadistic fantasies, and made descriptive comments about our process (for example, her responses of increased distress and hopelessness), our contact remained intact or was restored.

Pursuing the ebb and flow of our interactions, our process, disconfirmed Clara's expectations that she would be abandoned unless she pretended she was not an angry person and simultaneously betrayed herself. Continued attention throughout her analysis to her rigid self-regulation, her propensity to withdraw angrily, increased the range and flexibility of her participation in the analysis. Her complaints, a reflection of her rigid, angry withdrawal, became less intense and somewhat less frequent. She became more adventuresome in her life, permitted herself an occasional extravagance, and in the analysis revealed her shame-ridden sexual and sadistic fantasies. To me, the most welcome change was that she was far better able to tolerate my lapses in understanding her.

The dynamic issues in Clara's treatment centered on the killing of her horse and the loss of the beloved housekeeper. Both incidents qualify as traumatic. They altered her self-state in that she became increasingly depressed and emotionally depleted, and ruptured her selfobject ties to her parents and the housekeeper. They also combined aspects of traumatic strains and shocks. However, I have not made these traumatic events central to this discussion. Although they were crucial in her treatment, I want to emphasize the extent to which attention to the process carried therapeutic leverage. Furthermore, I have described this process in terms of self- and interactive regulations, not in traditional dynamic formulations. The perspective of self- and interactive regulations facilitates the shift to a systems theory. I believe that this perspective better captures the co-construction of treatment relationships, their affective nuances, and the form in which relevant dynamic content emerges in sessions.

Clara and I formed a unique pair. Similarly Gail Reed, Anna Ornstein, and Stephen Mitchell and their patients formed unique pairs, unique analyst–patient systems. Another therapist with those patients would have formed a different system, right from the first meeting. However, the extent to which a therapist–patient pair is limited by the theory or model that guides the treatment is fair game for discussion. With this in mind, I addressed the dangers of therapeutic rigidity as well as the chaos introduced by the use of the concepts of countertransference and projective identification. I believe these concepts impose straitjackets on the spontaneity and improvisational quality of enactments that celebrate the uniqueness of analyst–patient interactions. I have attempted to carve a path between the therapist's flexibility and freedom to improvise, and the therapist's respect for constraints that preserve the integrity of the patient and the safety of the analytic relationship (see also Hoffman 1998).

The four vignettes from Clara's treatment capture the shift from a singular analytic focus on confrontation, clarification, interpretation, and working through (Greenson 1967) to co-constructing affectively rich ways of being with another person. As Lyons-Ruth (1999) proposed, "this collaboration can create unique and idiosyncratic contexts" (p. 604) in which the experience of the interaction of both participants, analyst and patient, is elaborated and transformed as each gets to know the mind of the other.

Having criticized some of the mainstays of the psychoanalytic process, what alternatives can I propose? My answer is systems theory. In the course of the case discussion I have already introduced terms intrinsic to systems theory: *self-* and *interactive regulation, co-construction, perturbations,* and the *dialectic between repetition and transformation.*

A word about systems theories. In the preceding chapters, the term *system* has appeared in two contexts. In referring to the five motivational systems, systems refers to the properties of "self-organizing and self-stabilizing, dialectic tension and hierarchical arrangement for the formation and function of each system" (Lichtenberg et al. 1992, p. 35). System is used here as in nervous system or circulatory system. The other usage of system, as in analyst and patient forming a system, is actually quite similar. In this usage, system refers to the way in which components or parts interact, and thus form a new entity, a system.

When Beatrice Beebe and I began our study of self- and mutual regulation we found that the empirical studies that were used to support self-regulation could just as easily be used to illustrate mutual or interactive regulation (Beebe and Lachmann 1988a,b, 1994). The reverse was true as well. We realized that self- and interactive regulation were two sides of the same coin. Together, they formed, and are embedded in, a system of ongoing regulations. Each regulation influences and shapes the other. For each partner self-regulation affects the quality of the interaction and vice versa. I described this process in adult treatment in detail for David and Clara.

Self- and interactive regulation constitute an indivisible system that is established in the early weeks of life and persists throughout development. Beebe and I (1994) have proposed that the organization of experience in development and in psychoanalytic treatment is the property of this interactive system, as well as the property of the individual (Sander 1977, 1985). That is, both infant and caregiver, and patient and analyst, co-construct characteristic and expectable patterns of self- and interactive regulation.

Once the analytic interaction is seen as comprising two partners, both of whom regulate themselves in the context of regulating each other, privileging countertransference and projective identification becomes redundant. We now have a far more powerful set of constructs to cover this terrain: a system composed of interactive regulations in which each partner simultaneously self-regulates. Transferences on the part of both analyst and patient clearly remain. They contribute to the quality, affective intensity, and content of the interaction. More important, the transference of each partner provides the context for the experiences of the other.

A systems approach has been suggested or stated by numerous analysts. It is found in Winnicott's (1950, 1960) observation that there is no such thing as a baby, but rather a mother–baby unit. As Kohut (1983) observed, "the analyst-observer must acknowledge that therapist and patient form of necessity an indissoluble unit" (p. 395).

Stolorow and colleagues' (1987) formulation of intersubjectivity constitutes an overarching systems perspective. They conceive of the interplay between the subjective worlds of child and caregiver, patient and analyst, and of the processes of development, psychopathology, and therapeutic action, as intersubjectively organized.

The view of the analytic dyad as a system supersedes the concrete influences of patient on analyst implied in countertransference and projective identification. From a systems perspective, analyst and patient are constantly both influencing each other and being influenced by each other. This influence includes the range from silence to words, as well as each participant's rhythms, intonations, and gestures. Furthermore, describing the analytic interaction as co-constructed does not ensure a good outcome to the treatment. But it does enable the analyst to evaluate his or her self-regulatory requirements for maintaining a tolerable affective state as well as to assess the patient's self-regulation in the context of the analytic interaction.

The three systems perspectives—self- and interactive regulation, which is a dyadic system; intersubjectivity; and the five motivational systems—vary in their level of abstraction, in their use of empathy and introspection to understand clinical phenomena, and in their relationship to empirical data. The approach based on self- and interactive regulation is derived from empirical research and is studied as to goodness of fit with adult psychoanalytic treatment. The five motivational systems were derived from both empirical infant research and clinical psychoanalysis. The theory of intersubjectivity was derived from a philosophical tradition as well as from clinical psychoanalytic phenomena. Together, all three systems theories contribute significantly to the treatment of the difficult-to-reach patient. In these analyses, as for example in my work with Clara, the interaction between analyst and patient, the process, requires continual close attention. These are also the treatments in which analysts frequently resort to explanations and interventions that invoke or use countertransference and projective identification. These are the treatments that would benefit from a shift by analysts to a systems perspective, which can increase the analyst's flexibility and range of responsivity. In adhering to the countertransference–projective identification model, the analyst is tied to the repetitive aspect of the transference. Since systems are constantly reorganizing and updating, analysts can become more attuned to the dialectic between repetition and transformation that is inherent in the analyst–patient interaction.

Systems theory, a theory of therapeutic process, seeks principles of organization for the system as a whole. Systems theory studies the individual in relation to the interaction and the context, with respect to the construction of patterns, perturbation of patterns, and transformation of patterns.

A most sophisticated discussion of systems theory has been proposed by Esther Thelen and Linda Smith (1994). Their conceptualization of development as a process that is context sensitive is specifically relevant for psychoanalysis. "Context sensitive" means that behavior emerges as though it was unfolding according to a predetermined timetable. However, when examined more closely it is organized or shaped by the immediate context in which it has been embedded. I have been using this definition of context throughout the case discussions. However, there is a wrinkle. Systems theory applies to any system—from the formation of clouds to the analyst–patient system. For clouds the immediate context covers the interactions of winds, temperature, moisture, and other contributing factors. However, people have memories, and, unlike clouds, their immediate context includes their history. Both analyst and patient bring their histories to their immediate context, and these histories become differentially activated in that context.

Development as understood by dynamic systems theory is nonlinear, discontinuous, and self-organizing. It is nonlinear and qualitative because of its complexity. New forms and qualities are constantly but tentatively organized, assembled, and reassembled. Nonlinear means that small events can cause big reactions.

Discontinuity refers to the continual transformations that produce new organizations. For example, in the history of transportation there is a discontinuity between the automobile and the airplane. At no point are there miniature automobile-airplanes. A whole new set of discoveries and inventions was utilized that made a decisive impact in developing a new organization, the airplane. Stern's (1985) narrative points of origin for psychopathology and the model scenes construct are similarly based on the concept of discontinuities in development. Utilizing aspects of earlier experiences, they bring together and shape, in a unique way, a new organization. Acknowledging the contributions of later events in a person's development in terms of their impact, rather than searching for ever earlier causes, is based on the principle of discontinuity.

The self-organizing propensity of systems relates directly to this question: How do systems change? Or, in terms of our discussion, How do transformations occur? To understand the process of change in a system, how a system self-organizes by forming temporary stable states, the role of perturbations of the system are important.

In self-organizing, the system moves toward one preferred configuration out of many. For example, self- and interactive regulation in a child–caregiver system may lead to heightened positive affect for both participants. The child may develop expectations of being responded to, but may simultaneously feel responsible for the emotional stability of its caregivers. In Clara's development, she increasingly felt resentful that she was required to show her parents that they were good parents.

When systems self-organize they settle into a few states or patterns that place some constraints on the system. In the dialectic between repetitions and transformations, repetitions are more likely to be favored.

Clara's participation in the treatment interactions tilted the system toward repetition of patterns that were familiar to her. However, my presence added a perturbation to the system. The therapeutic process tiptoed away from following her usual patterns, such as familiar interactions in which she would feel criticized and in danger of abandonment. For perturbations to perturb effectively, they must be powerful enough to move the system but not so violent that they send the system into a disorganized state.

Perturbations are disturbances that stimulate the system to organize new patterns. They are the way in which a system can change. In the course of normal development, perturbations include the maturation of capacities, the development of symbolic thought, or a change of context. In the course of normal development, an open or flexible system responds to perturbations by forming new stable patterns. To do so, the perturbations must fall within a comfortable range. When perturbations fall outside of this range, we approach conditions under which pathology is organized. For example, intense perturbations may be experienced as overstimulating and traumatic. A change in context, for example, when a person enters psychoanalytic treatment, may in and of itself perturb the system so that it becomes momentarily more flexible.

At one extreme, a pathological system may be in equilibrium. It then has all the novelty and passion of a swinging pendulum. It does not vary. It repeats itself, cannot get out of its rut, and may eventually run out of steam. At the other extreme, a pathological system may be chaotic and have no predictability.

Psychoanalytic treatment provides the perturbations that disturb the system. Perturbing the system should not be equated with introducing strong affect or suggestive pressures, or with provoking a patient to outbursts of anger, anxiety, or negative affect toward the analyst. In some instances this may be unsettling; in others, these very attempts at introducing perturbation may repeat the conditions that maintain the analyst–patient equilibrium. They follow the path of old patterns and do not change the context.

When, in what I felt to be a self-constraining manner, I described to Clara the various processes of our interactions, I perturbed the ongoing analyst–patient system. Clara's experiences in prior analysis reinforced patterns that had been familiar to her. For example, as she reported, in her previous analyses she was either perturbed excessively or insufficiently. She left those analyses with her patterns of organization unchanged, and with the feeling of being a resistive and treatment-obstructing patient. Although she felt recognized by those descriptions, they did not perturb the analyst–patient system and promote the organization of new patterns.

From a systems perspective, psychoanalysis provides an overarching perturbation of the system by providing a new context. According to this view, empathy, sensing oneself into the experience of the patient, affirmation, acceptance voiced or silent, and leading-edge interpretations make their therapeutic impact, *not* because they fulfill thwarted, long-neglected developmental needs. Rather, in fulfilling those needs, the currently organized system is perturbed, thrown into disequilibrium (cf. transference symptoms as discussed by A. Ornstein 1974). How, whether, or when the specific input from the analyst has this effect is determined by past experience and the current psychoanalytic relationship. The patient's past is contained in the self-regulation of the patient and in the context of the interactive regulation of the analysis. The patient's past and the analyst's past are thus an intimately connected aspect of the analyst–patient interaction, the system.

The very interventions that retain the system in equilibrium for some patients may prove to be the ones that succeed in perturbing the analyst–patient system in other treatments. A systems point of view prizes the unique interplay between analyst and patient in which every moment of their interaction is co-constructed. I have always kept in mind a patient of Ralph Greenson's (1970), who complained to him that he wanted tailor-made interpretations, but received interpretations from Greenson that sounded to him as though they were pulled off the ready-to-wear rack. The interventions I made to Clara's threat to remain on my couch and to throw all my books off the shelves, or to Nick's "twisted shit," or to Julie's plea—"I'm caught in the headlights of a car"—were tailor-made just for them. At those moments these patients signaled their readiness for something more by shifting to a directly challenging and, in some instances, metaphoric form of communication. I could then join their readiness for further transformative rather than repetitive experiences. An ability to join in and play was novel and remarkable for each. The perturbations along the way to the park (the snowball fight), the toilet, and the open road perturbed the system and impacted each of us. We were all transformed.

12

Self Psychology and the Varieties of Aggression

In the course of these chapters I set out to respond to some misperceptions and criticisms of self psychology and to describe its basic principles for psychoanalytic treatment. Using this synthesis as a springboard, my aim has been to contribute to the continuity, evolution, and expansion of self psychology as a theory of treatment and a vision of human nature. The clinical and theoretical modifications I described emerged from my therapeutic work as I learned from my patients how better to understand them.

AN EXPANSION OF SELF PSYCHOLOGY

Through the treatments I described, I illustrated the fundamental assumptions of self psychology: the primacy of self-experience and its clinical application in the analyst's focus on the patient's sense of self; the analyst's empathy and introspection as the tools of observation in understanding a patient's self-experience; the engagement and maintenance of selfobject ties, and the analysis of their disruption and repair; and the distinction between leading- and trailing-edge interpretations as a guide in assessing how best to frame interventions.

I expanded the basic concepts of the selfobject tie and selfobject transferences by proposing that transference consists of a selfobject *and* a representational dimension. The selfobject tie includes the functions that the analyst serves in the experience of the patient. Its establishment, and the tracking of its disruptions and their repair, is a vital aspect of all treatments, but in particular in working with the more difficult-to-treat patients. This dimension of the transference is more directly influential in addressing the vicissitudes of self-experience. The representational dimension includes the so-called object-related transferences that capture fantasies and experiences in some admixture as in model scenes. Both of these dimensions of the transference include the dialectic between the repetitive patterns in a person's ongoing interactions and experience and their transformations into new patterns and organizations of experience. This dialectic is an inherent aspect of the psychoanalytic process. I examined the variety of transformations of self-states encountered in life, through trauma and through a person's creativity, and in psychoanalytic treatment, through interpretations and through improvisations that are uniquely co-constructed in and by each analyst–patient pair. These therapeutic interactions, sometimes referred to as enactments, can capture the intimacy of the analytic encounter without opening the door to the kinds of disclosures that I believe carry the risk of the analyst's appearing intrusive or seductive.

In place of motivations based on sexual and aggressive drives, or only on strivings for selfobject experiences, I outlined a system of five motivations organized between caregiver and child throughout development. These are motivations that fulfill basic needs for attachment and affiliation, assertion and exploration, sensual pleasure and sexual excitement, regulation of physiological requirements, and the need to react aversively by antagonism and withdrawal. In an analysis, these motivations are interactively engaged by analyst and patient as they co-construct the transference and model scenes.

Countertransference and projective identification, I argued, should be retired, and their duties assigned to systems theory. In describing analyst and patient as a system, characterized by self- and interactive regulation, I have also linked the organization of experience in development with the process of psychoanalytic treatment.

A systems theory includes the continual transformations that balance the traditional psychoanalytic emphasis on the repetitiveness of psychopathology. Systems theory recognizes that development, as well as the patient–analyst interaction, is in a constant state of reorganization and updating. At each stage of development, experience is reorganized. Thus, later stages of development can be acknowledged for the crucial impact they exert in the shaping of a person's life. Psychoanalysts in general, including self psychologists, have tended to assume that earlier influences are more instrumental than later ones in shaping behavior and psychopathology. From a systems perspective, later events, for example, shock and strain trauma, not just the earliest versions of these experiences, can be decisive and exert an impact on the rest of the person's life.

The contributions of transformations in a dialectic with repetitions were illustrated in the model scenes concept. For example, David's discovery during puberty of the pornography in his uncle's room was decisive in braiding together earlier experiences with his later discoveries into an enduring pattern of expectations. The model scene, in his uncle's room, incorporated rigid, solitary self-regulation and expectations of the unreliability of interactive regulations—the repetitive pattern—with the hope of catching his father's attention—a new organization—that continued throughout life and organized the transference.

Self- and interactive regulation cut across the selfobject and representational dimensions of the transference. Both of these dimensions are co-constructed through each partner's self-regulation as well as their interactive regulations. Thus, in the patient's transference expectations of the analyst, and the analyst's transference expectations of the patient, each partner is affected by his or her own behavior (self-regulation) as well as that of the partner (interactive regulation). The nature of each partner's self-regulation affects the interactive regulation and vice versa.

The four vignettes from the treatment of Clara, described in Chapter 10, illustrated these interactive influences, as well as Clara's and my requirements for self-regulation.

My aim in expanding the clinical theory of self psychology has been to offer a more comprehensive approach to the treatment problems raised by the varieties of aggression. The clinical material I presented covers aggressive reactions, from mild but chronic hostility and irritability, to eruptions of rage and murderousness. We are able to empathize with experiences of rage outbursts motivated by searing shame or feelings of vulnerability. I introduced the term *eruptive aggression* to describe those instances in which hostility, contempt, anger, rage, and murder burst forth like an erupting volcano, without warning, or circumstances that provide a basis for the eruption. When the outer limits of eruptive aggression are reached, the quality of our empathy is strained. That is, to enter the subjective state of murderers and serial killers, and understand their experience from within their perspective, tests our capacity for empathy to the limit.

Our empathy is engaged when we grasp the personal context to which, and in which, a person is reacting. For example, the self-betrayal described by Clara when she abandoned her horse when it was to be killed offered me entrée into her subjective experience. It depicted the context for further explorations of her motivations, life experiences, and the transference. However, from her point of view, in the course of her life, the connection to that context became increasingly attenuated. This occurred through the strain of repeated experiences in which she succumbed to parental pressures and pretended that she was not angry, while she felt enraged. Subsequently, she built her self-respect on her self-definition as bad, angry, and a murderer. Taken out of its organizing context, she was left with the sense that she had both killed her horse and betrayed herself. Her angry demands, rageful outbursts, pessimism, criticality, sadistic fantasies, and the "murder" of her horse had all acquired a life of their own. These behaviors and affect states had become familiar to her. They had become a relatively unquestioned part of her, the way in which she knew herself. Although she did not like that side of her, she felt convinced that it was an essential and undeniable aspect of herself. When I attempted to place these reactions into a context in which their meaning and implications would shift, she felt threatened and reacted with increased rage.

The clinical implication illustrated in this aspect of Clara's treatment is that aggression can both come to assume an energizing or vitalizing role and sustain the sense of self. That aggression can vitalize the sense of self follows Kohut's (1972) theory, but the role of aggression in sustaining the sense of self challenges Kohut's proposition that narcissistic rage is a breakdown product of the self. That is, from Kohut's perspective, by addressing the underlying self-vulnerability, the self is strengthened and the destructive quality of the rage will diminish. Instead, addressing the underlying self-vulnerability can threaten the sense of self, and rage will be expressed.

As I illustrated in case examples, feeling angry or being enraged can energize a person and be a crucial constituent of the sense of self. The analyst is then faced with these questions: Does this patient's aggression retain its elastic reactivity? Or has this patient's aggression become a rigid eruptive potential and an inextricable aspect of the sense of self? Through empathy and introspection a patient's rageful outbursts, sadistic provocations, and contempt can be understood, and made understandable, within the treatment and the context of the patient's life. However, placing murderousness into a context that includes feelings of vulnerability can elicit a patient's enraged self-protection against this threat. The analyst's flexibility in entertaining these possibilities through close attention to the process of treatment can guard against under- or overestimating the place of aggression in the life of a person.

Two further issues are closely connected with the requisite flexibility of the analyst: the relationship between shame and aggression, and the question of "owning" one's aggression. As illustrated in the Ornstein-Mitchell debate, aggression can be viewed as covering an underlying sense of inadequacy and shame or the reverse—shame can cover underlying aggression. Viewing this difference from the standpoint of treatment, I have argued that even when aggression is viewed as reactive to shame, its place in the organization of the self can still require direct or indirect acknowledgment by the analyst. Dealing only with the underlying shame experience may or may not be borne out clinically, depending on the extent to which the person has woven aggression into the fabric of his or her sense of self.

The central place of feeling oneself to be murderous, destructive, or sadistic was illustrated in the treatments of Julie and Clara as well as the patients described by Ornstein (1998a,b) and Gruenthal (1993). In each of these instances the treating analyst had to shift perspectives to grasp empathically the importance to the patient of being recognized as the proud owner of the aggression. In all of these cases, the patients had no difficulty owning the aggression; rather, they felt they could not and did not wish to let go of it. It had become an intrinsic aspect of them.

For murderers in prison, and for some of the serial killers I described, eruptions of violence restored self-esteem after the person had been shamed, disrespected, or otherwise subjected to narcissistic injuries. This group of men resorted to violence in the absence of any other face-saving, self-esteem–restorative resources. They certainly lacked Henrik Ibsen's creative capacity to transform a humiliating defeat into a triumph over the humiliators.

In the course of these chapters, I formulated numerous choices with respect to understanding and treating clinical issues. Anticipating the treatment stalemates that can arise, these choices can help avert standoffs, that is, impasses co-constructed by analyst and patient. The role occupied by an emphasis on co-construction of the analytic experience has been increasing in analytic discourse. This broadening of the procedures of treatment has been a mixed blessing for me. My burden as an analyst has increased, but at the same time dealing with these new perspectives has lightened the work. The increase in burden is directly related to my view that analyst and patient form an interacting system. This implicates the analyst in every aspect of the analysis. No moment during an analysis can be written off as only the patient's transferences or the patient's projections (or as the analyst's countertransferences or projective identifications). From a systems perspective, in each instance during treatment, transferences and projections are embedded in a context that, at the very least, contributes the crucial background to the analytic transactions. In many instances, however, the analyst–patient interaction reveals the context out of which the patient's reactions can be understood.

The pressures on the analyst are reduced by the increased analytic flexibility and spontaneity that I have also advocated. Such flexibility is found when the phenomena of the analytic interaction are looked upon from the vantage point of the selfobject and the representational dimensions of the transference. In addition, when interpretations are made with cognizance of leading- and trailing-edge perspectives, the analyst's attention can hover freely without lunging toward one extreme—a belligerent standoff—or the other extreme—sailing on a sea so calm that it is dead. The first extreme is occupied by those who recognize only object-related transferences. The other extreme is occupied by those who erroneously believe that selfobject transferences mean that the analyst provides the patient with the experience of living in a kinder, gentler world. A two-dimensional perspective guards against the treatment ambience becoming rigidly authoritarian in the first extreme, and hopelessly Pollyannaish in the second. This dual perspective can steer treatment away from the kind of dead end in which it can get stuck, even in the best of hands.

But wait, it's not quite that simple. Lest I give the impression that analysis is a breeze, think back on the treatments of Julie and Clara. They were by no means easy, simple, or straightforward. Although I would call the analysis of Clara relatively successful, I am much more guarded about my work with Julie.

There is a particular vexing problem that arises in the course of analysis to which I have only alluded so far. I am referring to those times in treatment when patients challenge the analyst to do something to change a persisting problem in their lives, or to disclose something about themselves.

Frequently such requests/demands/challenges/threats center on patients' imperative need to know whether the analyst did or did not have a particular feeling about them. Questions such as "Were you angry?" "Were you irritated?" are asked with the impression that unless the analyst answers, treatment may be over. Turning the question back to the patient ("What do you think?") or another delaying tactic ("How come you are raising this question at this time?" "How would you feel about having an angry or irritated analyst?") may be effective, but too often they take their toll. In these circumstances, the patient may escalate to make greater demands, or worse, capitulate and analyze his or her need to know and refrain from ever asking direct questions again. All of the above circumstances can be silent and jeopardize the outcome of the treatment. These ruptures may or may not be repaired by further investigation of the interactions in question. In the worst case scenario, they are swept under the couch.

Of course, we are familiar with reports in which investigating the meaning of patients' demands for disclosures led to valuable analytic insights. Yes, there is a best-case scenario. After informing the patient that before answering the question, it would be valuable to explore its meaning, there are patients who will take up the task of self-exploration at those crucial moments.

By the time Clara threatened to throw my books off the shelf, I knew that my offering her a verbal interpretation ("I would interpret this as your wanting me to hold you") required my simultaneous readiness to be able to back up my interpretation by literally restraining her. Similarly, offering to go to the park with her, as she lay on the couch, without my being ready literally to go with her, would have led to a futile session. I believed it would have led to another instance in which repetition in the representational dimension transference would have reigned supreme over possibilities for transformations. In addition, there was the danger that she would feel I did not take her threats seriously enough. Feeling that I treated her threat too cavalierly would have obliged her to turn up the heat of her demands. In effect, she would have felt challenged and would have escalated her threats. I learned from these incidents that unless I entertained the possibility of actively following through, I had no chance of maintaining communication with her.

In the closing days of her analysis, we revisited her threats. She told me that she always felt I took her seriously, no matter how far off the mark I was in my understanding of her. I told her of my concern if I had not taken her at her word. Had I not been ready to take her up on her threats, she told me, she would have continued to feel unsafe and would have quickly and directly translated her discomfort into the critical, dis-tancing, contemptuous, despairing stance that we knew so well from much of her treatment and that she knew so well.

A patient's questions about the analyst's feelings touch directly on the analyst's subjectivity and require the analyst's readiness to respond. Of course, the analyst's self-examination and self-reflections about the meaning of his or her response to the patient are essential. I am speaking here to analysts who view analytic self-revelation with considerable cau-tion, and who tend to err on the side of overrestraint and analytic ano-nymity. Of course there is a whole other group of analysts who do not wait to be asked how they are feeling, but will unzip their subjectivity in front of their patients.

In addition to the analyst's readiness to respond to personal ques-tions, and not use the analytic setup to parry, delay, or manipulate so as to avoid the question, of equal importance is the presence of mind of the analyst. The analyst's spontaneity and improvisational ability are crucial at these moments, a resource also endorsed by Bacal (1998) in his dis-cussion of the analyst's optimal responsiveness.

All this is easier said than done. At best, such spontaneity requires a relaxed dialogue rather than the tense, anxious confrontations that are, more likely than not, brewing just at those moments in treatment when some presence of mind is called for.

Prescriptive comments are useless in these situations. The specifics of the circumstances that challenge the subjectivity of the analyst are unique. Biding time and seizing a moment to reflect may help. I gener-ally reach for some humor, sometimes mildly directed at my predica-ment at that moment. For example, in several of the cases, I described interventions that would be difficult to classify. These include the "that's the worst kind" to Nick's twisted shit; the "I'm dancing as fast as I can" story for David; the parting comment, "If you think of yourself as a deer caught in the headlights of a car, think of him as a car without a driver" to Julie; and the snowball fight with Clara. I consider these to be my personal reactions. For me, they captured a moment with just this, and only this, patient. These comments could not be repeated in any other circumstance and carry the same affective charge. As I learned later, they

were memorable to the patients as well. These moments make a significant contribution to the transformation of rigid, repetitive patterns and
organize new expectations for both analyst and patient. For the patients
involved they provided perturbations of the expected pattern of threat
leading to retaliation, rejection, shaming, or abandonment. For me, they
organized expectations that I could regulate my own affective comfort
and simultaneously maintain my contact with patients in states of despair, shame, or anger. My interventions may indirectly disclose how I
try to get myself out of a sticky situation, but they are not explicit disclosures of how I feel about the patient. However, implicit in each of these
comments is, I believe, my affection for the patient.

The spontaneous comments I discussed in the treatments of Nick,
Julie, and Clara can be considered enactments, as they are in the terminology developed by the members of the Process of Change Study Group
of Boston (Lyons-Ruth 1998, Stern 1998). According to them, in the
course of therapy, analyst and patient gain implicit knowledge of their
relationship, of being with each other. In their ongoing interactions, as
the treatment moves along, there are opportunities for special moments—
"now moments." These tend to be remembered by patients as special
moments. I have already alluded to these in my discussion of Nick's
treatment as "turning points" (Wallerstein 1986), heightened affective
moments (Beebe and Lachmann 1994), surprise (Reik 1935), and humor (Kohut 1966). These "now moments" lead to a "moment of meeting" and constitute unique experiences for both analyst and patient. They
become part of a person's representation of procedures, and may or may
not be symbolized.

My patients and I got to know each other in a new way. Each of my
comments was ushered in by a momentary novel and spontaneous image or metaphor offered by the patient. My comments were surprising to
me and evoked heightened positive affect for both of us in our improvisational interaction. These were memorable moments for both participants in the analytic interaction as we came together, neither by the
book nor did we throw away the book (Hoffman 1998). Rather a new
book has been coauthored, or better still, an old narrative has been transformed into a new adventure.

Each of these improvisational comments occurred at moments when the treatments could have deteriorated into angry or stilted, dry, affectless standoffs, such as a repetitive series of complaints. But a bigger danger was averted. Without the improvisational moment, an opportunity for a special meeting would have been lost. In these potentially tense situations, the analyst's readiness to describe his or her feelings toward the patient and awareness of his or her affective participation in the analysis, whether with love, flirtatiousness, challenge, or restraint, help transform a potential stalemate into an opportunity.

These heightened affective moments, like all the patterns of our interactions that I described, occurred between these patients and me on the level of our procedural knowledge (see Clyman 1991, Grigsby and Hartlaub 1991, Sorter 1995). In contrast to declarative memory, which refers to symbolically organized recall for information and events, procedural memory refers to skills or action sequences that are encoded nonsymbolically and usually out of awareness. Over time, these procedures become automatic and influence processes that guide behavior. In adults, procedural memories are content-free, in the sense that they entail the learning of processes rather than information. Procedural memories guide the way in which we ride a bicycle and engage in a dialogue. But procedural knowledge also has come to include the way we joke around, express affection, and get attention (Lyons-Ruth 1998).

To back up a bit, in the course of this book I have frequently reversed figure and background in the description of psychoanalytic treatment by placing the dynamic content (declarative memory) that was explored and interpreted into the background and the unverbalized procedures of our interactions into the foreground. For example, how David and I addressed his self-regulation difficulties, how Nick and I addressed the effects of his toilet trauma, or how Clara and I engaged her propensity to erupt with rage constituted interactions on the level of procedural knowledge. Not until near the end of the treatments did we revisit these processes and reminisce about them. Putting them into words was not a crucial element in making them part of the ordinary, available repertoire of engaging with another person. The benefit that these patients derived from these heightened affective moments as they became part of their analytic experience was noted subsequently in their lives. Dynamic issues were of course also addressed throughout these analyses, for example, David's sexual identification with his father's women, or Nick's disappointment in the father who left him at the mercy of his mother, or Clara's competitiveness with her sisters and her desire to become her father's son. In the treatments in particular, these dynamic issues were necessary but not sufficient to bring about therapeutic change. The unverbalized transactions around these dynamics, our negotiations on a procedural level, clinched the deal.

REACTIVE AND ERUPTIVE AGGRESSION

In addition to outlining an analytic approach that can increase analytic flexibility in general, I specifically addressed the treatment of patients whose psychopathology was marked by a variety of expressions of aggression. I examined the concept of reactive aggression, the target of much criticism of self psychology from practitioners of other psychoanalytic approaches. I reassessed the way in which the phenomena of aggression are described from perspectives other than self psychology. There are instances where aggression appears, in Anna Freud's terms, for no apparent reason at all. These require a perspective that can account for the transformation of reactive aggression into aggression that appears to erupt from the person like a volcano.

A central treatment obstacle in the analysis of Clara was her distrust of verbal communication, in particular what was said to her. Her experience in her family of having to pretend that she had no angry thought in her head in order to be released from the chair and rejoin the family left her distrustful of words. In her distrust, there is a strange parallel to the violent men and serial killers. Their backgrounds also led them to be distrustful of, and uncommitted to, verbal communication. Although on vastly different scales, in these circumstances, expression of anger and violence erupt without a motivating and symbolized context. Clara's treatment was dominated by her repeatedly testing my reliability through enactments. For example, will I insist on following my agenda in contrast to attention to hers? Clara had to make sure that she had not once again lent herself to another self-betrayal. Among the few feelings of her own that she could trust were her rage, despair, and hopelessness. In the sequence leading up to and including the imagined snowball fight, her capacity for symbolic elaborations included experiences that previously had remained automatic procedures. Her ability to play with words had been enlarged or restored.

In the patients we treat, manifestations of eruptive aggression are still contained within limits that make them accessible to empathy and introspection. However, what appeared in limited form in the psychology of Clara, is, I believe, massively present as the basis for eruptive aggression in some murderers and in some serial killers. In these men, their histories and development as killers can be told from the point of view of a limited ability to communicate verbally and affectively, or, put differently, in their tendency toward rigidity and concreteness in their communications. Trauma dominated their backgrounds from their early years onward. Possibilities for sustained selfobject ties were quickly shattered, coupled with self-states of terror, rage, and hopelessness becoming rigidly established. But most important, the available histories are replete with depictions of their environments that failed to respond to their signals that something was dreadfully wrong. These signals ranged from feeble and disguised to blatant, but they were ignored by family and friends as well as by law enforcement officals.

In these circumstances, aggression becomes and appears eruptive. The context in which it had evolved and had failed to respond had thereby invalidated itself. The serial killings were then without a context, and the killings themselves appear disembodied, detached, and dissociated acts. The killings appear to come from nowhere. They seem cold-blooded, as compared to the murderers described by Gilligan, who were certainly violent but in a hot-blooded way. Their rage erupted.

In psychoanalytic treatment, when eruptive aggression is a prominent variety in a patient's repertoire, even for many years in the treatment of Clara, placing it into a context may have no meaning to the patient. However, in psychoanalytic treatment, a context that has meaning can be co-constructed through the analyst–patient interactions.

Perspectives on human nature as contained in Freudian, Kleinian, relational, or self psychological approaches can provide visions of human nature that can broaden analytic opportunities for empathic entry into a patient's subjective experience. Assuming that patients who are treated by good analysts from various theoretical approaches also improve, and that for a patient to feel understood is a sine qua non of treatment, we can learn from each other.

In investigating the subjective experience of aggression, one's theory as to the origin of aggression in development must be placed into a "blind trust." The analyst's approach to the experience of the patient can convey a tilt toward the favored theory of the origin of aggression. In my discussion of eruptive aggression in murderers and serial killers, I reported evidence that the question of the origin of aggression is far more complex than either/or formulations can capture. That is, either an abusive, depriving environment or a neurological predisposition can eventuate in the person's becoming a murderer.

When the role of eruptive aggression dominates a patient's life and treatment, analysts encounter a special challenge. Even though in different ways, different theories—Freudian, Kleinian, relational, self psychological—attempt to grasp such psychopathology, the challenges are to the person of the analyst. For these patients, the distance between their aggressive eruptions and the conditions, past and present, from which rage erupts challenges the analyst's capabilities, integrity, sensitivity, commitment, intelligence, stability, affective attunement, capacity for empathy, and capacity to relate. Should this challenge be experienced as a disconfirmation of a preferred theory, no matter what it is, in reaction the analyst can cling ever more tenaciously to it. The ensuing stalemate is then co-constructed.

When the role of eruptive aggression dominates a patient's life and treatment, another question is raised for me: How does this view of eruptive aggression affect the self psychological vision of human nature?

Kohut (1984) described the vision of human nature that is implicit in Freud's theory as "guilty man" and in his own theory as "tragic man."

He thereby placed the two visions of human nature, and thus their two theories of aggression, into vastly different perspectives. Kohut depicted Freud's man as having to deal with a propensity for aggression, and hence guilt over murderous (oedipal) desires. Kohut depicted his man as reacting to experiences of failing to have vital needs, selfobject needs, met phase appropriately.

Tragic man is essentially a narcissistic person who has been understood from an empathic vantage point. To understand the narcissism of tragic man, we can extend our empathy to encompass the slights, hurt, failures in acknowledgment, experiences of dashed hopes, and disappointment that are their daily bread. More or less we can access those feelings in ourselves.

In my clinical illustrations I have taken Kohut's man as far as I could, to the outer limits of my capacity to understand the experiences of another person through empathy and introspection. I can understand the variations of rage, contempt, or hostility that my patients expressed toward me, toward others, and toward themselves. I can even stretch my empathy to grasp murderousness and even the Vietnam veteran having an orgasm when killing Vietcong. To do that I imagine the context of his army experience, peer pressure, sanctioning of killing, terror, and whatever personal past experiences were activated in that moment. Can we empathize with the murderers whom James Gilligan interviewed? Perhaps. How about the serial killers stalking and mutilating anonymous victims? The horrendous childhoods that characterize some, but by no means all, of the serial killers I described evoke horror and, simultaneously, compassion for the victims. But these histories do not explain or place the killings that were committed into a context that we can enter and thereby sense the quality of their experience. Their history and the immediate context of the crimes do not bring us closer to understanding their experience from within the context of their lives. Beyond serial killing, can we grasp, empathically, the Nazis who ran the concentration camps, who watched the gassing of millions of Jews, and then went home and played with their children? Here is a domain that extends beyond my empathic reach. From my perspective, its inhabitants qualify neither as guilty nor as tragic men. In these instances we tend to remain outside the subjective frame of reference. We describe them as evil, a literary term, not a psychoanalytic one.

Think, again, of Shakespeare's *Othello*. Othello is a tragic character. His decline, his flawed humanity, evokes our compassion and sympathy. We can empathize with his experience of becoming Iago's victim as we recall milder versions of victimization in our own lives. But what about Iago? What is he? Not a tragic figure, by no means a guilty man. If we characterize him as, for example, an evil man, we have left the perspective of viewing human nature from within the subjectivity of the person, and have resorted to a moral judgment about the behavior of a person. We are on a different level of discourse where empathy fails, and at best we can only describe.

Serial killers try desperately to retain some hold on the world around them. Some live an overtly conventional life in which they seem to function in an unremarkable way. Typical, as well, is the rigid pattern of their killings. For example, Arthur Shawcross always placed the bodies of his victims in a particular position, as though to leave his signature on the body, like an artist who signs his work. Pride in exhibiting their productions may be part of serial killers' motivations, but their rigid, concretely expressed need for order can provide them with continuity and stability through their murders in their lives. Repetitively, they try to approximate a context to contain their experiences, and contain the deadness and chaos that characterize their subjective world. Beyond tragic man, there is life without a context. It is in this variant that aggression becomes eruptive, and our ability to empathize gradually evaporates.

From these studies I emerged with two convictions: (1) the primacy of self-experience, when threatened, evokes aggression (and/or withdrawal) as a response; and (2) the reactive nature of aggression does not define its place in a person's life. Reactive aggression can be transformed into eruption of aggression, a phenomenon that was noted in several of the patients I described but is most dramatically found in those people whose early life was suffused with physical and emotional trauma, abuse, neglect, and a nonresponse to signals that something was felt by them to be dreadfully wrong.

Having established a place for aggression as a reaction to various noxious experiences, and having outlined varieties of aggression, linked to, embedded in, or detached from contexts, and accessible to empathy and introspection to varying degrees, I have opted to remain in the arena of clinical psychoanalysis. Rather than trying to settle questions about the nature of aggression, I have tried to capture the unsettling place of aggression in psychoanalytic treatment.

References

Adler, E., and Bachant, J. L. (1998). *Working in Depth*. Northvale, NJ: Jason Aronson.

Ainsworth, M., Blehar, M., Waters, E., and Wall, S. (1978). *Patterns of Attachment*. Hillsdale, NJ: Lawrence Erlbaum.

Atwood, G., and Stolorow, R. D. (1984). *Structures of Subjectivity*. Hillsdale, NJ: Analytic Press.

Bacal, H. (1998). Is empathic attunement the only optimal response? In *Optimal Responsiveness: How Therapists Heal Their Patients,* ed. H. Bacal, pp. 289–302. Northvale, NJ: Jason Aronson.

Bacal, H., and Newman, K. (1990). *Theories of Object Relations: Bridges to Self Psychology*. New York: Columbia University Press.

Balint, M. (1969). Trauma and object relations. *International Journal of Psycho-Analysis* 50:429–435.

Beebe B., and Lachmann, F. M. (1988a). Mother–infant mutual influence and precursors of psychic structure. In *Frontiers of Self Psychology: Progress in Self Psychology*, vol. 3, ed. A. Goldberg, pp. 3–26. Hillsdale, NJ: Analytic Press.

———— (1988b). The contributions of mother–infant mutual influence to the origins of self and object representations. *Psychoanalytic Psychology* 5:305–337.

———— (1994). Representation and internalization in infancy: three principles of salience. *Psychoanalytic Psychology* 11:127–165.

Beebe, B., and McCrorie, E. (in press). A model of love for the 21st century: literature, infant research, romantic attachment, and psychoanalysis. *Psychoanalytic Inquiry*.

Beebe, B., and Stern, D. (1977). Engagement-disengagement and early object experiences. In *Communicative Structures and Psychic Structures*, ed N. Freedman and S. Grand, pp. 35–55. New York: Plenum.

Bollas, C. (1995). *Cracking Up*. New York: Hill and Wang.

Bowlby, J. (1969). *Attachment and Loss, Vol. I. Attachment*. New York: Basic Books.

Brazelton, T. B. (1992). *Touch and the fetus*. Paper presented at the Touch Research Institute, Miami, FL, May.

Bromberg, P. (1998). Interpersonal psychoanalysis and self psychology: a clinical comparison. In *Standing in the Spaces: Essays on Clinical Process, Trauma, and Dissociation*, pp. 147–162. Hillsdale, NJ: Analytic Press.

Clyman, R. (1991). The procedural organization of emotions: a contribution from cognitive science to the psychoanalytic theory of therapeutic action. *Journal of the American Psychoanalytic Association* (Supplement) 39:349–383.

Curtis, H. (1983). Review of *The Search for the Self: Selected Writings of Heinz Kohut, 1950–1978. Journal of the American Psychoanalytic Association* 31:272–285.

———— (1985). Clinical perspectives on self psychology. *Psychoanalytic Quarterly* 54:339–378.

Dowling, S. (1990). Fantasy formation: a child analyst's perspective. *Journal of the American Psychoanalytic Association* 38:93–112.

Eissler, K. R. (1953). The effect of the structure of the ego on psychoanalytic technique. *Journal of the American Psychoanalytic Association* 1:104–143.

Erikson, E. (1959). Identity and the life cycle. *Psychological Issues*, Monograph 1. New York: International Universities Press.

Fairbairn, W. R. D. (1952). *An Object Relations Theory of Personality*. New York: Basic Books.

Fenichel, O. (1925). The clinical aspect of the need for punishment. In *The Collected Papers of Otto Fenichel*, Vol. 1, ed. H. Fenichel and D. Rapaport, 2nd ed., pp. 71–92. New York: Norton.

Ferenczi, S. (1919). Technical difficulties in the analysis of a case of hysteria. In *Further Contributions to the Theory and Technique of Psychoanalysis*, ed. S. Ferenczi, pp. 189–197. London: Hogarth.

———— (1933). Confusion of tongues between adults and the child. In *Final Contributions to the Theory and Technique of Psychoanalysis*, ed. S. Ferenczi, pp. 156–167. London: Hogarth.

Field, T. (1981). Infant gaze aversion and heart rate during face-to-face interactions. *Infant Behavior and Development* 4:307–315.

Fonagy, P. (1991). 'Thinking about thinking': some clinical and theoretical considerations in the treatment of a borderline patient. *International Journal of Psycho-Analysis* 72:639–654.

———— (1999). *The process of change and the change of processes: What can change in a "good" analysis?* Paper presented at the Spring Meeting, Division 39 of the American Psychological Association, New York, April.

Freud, A. (1936). *The Ego and the Mechanisms of Defence. Writings 2.* Madison, CT: International Universities Press.

———— (1972). Comments on aggression. *International Journal of Psycho-Analysis* 53:163–171.

Freud, S. (1893). On the psychical mechanisms of hysterical phenomena. *Standard Edition* 3:25–42.

———— (1905). Jokes and their relation to the unconscious. *Standard Edition* 8:59–137.

———— (1910). Leonardo da Vinci and a memory of his childhood. *Standard Edition* 11:59–138.

———— (1914a). Remembering, repeating, and working through. *Standard Edition* 13:145–155.

—————— (1914b). On narcissism. *Standard Edition* 14:67–104.

—————— (1916–1917). Fixation to trauma: the unconscious. *Standard Edition* 18:273–285.

—————— (1920). Beyond the pleasure principle. *Standard Edition* 18:7–66.

—————— (1924). The economic problem of masochism. *Standard Edition* 19:157–172.

—————— (1930). Civilization and its discontents. *Standard Edition* 21:59–145.

Gill, M. (1982). Analysis of the transference, Vol. 1, *Psychological Issues*, Monograph 53. Madison, CT: International Universities Press.

—————— (1994). *Psychoanalysis in Transition*. Hillsdale, NJ: Analytic Press.

Gilligan, J. (1996). *Violence*. New York: Putnam.

Gladwell, M. (1997). Damaged. *The New Yorker*, February 24, March 3, pp. 132–147.

Goldberg, A. (1995). *The Problem of Perversion*. New Haven: Yale University Press.

Greenacre, P. (1957). The childhood of the artist: libidinal phase development and giftedness. *Psychoanalytic Study of the Child* 12:47–72. New York: International Universities Press.

Greenson, R. R. (1965). The working alliance and the transference neurosis. *Psychoanalytic Quarterly* 34:155–181.

—————— (1967). *The Technique and Practice of Psychoanalysis*. Madison, CT: International Universities Press.

—————— (1970). The exceptional position of the dream in psychoanalytic practice. *Psychoanalytic Quarterly* 39:519–549.

Grigsby, J., and Hartlaub, G. (1991). *Procedural learning and the development and maintenance of character*. Paper presented at the Sixth International Conference on Psychological Development, Prague, August.

Gruenthal, R. (1993). The patient's experience of the analyst's gender: projection, factuality, interpretation, or construction. *Psychoanalytic Dialogues* 3:323–342.

Harris, A. (1998). Aggression: pleasures and dangers. *Psychoanalytic Inquiry* 18:31–44.

Hartmann, H., Kris, E., and Loewenstein, R. (1949). Notes on the theory of aggression. *Psychoanalytic Study of the Child* 3/4:9–36. New York: International Universities Press.

Hofer, M. (1990). Early symbiotic processes: hard evidence from a soft place. In *Pleasure Beyond the Pleasure Principle*, ed. R. A. Glick and S. Bone, 2nd ed., pp. 55–80. New Haven: Yale University Press.

Hoffman, I. (1998). *Ritual and Spontaneity in the Psychoanalytic Process: A Dialectical Construction*. Hillsdale, NJ: Analytic Press.

Ibsen, H. (1881). *Ghosts*. In *The Plays of Ibsen, Vol. 3*, ed. M. Meyer, pp. 3–101. New York: Washington Square Press, 1986.

——— (1882). *An Enemy of the People*. In *The Plays of Ibsen, Vol. 3*, ed. M. Meyer, pp. 375–506. New York: Washington Square Press, 1986.

Joseph, B. (1985). Transference: the total situation. *International Journal of Psycho-Analysis* 66:447–454.

——— (1987). Projective identification: some clinical aspects. In *Projection, Identification, Projective Identification*, ed. J. Sandler, pp. 65–76. Madison, CT: International Universities Press.

——— (1992). Psychic change: some perspectives. *International Journal of Psycho-Analysis* 73:237–243.

Kaplan, S. (1990). *American Studies in Black and White: Selected Essays, 1949–1989*. Amherst, MA: University of Massachusetts Press.

Kernberg, O. (1974). Further contributions to the treatment of narcissistic personalities. *International Journal of Psycho-Analysis* 55:215–240.

——— (1975). *Borderline Conditions and Pathological Narcissism*. New York: Jason Aronson.

Klein, M. (1975). *Envy and Gratitude and Other Works 1946–1963*. New York: Dell.

Kohut, H. (1966). Forms and transformations of narcissism. In *The Search for the Self, Vol. 1*, ed. P. Ornstein, pp. 427–460. Madison, CT: International Universities Press, 1978.

———— (1971). *The Analysis of the Self*. Madison, CT: International Universities Press.

———— (1972). Thoughts on narcissism and narcissistic rage. In *The Search for the Self, Vol. 2*, ed. P. Ornstein, pp. 615–659. New York: International Universities Press, 1978.

———— (1977). *The Restoration of the Self*. Madison, CT: International Universities Press.

———— (1980). Selected problems in self psychological theory. In *The Search for the Self, Vol. 4*, ed. P. Ornstein, pp. 489–523. Madison, CT: International Universities Press, 1991.

———— (1981). On empathy. In *The Search for the Self, Vol. 4*, ed. P. Ornstein, pp. 525–535. Madison, CT: International Universities Press, 1991.

———— (1983). Selected problems in self psychological theory. In *Reflections on Self Psychology*, ed. J. D. Lichtenberg and S. Kaplan, pp. 387–416. Hillsdale, NJ: Analytic Press.

———— (1984). *How Does Analysis Cure?* Chicago: University of Chicago Press.

Kramer, S. (1994). The influence of Mahler and Kohut on psychoanalytic practice. In *Mahler and Kohut: Perspectives on Development, Psychopathology, and Technique*, ed. S. Kramer and S. Akhtar, 2nd ed., pp. 1–16. Northvale, NJ: Jason Aronson.

Kris, E. (1956). The recovery of childhood memories in psychoanalysis. In *Selected Papers of Ernst Kris*, pp. 301–340. New Haven: Yale University Press, 1975.

Krystal, H. (1976). On trauma and affect. *Psychoanalytic Study of the Child* 33:81–116. New Haven, CT: Yale University Press.

Lachmann, A. (1999). *The theme of cuckoldry in* Othello. Paper presented at the 22nd Annual Conference of the Psychology of the Self, Toronto, Canada, October.

Lachmann, A., and Lachmann, F. M. (1994). The personification of evil: motivations and fantasies of the serial killer. *International Forum of Psychoanalysis* 4:17–23.

————— (1997). The evil self of the serial killer. In *Progress in Self Psychology, Vol. 13*, ed. A. Goldberg, pp. 327–340. Hillsdale, NJ: Analytic Press.

Lachmann, F. M. (1986). Interpretation of psychic conflict and adversarial relationships: a self-psychological perspective. *Psychoanalytic Psychology* 4:341–355.

————— (1996). How many selves make a person? *Contemporary Psychoanalysis* 32:595–614.

————— (1998). From narcissism to self pathology to . . . ? *Psychoanalysis and Psychotherapy* 15:5–27.

————— (2001). Some contributions of infant research to adult psychoanalysis. What have we learned? How can we apply it? *Psychoanalytic Dialogues* 11.

Lachmann, F. M., and Beebe, B. (1989). Oneness fantasies revisited. *Psychoanalytic Psychology* 6:137–149.

————— (1992). Representational and selfobject transferences: a developmental perspective. In *Progress in Self Psychology Vol. 8*, ed. A Goldberg, pp. 3–15. Hillsdale, NJ: Analytic Press.

————— (1993). Interpretation in a developmental perspective. In *Progress in Self Psychology, Vol. 9*, ed. A. Goldberg, pp. 47–52. Hillsdale, NJ: Analytic Press.

————— (1996a). Three principles of salience in the organization of the analyst–patient interaction. *Psychoanalytic Psychology* 13: 1–22.

————— (1996b). The contribution of self- and mutual regulation to therapeutic action: a case illustration. In *Progress in Self Psychology, Vol. 12*, ed. A. Goldberg, pp. 123–140. Hillsdale, NJ: Analytic Press.

————— (1998). Optimal responsiveness in a systems approach to representational and selfobject transferences. In *Optimal Responsiveness*, ed. H. Bacal, pp. 305–326. Northvale, NJ: Jason Aronson.

Lachmann, F. M., and Lichtenberg, J. D. (1992). Model scenes: implications for psychoanalytic treatment. *Journal of the American Psychoanalytic Association* 40:117–137.

Laplanche, J., and Pontalis, J.-B. (1973). *The Language of Psychoanalysis.* New York: Norton.

Leider, R. J. (1998). In the belly of the beast: the vicissitudes of aggression. *Psychoanalytic Inquiry* 36:560–564.

Lewis, D. O. (1999). *Guilty by Reason of Insanity.* New York: Ivy Books.

Lichtenberg, J. D. (1989). *Psychoanalysis and Motivation.* Hillsdale, NJ: Analytic Press.

Lichtenberg, J. D., Lachmann, F., and Fosshage, J. (1992). *Self and Motivational Systems.* Hillsdale, NJ: Analytic Press.

——— (1996). *The Clinical Exchange.* Hillsdale, NJ: Analytic Press.

Loewald, H. (1980). *Papers on Psychoanalysis.* New Haven: Yale University Press.

Lyons-Ruth, K. (1991). Rapprochement or approchement: Mahler's theory reconsidered from the vantage point of recent research on early attachment relationships. *Psychoanalytic Psychology* 8:1–23.

——— (1998). Implicit relational knowing: its role in development and psychoanalytic treatment. *Infant Mental Health Journal* 19:282–289.

——— (1999). The two-person unconscious: intersubjective dialogue, enactive relational representation, and the emergence of new forms of relational organization. *Psychoanalytic Inquiry* 19:576–617.

Maher, A. (1993). Creativity: a work in progress. *Psychoanalytic Quarterly* 62:239–261.

Mahler, M. S., Pine, F., and Bergman, A. (1975). *The Psychological Birth of the Human Infant.* New York: Basic Books

McDevitt, J. B., (1980). *Separation-individuation and aggression.* A. A. Brill Memorial Lecture, New York Psychoanalytic Institute, November.

Meyer, B. C. (1967). *Joseph Conrad: A Psychoanalytic Biography.* Princeton, NJ: Princeton University Press.

Meyer, M. (1967). *Henrik Ibsen: The Making of a Dramatist 1828–1864.* London: Rupert Hart-Davis.

——— (1971). *Henrik Ibsen: The Farewell to Poetry 1864–1882.* London: Rupert Hart-Davis.

———— (1986). Introduction to *Ghosts*. In *The Plays of Ibsen Vol. III*, pp. 3–22. New York: Washington Square Press.

Miller, A. (1981). *Prisoners of Childhood*. New York: Basic Books.

———— (1990). *For Your Own Good*. New York: Noonday.

Miller, J. P. (1985). How Kohut actually worked. In *Progress in Self Psychology, Vol. 1*, ed. A. Goldberg, pp. 13–32. New York: Guilford.

Milrod, D. (1982). The wished-for self image. *Psychoanalytic Study of the Child*. 37:95–120. New Haven: Yale University Press.

Mitchell, S. (1993). *Hope and Dread in Psychoanalysis*. New York: Basic Books.

———— (1998a). Aggression and the endangered self. *Psychoanalytic Inquiry* 18:21–30.

———— (1998b). Commentary on case. *Psychoanalytic Inquiry* 18:89–99.

Modell, A. (1986). The missing elements in Kohut's cure. *Psychoanalytic Inquiry* 6:367–385.

Moes, E. (1991). Ted Bundy: a case of schizoid necrophilia. *Melanie Klein and Object Relations* 9:54–72.

Morrison, A. (1989). *Shame: The Underside of Narcissism*. Hillsdale, NJ: Analytic Press.

Murray, H. A. (1967). Dead to the world. *In Essays in Self Destruction*, ed. E. S. Shneidman. New York: Science House.

Newton, M. (1992). *Hunting Humans: The Encyclopedia of Serial Killers, Vol. 1*. New York: Avon.

Norris, J. (1988). *Serial Killers*. New York: Dolphin.

Ogden, T. H. (1979). On projective identification. *International Journal of Psycho-Analysis* 60:357–374.

———— (1982). *Projective Identification and Psychotherapeutic Technique*. New York: Jason Aronson.

Olsen, J. (1993). *Misbegotten Son*. New York: Dell.

Ornstein, A. (1974). The dread to repeat and the new beginning: a contribution to the psychoanalysis of narcissistic personality disorders.

Annual of Psychoanalysis, pp. 231–248. Madison, CT: International Universities Press.

———— (1991). The dread to repeat: comments on the working through process in psychoanalysis. *Journal of the American Psychoanalytic Association* 39:377–398.

———— (1998a). The fate of narcissistic rage in psychotherapy. *Psychoanalytic Inquiry* 18:55–70.

———— (1998b). Response to the discussants: the fate of narcissistic rage in psychotherapy. *Psychoanalytic Inquiry* 18:107–119.

Ornstein, P. H. (1985). Clinical understanding and explaining: the empathic vantage point. In *Progress in Self Psychology, Vol. 1*, ed. A. Goldberg, pp. 43–61. Hillsdale, NJ: Analytic Press.

Ornstein, P. H., and Ornstein, A. (1993). Assertiveness and destructive aggression: a perspective from the treatment process. In *Rage, Power, and Aggression*, ed. R. A. Glick and S. P. Roose, 2nd ed., pp. 102–117. New Haven: Yale University Press.

Oxford English Dictionary (1982). Oxford: Oxford University Press.

Parens, H. (1979). *The Development of Aggression in Early Childhood*. New York: Jason Aronson

———— (1990). On the girl's psychosexual development: reconsiderations suggested from direct observations. *Journal of the American Psychoanalytic Association* 38:743–772.

Pine, F. (1981). In the beginning: contributions to a psychoanalytic developmental psychology. *International Review of Psycho-Analysis* 8:15–33.

———— (1990). *Drive, Ego, Object, and Self*. New York: Basic Books.

Psychoanalytic Dialogues. (1995). Self psychology after Kohut: a polylogue. 5:351–434.

Raine, A. (1999). Murderous minds: Can we see the mark of Cain? *Cerebrum* 1:15–30.

Raphling, D. L. (1998). The narcissistic basis of aggression. *Psychoanalytic Inquiry* 18:100–106.

Reed, G. (1996). *Clinical Understanding*. Northvale, NJ: Jason Aronson.

Reik, T. (1935). *Surprise and the Psychoanalyst: On the Conjecture and Comprehension of Unconscious Processes.* New York: Dutton, 1937.

Ressler, R. K., Burgess, A. W., and Douglas, J. E. (1988). *Sexual Homicide: Patterns and Motives.* New York: Lexington.

Rothstein, A. (1980). Toward a critique of the psychology of the self. *Psychoanalytic Quarterly* 49:423–455.

Rule, A. (1987). *The I-5 Killer.* New York: Signet.

——— (1989). *The Stranger Beside Me.* New York: Signet.

Sameroff, A. (1983). Developmental systems: context and evolution. In *Mussen's Handbook of Child Psychology, Vol. 1,* ed. W. Kessen, pp. 237–294. New York: Wiley.

Sameroff, A., and Chandler, M. (1976). Reproductive risk and the continuum of caretaking casualty. In *Review of Child Development Research, Vol. 1,* ed. F. D. Horowitz, pp. 187–244. Chicago: University of Chicago Press.

Sander, L. (1977). The regulation of exchange in the infant–caretaker system and some aspects of the context-content relationship. In *Interaction, Conversation, and the Development of Language,* ed. M. Lewis and L. Rosenblum, 2nd ed., pp. 133–156. New York: Wiley.

——— (1983a). To begin with—reflections on ontogeny. In *Reflections on Self Psychology,* ed. J. Lichtenberg and S. Kaplan, 2nd ed., pp. 85–104. Hillsdale, NJ: Analytic Press.

——— (1983b). Polarity paradox, and the organizing process in development. In *Frontiers of Infant Psychiatry,* ed. J. D. Call, E. Galenson, and R. Tyson, pp. 315–327. New York: Basic Books.

——— (1985). Toward a logic of organization in psychobiological development. In *Biologic Response Styles: Clinical Implications,* ed. K. Klar and L. Siever, pp. 20–36. Washington, DC: Monograph of the American Psychiatric Association.

Sandler, J. (1960). The background of safety. *International Journal of Psycho-Analysis* 41:352–356.

——— (1967). Trauma, strain, and development. In *Trauma,* ed. S. Furst, pp.154–176. New York: Basic Books.

Sands, S. (1997). Self psychology and projective identification—Whither shall they meet? *Psychoanalytic Dialogues* 7:651–658.

Schafer, R. (1972). Internalization: Process or fantasy? *Psychoanalytic Study of the Child* 27:411–436. New Haven: Yale University Press.

——— (1976). *A New Language for Psychoanalysis*. New Haven: Yale University Press.

——— (1980). Action language and the psychology of the self. *Annual of Psychoanalysis* 18:83–92. Madison, CT: International Universities Press.

——— (1997). *The Contemporary Kleinians of London*. Madison, CT: International Universities Press.

Schwaber, E. A. (1992). Countertransference: the analyst's retreat from the patient's vantage point. *International Journal of Psycho-Analysis* 73: 349–362.

——— (1998). The non-verbal dimension in psychoanalysis: 'State' and its clinical vicissitudes. *International Journal of Psycho-Analysis* 79: 667–679.

Sears, D. (1991). *To Kill Again*. Wilmington, DE: Scholarly Resources Books.

Sedgwick, W. E. (1967). Ishmael vs. Ahab. In H. Melville, *Moby Dick*, pp. 640–648. New York: Norton.

Silverman, L. D., Lachmann, F. M., and Milich, R. (1982). *The Search for Oneness*. Madison, CT: International Universities Press.

Simon, B. (1991). Psychoanalysis and severe trauma. a longstanding and uneasy relationship. Transactions of the Topeka Psychoanalytic Society, recorder M. Berg. *Bulletin of the Menninger Clinic* 55:517–519.

Singer, M. (1999). How central is aggression to clinical psychoanalysis? *Journal of the American Psychoanalytic Association* 4:1179–1189.

Sorter, D. (1995). Therapeutic action and procedural knowledge. *International Forum of Psychoanalysis* 4:65–70.

Spitz, R. (1965). *The First Year of Life*. Madison, CT: International Universities Press.

Stechler, G. (1987). Clinical applications of a psychoanalytic systems model of assertion and aggression. *Psychoanalytic Inquiry* 7:348–363.

Steiner, J. (1994). Patient-centered and analyst-centered interpretations: some implications of containment and countertransference. *Psychoanalytic Inquiry* 14:406–422.

Stepansky, P. (1977). A history of aggression in Freud. *Psychological Issues, Monograph 39*. Madison, CT: International Universities Press.

Stern D. (1977). *The First Relationship*. Cambridge, MA: Harvard University Press.

———— (1983). The early development of schemas of self, of other, and of "self with other." In *Reflections on Self Psychology*, ed. J. Lichtenberg and S. Kaplan, pp. 49–84. Hillsdale, NJ: Analytic Press.

———— (1985). *The Interpersonal World of the Infant*. New York: Basic Books.

———— (1995). *The Motherhood Constellation*. New York: Basic Books.

———— (1998). The process of therapeutic change involving implicit knowledge: some implications of developmental observations for adult psychotherapy. *Infant Mental Health Journal* 19:300–308.

Stern, D., Sander, L., Nahum, J., et al. (1998). Non-interpretive mechanisms in psychoanalytic therapy: the "something more" than interpretation. *International Journal of Psycho-Analysis* 79:903–922.

Stewart, H. (1998). Commentary on paper by Paul Williams. *Psychoanalytic Dialogues* 8:501–506.

Stolorow, R. D. (1986). Critical reflections on the theory of self psychology: an inside view. *Psychoanalytic Inquiry* 6:387–402.

———— (1994). Aggression in the psychoanalytic situation. In *The Intersubjective Perspective*, ed. R. D. Stolorow, G. E. Atwood, and B. Brandchaft, pp. 113–120. Northvale,, NJ: Jason Aronson.

Stolorow, R. D., Brandchaft, B., and Atwood, G. (1987). *Psychoanalytic Treatment: An Intersubjective Approach*. Hillsdale, NJ: Analytic Press.

Stolorow, R. D., and Lachmann, F. M. (1980). *Psychoanalysis of Developmental Arrests*. Madison, CT: International Universities Press.

———— (1984/1985). Transference: the future of an illusion. *Annual of Psychoanalysis* pp. 19–37. Madison, CT: International Universities Press.

Stolorow, R. D., Orange, D., and Atwood, G. (1998). Projective identification be gone!: commentary on paper by Susan H. Sands. *Psychoanalytic Dialogues* 8:719–726.

Stone, L. (1961). *The Psychoanalytic Situation*. Madison, CT: International Universities Press.

Teicholz, J. G. (1999). *Kohut, Loewald, and the Postmoderns*. Hillsdale, NJ: Analytic Pess.

Thelen E., and Smith, L. (1994). *A Dynamic Systems Approach to the Development of Cognition and Action*. Cambridge, MA: MIT Press.

Tuch, R. H. (1997). Beyond empathy: confronting certain complexities in self psychological theory. *Psychoanalytic Quarterly* 66:259–282.

Waelder, R. (1936). The principle of multiple function: observations on over-determination. In *Psychoanalysis: Observation, Theory, Application*, ed. S. A. Guttman, pp. 68–83. Madison, CT: International Universities Press.

Wallerstein, R. (1986). *Forty-Two Lives in Treatment*. New York: Guilford.

Watts, P. (1964). Introduction. In *Henrik Ibsen—Ghosts and Other Plays*. London: Penguin.

Weiss, J., and Sampson, H. (1986). *The Psychoanalytic Process*. New York: Guilford.

Wilson, C. (1990). *The Mammoth Book of True Crime 2*. New York: Carroll and Graf.

Winnicott, D. W. (1950). Aggression in relation to emotional development. In *Through Paediatrics to Psychoanalysis*, pp. 204–218. New York: Basic Books, 1958.

———— (1960). The theory of parent–infant relationship. In *The Maturational Processes and the Facilitating Environment*, pp. 37–55. Madison, CT: International Universities Press, 1965.

Wolff, P. (1991). The causes, controls, and organization of behavior in the neonate. *Psychological Issues Monograph 5*. Madison, CT: International Universities Press.

Zetzel, E. (1956). The concept of transference. In *The Capacity for Emotional Growth*, pp. 168–181. Madison, CT: International Universities Press, 1970.

Credits

Index

Abusive relationships, negative
  therapeutic reaction, 168–172
Adler, E., x
Aggression
  countertransference as expression
    of analyst's, 194–201
  defined, 2
  destructive and nondestructive,
    32–33
  developmental factors, 25–45 (See
    also Developmental factors)
  motivational systems theory, 47–
    72 (See also Motivational
    systems theory)
  narcissistic injury and, 3–4, 8–9
  reactive to eruptive, 119–147 (See
    also Reactive to eruptive
    aggression)
  self psychology and, 2–5
    debate over, 5–9
Ainsworth, M., 79
Ambition, self psychology, 14–17
Arlow, J., ix

Assertion
  aggression and, motivational
    systems theory, 49–50
  self psychology, 14–17
Atwood, G., 22

Bacal, H., 62, 90
Bachant, J. L., x
Balint, M., 89, 90, 91
Barnett, B., 149–166, 169
Beebe, B., x, 4, 33, 34, 62, 67,
    75, 82, 93, 140, 206, 214,
    230
Bergmann, M., viii
Bernfeld, S., 6
Blake, J., 131, 132
Bollas, C., 137
Bowlby, J., 79
Brain, violence and, 133–135
Brazelton, T. B., 4
Brenner, C., ix
Bromberg, P., 12, 13
Bundy, T., 124–126, 127

Calamandrei, M., 119
Chandler, M., 75
Childhood abuse, violence, 133–134
Clyman, R., 231
Conflict model, self psychology, ix
Countertransference, 191–208
    as Catch-22, 192–194
    as expression of analyst's
        aggression, 194–201
    overview, 191–192
    projective identification, 201–208
    self psychology, 21
Creativity (Ibsen example), 103–117
    biographical roots, 112–117
    creative transformation, 108–112
    overview, 103–104
    plots, 105–107
    transformation through, 107–108
Curtis, H., 7, 13

Deprivation, aggression and, 6
Destructive aggression, 32–33
Developmental factors, 25–45
    aggression
        destructive and nondestructive,
            32–33
        self- and interactive regulation,
            33–34
            case illustration, 35–45
    gender differences, 30–31
    historical perspective, 27–30
    overview, 25–27
    reactive aggression, transformation
        of, 140–143
Distortion, projection and, self
    psychology, 12–14
Dowling, S., 90

Drive theory, aggression, 4, 6–7, 27–
    30

Eissler, K. R., 204
Empathy, self psychology, criticism
    of, 11–12
Empathy (enraging, case
    illustration), 173–190
    case history, 176–179
    chair and couch, 180–182
    enactments and transformations,
        186–190
    overview, 173–174
    presentation, 174–175
    regulations, 182–185
Enactments, transformations and,
    enraging empathy, 186–190
Enraging empathy, 173–190. See also
    Empathy
Erikson, E. H., 90
Eruptive aggression, 137–139, 232–
    237. See also Reactive to
    eruptive aggression
Expectancies, trauma, 92–94

Fairbairn, W. R. D., 8
Fenichel, O., 76
Ferenczi, S., 76, 90
Fetus, psychology of, 4
Field, T., 4
Fonagy, P., 17, 18, 40, 67, 99
Fosshage, J., 50, 67, 82
Freud, A., 25–26, 27, 28, 30, 31, 44,
    75, 120, 138
Freud, S., 5, 6, 8, 13, 22, 24, 67, 75,
    76, 78, 81, 89, 91, 104, 235
Frustration, aggression and, 6

Gender differences, developmental
    factors, 30–31
Gill, M., 2, 3, 193, 205, 206, 207
Gilligan, J., 144, 145, 233
Gladwell, M., 133, 134
Goldberg, A., 140
Greenacre, P., 104
Greenson, R. R., ix, 51, 213, 219
Grigsby, J., 231
Gruenthal, R., 196, 226

Harris, A., 9
Hartlaub, G., 231
Hartmann, H., 5
Heine, H., 24
Hill, K., 132
Hofer, M., 79
Hoffman, I., 230
Humor, narcissistic rage transformed
    through, motivational systems
    theory, 67–70

Ibsen, H., 103 passim
Individual differences, self
    psychology and, ix–x
Interactive regulation, self-
    regulation and, aggression, 33–
    34
  case illustration, 35–45
Interpretation
  self psychology, leading and
    trailing edge, 17–18
  state transformations, case
    illustration, 82–86

Jacobson, E., ix
Joseph, B., 8, 202

Kaplan, S., 89
Kernberg, O., 9, 12, 193, 202
King, P., 149
Klein, M., x, 8, 13, 202, 206
Kohut, H., viii, ix, x, 2, 3, 5, 6, 7,
    10, 11, 13, 14, 15, 16, 17, 23,
    28, 40, 44, 47, 48, 67, 78, 79,
    81, 90, 91, 104, 107, 140, 179,
    199, 201, 215, 225, 234–235
Kramer, S., 7
Kris, E., 55
Krystal, H., 93

Lachmann, A., 120, 121
Lachmann, F. M., 4, 14, 33, 34, 40,
    51, 55, 62, 67, 75, 82, 93, 121,
    149–166, 170, 206, 214, 230
Laplanche, J., 88
Leading edge, interpretation, self
    psychology, 17–18
Leider, R. J., 5
Lewis, D., 133, 134
Lichtenberg, J. D., 23, 50, 55, 64, 67
Loewald, H., 40
Lucas, H. L., 122–123, 126, 137,
    139
Lyons-Ruth, K., 28–30, 33, 213,
    230, 231

Maher, A., 104
Mahler, M., 28, 29
McCrorie, E., 33
Melville, H., 88, 89, 90, 93
Meyer, B., 104
Meyer, M., 107, 108, 112, 113, 114
Miller, A., 90, 137
Miller, J. P., 17

Mitchell, S., 9, 55, 195, 197, 198, 199, 200, 201, 227
Modell, A., 13
Model scenes, screen memories and, motivational systems theory, 54–56
  case illustration, 56–66, 71–72
Moes, E., 125
Morrison, A., 144
Motivational systems theory, 47–72. *See also* Systems theory
  aggression
    assertion and, 49–50
    experience of, 48–49
    enumeration of, 50–54
    model scenes and screen memories, 54–56
    case illustration, 56–66, 71–72
    narcissistic rage, transformation through humor, 67–70
    negative therapeutic reaction, 166–168
    overview, 47–48
Murray, H., 93

Narcissistic injury, aggression and, 3–4, 8–9
Narcissistic rage
  self psychology, 14–17
  transformation through humor, motivational systems theory, 67–70
Negative therapeutic reaction
  abusive relationships, 168–172
  correspondence on, 149–166
  motivational systems, 166–168
Newman, K., 62, 90

Newton, M., 122, 123
Nondestructive aggression, 32–33
Norris, J., 122

Object relations theory, aggression and, 4
Oedipus complex, self psychology, 5
Ogden, T. H., 202, 207
Olsen, J., 127, 128, 130
Ornstein, A., 48, 74, 177, 194, 195, 196, 197, 198, 199, 200, 201, 219, 225, 226
Ornstein, P. H., 11, 48, 74, 80
Oscar II (k. of Sweden), 108

Parens, H., 8, 32–33
Pine, F., 139
Pines, M., 149
Pontalis, J.-B., 88
Projection, distortion and, self psychology, 12–14
Projective identification, countertransference, 201–208
Psychoanalytic Dialogues, x

Raine, A., 134, 135
Raphling, D. L., 7, 8
Raynor, E., 149
Reactive to eruptive aggression, 119–147
  eruptive aggression, 137–139
  overview, 119–121
  self psychology, 232–237
  serial killers
    profile of, 122–127
    Shawcross case, 127–133, 135–137

shame and violence, 143–147
transformation of reactive
    aggression, 140–143
violence, neurological basis for,
    133–135
Reed, G., 19, 20, 21, 194
Reik, T., 67, 230
Ressler, R. K., 136
Rothstein, A., 6, 7
Rule, A., 123, 124

Sadism, aggression and, 7
Sameroff, A., 75, 78
Sampson, H., 175, 206
Sander, L., 27, 33, 79, 214
Sandler, J., 64, 87
Sands, S., 203, 207
Schafer, R., x, 206, 207
Schwaber, E. A., 82, 207
Screen memories, model scenes and,
    motivational systems theory,
    54–56
  case illustration, 56–66, 71–72
Sears, D., 124
Selfobject transference, self
    psychology, criticism of, 10
Self psychology, 1–24, 221–237
  aggression and, debate over, 5–9
  comparisons of, 19–24
  conflict model, ix
  criticism of, viii, 9–12
    empathy, 11–12
    selfobject transference, 10
  developmental factors, 25–45 (See
    also Developmental factors)
  expansion of, 221–232
  individual differences and, ix–x

interpretation, leading and trailing
    edge, 17–18
narcissistic rage, ambition, and
    assertion, 14–17
projection and distortion, 12–14
reactive and eruptive aggression,
    232–237
Self- regulation, interactive
    regulation and, aggression, 33–
    34
  case illustration, 35–45
Self-states
  case illustration, 79–82
  states and, state transformations,
    79–82
Serial killers, 236
  defined, 120–121
  profiles of, 122–127
Shawcross, 127–133
Shakespeare, W., 119–120, 236
Shame, violence and, reactive to
    eruptive aggression, 143–147
Shawcross, A., 127–133, 134, 135–
    137, 138, 139, 141, 142, 144,
    236
Silverman, L. D., 206
Simon, B., 91
Singer, M., 7
Single-event trauma, case
    illustration, 94–101
Smith, L., 4, 216
Sorter, D., 231
Spitz, R., 27–28
State transformations, 73–86
  case illustration, 82–86
  creativity and, 103–117 (See also
    Creativity)

State transformations (*continued*)
  model of, 74–78
  overview, 73–74
  states and self-states, 79–82
  trauma and, 87–101 (*See also*
    Trauma)
Stechler, G., 25, 26–27, 30, 31, 49, 51
Steiner, J., 202
Stepansky, P., 6
Stern, D., 27, 47, 63, 67, 68, 75, 79,
    80, 81, 92, 93, 217, 230
Stewart, H., 149
Stolorow, R. D., viii, 11, 14, 16, 22,
    40, 49, 215
Stone, L., 51
Systems theory, 209–220. *See also*
    Motivational systems theory
  case examples, 209–213
  described, 213–220

Teicholz, J., 195, 199
Thelen, E., 4, 216
Trailing edge, interpretation, self
    psychology, 17–18
Transformational model, state
    transformations, 74–78. *See also*
    State transformations

Transformations, enactments and,
    enraging empathy, 186–190
Trauma, 87–101
  expectancies, 92–94
  overview, 87–92
  single-event, case illustration, 94–
    101
Tuch, R. H., 12

Violence
  neurological basis for, 133–135
    (*See also* Aggression; Reactive to
    eruptive aggression)
  shame and, reactive to eruptive
    aggression, 143–147

Waelder, R., 75
Wallerstein, R., 67, 230
Watts, P., 108
Weiss, J., 175, 206
Wilson, C., 122
Winnicott, D. W., 51, 173, 215
Woodfield, R., 123–124, 126, 127,
    137, 139, 142

Zetzel, E., 51

About the Author

Frank M. Lachmann, Ph.D., is a member of the Founding Faculty of the Institute for the Psychoanalytic Study of Subjectivity; Clinical Assistant Professor, New York University Postdoctoral Program in Psychotherapy and Psychoanalysis; and Training and Supervising Analyst, Postgraduate Center for Mental Health. A member of the advisory boards of psychoanalytic institutions in Boston, Chicago, Kansas City, Minneapolis, Los Angeles, San Francisco, and Toronto, he is author or co-author of more than 75 publications in the areas of self psychology; empirical infant research; the implications of empirical infant research for the analysis of adults; and aspects of the therapeutic relationship such as transference, therapeutic alliance, interpretation, and non-interpretive interventions.

Dr. Lachmann was co-author with Robert Stolorow of *Psychoanalysis of Developmental Arrest*, and with Lloyd Silverman and Robert Milich of *The Search for Oneness*. His most recent publications include *Self and Motivational Systems* and *The Clinical Exchange: Techniques Derived from Self and Motivational Systems*, both co-authored with Joseph Lichtenberg and James Fosshage. In the applied psychoanalytic literature, he has authored or co-authored papers on Eugene O'Neill, Henrik Ibsen, serial killers, and what music can contribute to psychoanalysis.

Dr. Lachmann received the Division 39 of the American Psychological Association Distinguished Scientist Award in 1998, and delivered the Kohut Memorial Lecture at the 22nd Annual International Conference on the Psychology of the Self in 1999.